# The Ethnography of
# Charles Darwin

ALSO BY CHARLES DE PAOLO

*Epidemic Disease and Human Understanding: A Historical Analysis of Scientific and Other Writings* (McFarland, 2006)

*Human Prehistory in Fiction* (McFarland, 2003)

# The Ethnography of Charles Darwin

## A Study of His Writings on Aboriginal Peoples

CHARLES DE PAOLO

McFarland & Company, Inc., Publishers

*Jefferson, North Carolina, and London*

**ACKNOWLEDGMENTS.** Extracts from *Charles Darwin's Beagle Diary*, edited by R. D. Keynes, 1988, 2001, © Cambridge University Press. Reprinted with the permission of Cambridge University Press. Extracts from *Charles Darwin's Notebooks, 1836–1844, Geology, Transmutation of Species, Metaphysical Enquiries*, edited by Paul H. Barrett, Peter J. Gautrey, Sandra Herbert, Davd Kohn, and Sydney Smith, 1988, 2008, © The Committee for the Publication of Charles Darwin's Notebooks, 2008, published by Cambridge University Press, reproduced with permission.

   I would like to thank Victoria Oriana DePaolo for helping me to prepare this manuscript.

LIBRARY OF CONGRESS CATALOGUING-IN-PUBLICATION DATA

De Paolo, Charles, 1950–
   The ethnography of Charles Darwin : a study of his writings on aboriginal peoples / Charles De Paolo.
      p.    cm.
   Includes bibliographical references and index.

   ISBN 978-0-7864-4877-7
   softcover : 50# alkaline paper ∞

   1. Darwin, Charles, 1809–1882 — Political and social views.
2. Darwin, Charles, 1809–1882 — Criticism and interpretation.
3. Indigenous peoples — Public opinion.   4. Indigenous peoples —
Philosophy.   5. Human evolution — Philosophy.   6. Racism in
anthropology.   I. Title.
GN380.D468   2010
305.8 — dc22                                              2009051801

British Library cataloguing data are available

On the cover: (top) Portrait of Charles Darwin, 1869; (bottom) illustration of native Fuegians by H.H. Nichols

Manufactured in the United States of America

*McFarland & Company, Inc., Publishers*
   *Box 611, Jefferson, North Carolina 28640*
   *www.mcfarlandpub.com*

# Table of Contents

# Introduction

Charles Darwin contributed to a century-long scientific enterprise to define man's place in nature. Modern scholars have recognized his efforts, but there is a difference of opinion in regard to his position on the dignity of native man and on indigenous cultures. A review of the scholarship will show that there are three perspectives on this position: the first portrays Darwin as a fervent humanitarian whose opinions on extant primitives was consistent, despite the occasional ambiguous or petulant statement; the second takes his intermittent comments on nonwhites as unequivocal evidence of racist tendencies; and the third, recognizing the validity of previous perspectives, finds his discourse on race relations to be contradictory. This contradiction and Darwin's subtle attempt at a resolution will be the focus of this study. Although Darwin's ethnographic writings are fragmentary, if consolidated they reveal a lifelong intellectual and conscientious struggle to understand native man's place in natural history and, more generally, the relationship between Europeans and aboriginal people worldwide.

Two scholars who have written informatively on Darwin's anthropology subscribe to the humanitarian perspective described above. Howard S. Gruber shows that Darwin defended the humanity of black people, praised their intelligence and moral sensibility, condemned slavery vociferously, and recognized the unity of humankind in the context of evolutionary history (65–70). Janet Browne, in a superb biography, situates Darwin's humanistic sensibility in its cultural and familial contexts and attempts to account for ethical inconsistencies in his discourse. She explains, for example, that while Darwin depicted Fuegians in dark metaphors, and though natives were generally thought of in British society as "specimens," both he and Robert FitzRoy, Captain of H.M.S. *Beagle*, remained "absolutely certain that all human beings came from the same stock," and that there was only one original species of diverse mankind; moreover, they rejected the idea that primitive people were different from Europeans. These propositions were, for both men, fundamentally "humanitarian and biblical." Both took their mandate to establish missions and to explore new worlds seriously (241). Although politically unlike in their humanitarian and philanthropic sentiments, neither subscribed to racist theories.

A second interpretation questions the consistency of Darwin's compassion for and optimism about native peoples. Patrick Brantlinger, in an extensively researched book, points out that, although Darwin rejected the idea of racial degeneration, he was not very hopeful about the prospects of uncivilized man: "From the 1830s, Darwin believed that, though humanity formed a single species, certain primitive races were so far behind civilization — so lost in the immense past of social evolution — that their extinction was likely if not inevitable" (165). Thus, it appears that Darwin had misgivings about the possibility of civilizing savages. On the one hand, he was genuinely impressed by "the intelligence and progress toward civilization of the Fuegians whom Captain FitzRoy was returning to their homeland," and he was reasonably confident the repatriates, along with missionaries, could civilize their fellow Fuegians. On the other hand, he was astonished "at how subhuman the indigenous Fuegians seemed, and his opinion of all 'savages' remained quite negative" (166). More concerned with human extinction than with human origins, in the *Journal* and in later writings Darwin at times "looked forward to the complete triumph of civilized over primitive or 'lower' races" (167). Thus, one of two possibilities presented itself: either "the peaceful transformation of 'savagery' into its opposite or 'its violent liquidation'" (167). Darwin recurrently spoke of "the great, chronological, and cultural distance between the savage and the civilized conditions of human existence"; and the "survival of the fittest" theoretically accounted for the destruction of "supposedly less fit or less adaptable" human beings (168). All savages, in Darwin's view, were lost in time: "a vast temporal difference" separated history from prehistory and civilization from savagery (168). On the branching evolutionary tree, one could say that "modern savages were like dead branches ... born out of their due time" (168).

Though several scholars have identified the intellectual and moral contradictions in Darwin's ethnology, none has developed its implications fully. In 1958, Loren Eiseley hinted that Darwin's depiction of aborigines was inconsistent. With the scientific wisdom of the age classifying living men in terms of their cultural achievements and judging these works by Western standards, it is no surprise that Darwin was acutely aware of the enormous disparity between savage and civilized man. However, his personal contacts with Fuegians on board the *Beagle* and with natives throughout South America and the Pacific challenged stereotypes about savage man. These experiences, Eiseley believes, brought Darwin to a point where he began to revaluate "the problem of culture" as an evolutionary and global phenomenon. Ultimately, however, he was not able to solve "both sides of the human mystery"—that is, man's character as a biological and a socio-cultural being (264–65).

Surveying the anti-slavery activism of Darwin's youth under the influence of Erasmus Darwin and of Josiah Wedgwood and family at Maer Hall, as well as of the Cambridge University years when he embraced a belief in the brotherhood of all races, Adrian Desmond and James Moore articulate the humanitarian side of the ethnology comprehensively (xviii–xix, 111). Darwin's commitment to human dignity was reinforced by his visits to slave countries, such as Brazil, and his ethical indignation was genuine. He had faith in the morality and intelligence of many indigenous people, even though he viewed natives as would a condescending philanthropist who believed that their progress depended on European intervention (101).

The moral contradiction in Darwin's thinking, according to Desmond and Moore, was the consequence of his applying laissez-faire policy and evolutionary principles to the colonization of tribal lands. In their view, Darwin appears to have accepted, or was hesitant to denounce, the exploitative consequences of colonialism. Darwin, therefore, appeared to rationalize, and thereby to sanction, colonial advancement as inexorable and as perfectly consistent with the natural laws governing demography (147–48). According to natural selection, only the fittest human beings were expected to survive and to dominate the natural and socio-cultural history of the species. Contrary to Darwin's feelings, expressed in private discourse, this theory further implied that colonialism and the slave trade, though reprehensible in their effects on native people, were nonetheless consonant with the natural laws governing competition, selection, and extinction. In the realm of human activity, native or uncivilized man, when confronted by strong invaders, became a maladapted organism, destined either to be assimilated or to be extinguished by the newcomers, whether white or nonwhite. Desmond and Moore contend that, ultimately, Darwin's scientific enterprise had been redirected by "the race-judging attitudes of his culture," which considered civilization an inexorably progressive goal (148). Because natural selection did not favor isolated human communities, Darwin had made racial extinction "an inevitable evolutionary consequence" (149).

The present study has a twofold purpose: to survey Darwin's opinions on indigenous society and his relationships with aborigines whom he met as he circumnavigated the globe on the *Beagle*, from 1832 to 1836; and, more importantly, to examine his coming to terms with the humanity of nonwhite people in the context of, and in opposition to, prevailing racist ideas and the theory of evolution by natural selection.

It would be incorrect to assume that, while on board the *Beagle,* Darwin was a humanitarian who subsequently abandoned this commitment for one that ascribed authority to scientific and to economic principles oppressing aborigines. With the concept of the struggle for life, so prominent in Malthusian demography, came the problem of human victimization and of pessimism regarding the prospects of uncivilized people. Darwin's humanistic thought, unlike that of Malthus, did not simply accept the vicissitudes and suffering of uncivilized life as natural and inevitable; rather, he struggled, intellectually and morally, to reconcile his humanistic sensibility with biology and with national policy, so as to maintain the dignity of people who lived under uncivilized conditions.

Darwin's reaction to the ethnic groups he encountered varied from region to region and from tribe to tribe. In certain instances and for reasons we shall consider, he expressed derogatory opinions about particular communities, whereas in others he perceived inherent nobility. Negative reactions usually arose spontaneously when he met isolated tribes on distant shores. In his mind, these first impressions seemed to validate contemporary stereotypes. Through observation, social contact, and deductive reasoning, he gradually realized that conventional thinking on primitive man failed to illuminate and in some contexts distorted their humanness. Intermittently in his public and private discourse, he articulated concepts that more realistically defined the complexity of the human character and, particularly, native man's place in nature. He pursued this complex end, not by employing the fixed terms or hierarchies of eighteenth-century biology, such as the Scale of Nature and Linnaean taxonomy, but rather through evolutionary concepts, such as transmutation, descent, divergence, migration, and selection. Darwin defined his humanism over five decades. This reflective and analytical process, although fragmentary, discontinuous, and in places inconsistent, is documented in his personal and public discourse.

From his study of plant and animal life, and from his observations of the relentless competition between human communities worldwide, Darwin inferred that aborigines were subject to a kind of amoral selection at the hands of rival tribes, enslavers, or colonists. His reaction to this moral contradiction varied: at times, he subscribed to the status quo, while, at other times, he reaffirmed the common origin and equality of all races and recognized their hardships. Although he did not often advocate the plight of tribes openly, he eventually resolved his moral ambivalence. Unlike Malthus, who presented life in pre-agricultural communities as irremediably unstable and as regularly depopulated by disease, famine, and war, Darwin tried to discover why these conditions obtained and what could be done to ameliorate them.

In the private discourse of the early 1830s, Darwin wrote anecdotes and acerbic remarks defending human rights. From the late 1830s to the early 1870s, in need of an effective polemical strategy, Darwin collected population statistics in *Descent* to prove that societies in the Pacific were being systematically destroyed through attrition, as the influx of colonists altered the environments to which they had become adapted over time. Maoris and aborigines in Australia and Tasmania, in effect, had been rendered the maladapted victims of human selection. As Darwin's evolutionary biology developed, he consistently criticized the immoral consequences of the survival of the fittest, whether the dominant or fittest tribe was Malayan, Onan, or European.

This study is subdivided into three parts. Part I is concerned with precursors and possible influences on Darwin's ethnological writings. I examine ethnological elements of three texts that had a bearing on Darwin's later experience. He read and commented on Alexander von Humboldt's *Personal Narrative*, on the Reverend Thomas Robert Malthus' *Essay on the Principle of Population*, and on the literature of maritime history, with special emphasis on the *Beagle Narrative* of 1826–1830, by Captain Philip Parker King and others.

Darwin had the highest regard for Humboldt, especially for the latter's natural descriptions. Although it is difficult to document Darwin's direct indebtedness to Humboldt's writings on the natives whom he met in the equinoctial regions of America, circumstantial evidence, reviewed in chapter 1, suggests that his liberal and relativistic approach to native society was similar to Humboldt's. We know that Darwin read and annotated the *Personal Narrative* while on board the *Beagle* and that he was familiar with Humboldt's writings on man. They shared certain ideas. Although Darwin's discourse on the Fuegian tribes tends to be impressionistic and fragmentary, both he and Humboldt were consistently interested in how colonialism and the missions affected native populations. Humboldt described and compared native cultures. Once Darwin had familiarized himself with the Fuegian tribes, he, too, began to observe and record matters pertaining to indigenous civilization, culture, and geography.

Humboldt, unlike Darwin, was not heavily burdened by preconceptions about savage man. His critical anthropology questioned, with greater freedom and relativity, conventional theories about the origin and nature of primitive man, and he consistently supported the idea of human dignity. He criticized slave labor in Venezuela, in Guatemala, and in upper Peru, and the sugar, indigo, and cotton industries that fostered the practice. Darwin, too, was a humanist and anti-slavery proponent. But, unlike Humboldt, the pseudo-scientific theories supporting racism, as we shall see, interfered to a greater degree with the development of his mature thinking on man.

Along with Humboldt's *Narrative*, Malthus' *An Essay on the Principle of Population*, the focus of chapter 2 ("Malthus' Theological Demography"), is a comparative resource for the understanding of Darwin's ethnology. Malthus and Darwin faced complicated ethical, anthropological, and biological problems, the most difficult of which to define and to solve was the moral obligation Western man owed to isolated human communities. In the 1798 edition of the *Essay*, Malthus proposed that the relation between population growth and subsistence, along with factors that checked overpopulation, was determined by nature's fixed laws, preordained by God to fulfill a theological design in history. God established the laws of population precisely for the advantage of His creatures and could suspend these laws by fiat. The ethical dilemma confronting Malthus was that his design argument allowed for the destruction of maladapted or of severely deprived *human beings*. Malthus circumvented this dogmatic problem by invoking the doctrine of free will. Even though uncivilized societies incurred the hardship of population checks more severely than did civilized nations, they nevertheless had the potential ability to make decisions and to improve their own way of life. Despite this acknowledgment, Malthus failed to explain in practical terms how the trepidations of savage life, which he surveyed in North America, in South America, in Africa, and in the South Pacific islands, might be sufficiently allayed so as to permit natives to control population, to preclude destabilizing conditions, and to build a better society.

Malthus implied that God's providential objective was twofold: to allow the fittest to survive and the unfit, through conscience and discipline, to join the elect. For the unfit to survive in the long run, however, they had to cultivate the earth and to exercise the reasoning faculties. Only in this way would they be able to discern the natural order and the Wisdom and foreknowledge of God. In *1803*, Malthus shifted the locus of creative power, emphatically, from Divine Providence to humanity. Of the positive checks on population, such as famine and disease, all were attributable to the laws of nature. But the exercise of rational thought and of conscience, he reiterates, could efficiently control population before natural disasters and man-made events were unleashed to reduce human numbers. In keeping with orthodox doctrine on the character of God and human responsibility, he argued that the misery so acutely experienced in everyday life in uncivilized regions could not be blamed on God, for man had been given the potential to solve his own problems. Malthus' historical readings suggest that the intellectual cultures of indigenous societies in Africa, in North and South America, and in the South Pacific, were seriously limited by unremitting warfare, by slavery, and by material inadequacies. Political discord, tribal warfare, and slavery, in turn, contributed to the disintegration of the family, to the shortening of life spans, and to a high rate of infant mortality. These combined factors inhibited the founding of agricultural communities. For Africans, Native Americans, and Pacific Islanders, these were chronic conditions. Wherever a population approached or exceeded the level of subsistence, preventive checks (famine, war, disease, and immoral customs like forced labor and infanticide) came into effect and with devastating consequences. Though Malthus understood that primitive man struggled to exist, he neither expressed the need for, nor a method of, reclaiming primitive societies.

Captain Philip Parker King's *Narrative* of the *Beagle*'s 1826–1830 circumnavigation of the globe, which I review in chapter 3, provides background to Darwin's voyage and has comparative value as we consider the ethnology. The *Beagle* had traveled to Tierra del Fuego in 1826. The King narrative, existing in manuscript at the outset of Darwin's voyage, includes episodes involving natives in South America and in the Pacific; the manuscript was in the *Beagle*'s library, but Darwin did not read it while on board. He did read it upon its publication, and he criticized it briefly in correspondence and notebook entries.

The King narrative raises several issues having to do with communication and cognition. One involved miscommunication between tribes and ship's company, sometimes leading to dangerous skirmishes; another issue, appearing in both King's and FitzRoy's writings (primarily in *Narrative* 2), was the use of pseudo-scientific modalities, such as phrenology, to claim unjustifiably that aborigines were by nature impulsive and unpredictable; and that their characters, customs, and material cultures, were anomalous. It is true that King, FitzRoy and others were sympathetic to individual natives and concerned about their difficulties. They described physical features, contrasted native physiology and behaviors, and classified people ethnologically. But these progressive activities were undermined by phrenology and by what it claimed to prove about native cognition and behavior. Its findings reinforced ethnic assumptions about Native South Americans as being helpless barbarians, disposed to cannibalism, and reclaimable to humanity only if converted to Christianity and only if educated.

Part II, comprising chapters 4, 5, 6, and 7, charts the voyage from region to region and from one native society to another. In chapter 4, Darwin expressed sympathy and respect for black slaves whom he encountered in Chile and Brazil, from January to August 1832. Anecdotes and descriptions in the *Diary* convey the plight of runaway slaves, the mendacious cruelty of the slave-hunters who pursued them, and the mistreatment that was part of everyday life. In Brazil, he boldly contrasted the lifestyle of the rich plantation owners with that of slaves. Although plantations differed from one another in terms of material want and intensity of suffering, Darwin condemned all slave civilizations as abominations. Savagery, he concluded, was defined in moral not ethnic terms: the true savages were those who created and promulgated the system. Both Darwin and FitzRoy agreed that slavery destroyed the fabric of a nation, fomented rebellion, and was, in the long term, politically and economically disastrous.

In chapter 5, I look at Darwin's initial encounters with indigenous cultures in Tierra del Fuego. Fuegian societies were, for him, as anomalous as slave plantations, but with a very important distinction. Whereas African slaves retained their resourcefulness and dignity while enduring the enormities of servitude, Darwin felt that Fuegian tribes were slaves to the natural world, and he belittled them for their perceived failure to overcome the challenges, and to develop the resources, of their natural habitat. Though accommodated to nature in their basic needs, they had not, or could not, exercise their reasoning faculties to transform their world advantageously. Perhaps, for this reason, Darwin initially derogated the Alacaluf tribe. His opinions, in 1832, differed from those of Captain FitzRoy, for whom this was a return visit. FitzRoy, in December of 1832, saw the Fuegians as human beings living under savage conditions rather than as sub-human creatures or throwbacks. He rejected preconceptions and promoted feelings of brotherhood. Darwin's first impression of the natives on 18 December 1832, on the other hand, was emotionally charged. In the tribesman he saw wild men, devoid of language and culture, and he used unbecoming language to describe them in his *Diary* and in his correspondence.

Despite the excitement of the first encounter, Darwin eventually tried to understand the people, ethnologically, but the method he employed in order to relate Fuegians, Eskimos, and South Sea Islanders to one another was contrived and simplistic, although he made several thought-provoking comments. He compared Fuegian aborigines to the repatriates. Those who had been educated in England, he believed, not only dramatized the great difference between civilized and uncivilized life, but also the validity of FitzRoy's observation that savagery was a circumstantial condition and not a trait inherent to some human beings and not to others. The difference between the anglicized and indigenous natives was even more demonstrable in their interactions: the repatriates, dressed in British clothing and speaking English, approached their families but were received unsympathetically, much to the consternation of FitzRoy.

FitzRoy's long-range plan was to establish a settlement in Jemmy Button's homeland, and he was confident that the three Fuegian repatriates would remain to work as liaisons between Britain and the local population. By 27 January, natives unexpectedly threatened the crew, along with Jemmy and companions, and the indigenes went so far as to harass the missionary Rev. Matthews. Though the acculturation of the repatriates appeared successful, Darwin had second thoughts about the long-term effects of British education, and about the possibility of his wards' resistance to backsliding. Letters of 30 March and of 11 April 1833 reflect his doubts about the civilizing process and about aboriginal cooperation with the mission. His tone changed as he described aborigines there as miserable barbarians. The reason for this change of heart was his acceptance of rumors about cannibalism (based as they were on dubious evidence), along with the natives' mistreatment of the Reverend Matthews.

On the return to Tierra del Fuego, on 24 February 1834, Darwin once again encountered Alacaluf tribesmen in the canoes. He reverts to derogatory language to describe their physical appearance and speculates in the *Diary* about how these "gifted animals" were able to survive in so inhospitable a region. Exhibiting genuine interest in their migratory history and in their day-to-day survival, he conjectured that the Fuegian inhabitants had become mentally adapted to the demands of the environment, not through their own initiatives, but because natural pressures had fitted them, like any other animals, to the rigors of climate and to the paucity of resources. Though they seemed to be hopeless, their very existence as gatherers was a testament to human adaptability. The idea that man could be absorbed into his habitation became startlingly clear on 5 March 1834, when the *Beagle* met Jemmy for the last time. They were shocked at how the accoutrements of civilization were gone (his companions had fled after stealing his clothes), as he stood self-consciously in a canoe, dressed in animal skins. Jemmy had even lost his English-language skills. This traumatic experience confirmed Darwin's worst fears, and he expressed his feelings candidly in correspondence of 30 March and of 6 April 1834 about the apparent regression of their protégé, of whom they were so proud.

Chapter 6, "The 'Barbarians' of Argentina," gathers Darwin's ethnological anecdotes and comments made from the summer of 1833 to the winter of 1834. As a guest of General Juan Manuel de Rosas (1793–1877), notorious cattle rancher and dictator, Darwin undertook naturalistic excursions but had unknowingly entered into a war of extermination, waged by the Spanish cattle interests against indigenous Indian tribes whose vast land was essential to the ranchers for cattle grazing and for the building of *estancias* or colonial mansions. The expulsion of the Indians led to a sequence of battles, the most notorious of which occurred in the autumn of 1833 and resulted in the massacre of hundreds of natives.

In his private discourse, Darwin at times sardonically rejected the premise that de Rosas was pursuing a just war on the Pampas and that the natives were barbarians. Although he found the idea of the cattle industry migrating westward towards the Andes as a grand enterprise, at the same time he found the displacement of Native South Americans and their mistreatment at the hands of gauchos to be immoral. The brutality of the campaign knew no bounds: women were killed so as not to breed, and children were sold into slavery. Rival tribes were pitted against one another, and inter-tribal enmity was used to the colonists' advantage. Darwin acerbically criticized the "glorious campaign" and its inhumanity. In Argentina, Darwin's humanism — his sympathy for the natives — was genuine, though its expression was limited to personal discourse in the form of ironic invective.

Darwin's ethnological sensibilities were also evident during his visit to Argentina. He wrote descriptions of various tribes, recorded details of costume and behavior, wondered about religious beliefs, considered the interaction of physiology and environment with respect to various tribes, consistently considered how indigenous communities related to each other and spoke of their descent from original, northern nations. He was acutely aware of antiquarian artifacts and of what they could disclose about equestrianism, about tool and weapon technology, and about ethnic culture. On one occasion, he extrapolated from a fragmented arrowhead to perceptive conclusions about tribal origin and geography.

Adumbrating his use of census data in 1871/74 to demonstrate the adverse effects of colonialism on indigenes of the South Pacific was his study of population statistics in November 1834, while on the island of Chiloé, off the coast of Chile. These data were interesting for what they disclosed about ethnicities in the region and about the *mestizos* or mixed races. Ambivalence over the integrity of tribal residents, however, appears in the *Diary*; for example, Darwin expressed visceral contempt for mixed-race soldiers and for gauchos, while unconscionably taking part in a raid on a native burial site on 1 and 2 January 1834, while on Guanaco Island. Nonetheless, during his stay in Argentina and in its environs, Darwin was more humanist than racist and more ethnologist than vandal.

Darwin's experience in the South Pacific, autumn 1835 to spring 1836, is the focus of chapter 7. The private discourse reveals that his ethnological perceptions were maturing but that conventional assumptions remained stubborn. In the autumn of 1835, for example, he considered Tahitians to be noble savages, in the tradition of Rousseau, while FitzRoy attributed their intelligence, not to rich cultural tradition, but to the shape of their skulls and to their physiological characteristics. With his criteria of judgment and his definitions of terms lacking clarity, Darwin claimed that Australian natives were a few degrees higher on the scale of civilization than the Fuegians; but, on the scale of barbarism, a few degrees lower. While touring the Bay of Islands in New Zealand, he noticed the physical similarities of Maoris and Tahitians, but, without explaining why, declared the former to be savage; the latter, truly civilized.

The old ethnology, with its categorical and dialectical features, is intermingled in the *Diary*, with observations and insights having a modern air. Perhaps discussions with FitzRoy helped Darwin to see the superficiality of ethnic paradigms and that more could be learned by viewing the relationship between native people in terms of migration and heritage. Whereas Darwin conjectured that the Maoris occupied an intermediate position between Tahitians and Fuegians, FitzRoy asserted that they, along with the Fuegians, probably had descended from a single race in the northern hemisphere and had subsequently migrated to tropical regions. Despite FitzRoy's faith in phrenology, he, rather than Darwin, suggested that physical differences between natives could be explained, in part, by differences in climate, habit, and diet.

Gradually, as exceptions to arcane methods of classification accumulated, Darwin relied less on them and adopted a more relativistic approach to his experiences. Rather than to degrade the body-art, customs, music, and singing of native people, he began to appreciate these things as expressions of cultural identity — as what truly distinguished one society from another, irrespective of race. And, on a zoological level, he learned that varieties of human beings acted on each other in the same way as did different species of animals. The stronger race or ethnicity, whether Malayan, Ona (a northeastern tribe in Tierra el Fuego), or European, always dominated or extirpated the weaker; and this kind of competitiveness transpired between communities of the same ethnicity, as in the inter-tribal warfare of Maori against Maori, of Australian aborigines against Australian aborigines, and of both against white settlers. By 1836, though not absolutely free of intemperate statements, of racist assumptions, and of obsolete concepts, Darwin no longer doubted the humanity of native people, nor did he devaluate their lifestyles. Chapter 8 recapitulates the complex emergence of Darwin's Humboldtian ethnology, and this summary segues to Part III (chapters 9, 10, 11, and 12), which considers the interrelationship between the voyage experiences and the development of Darwin's evolutionary theory in the post-voyage years.

In chapter 9, I consider the persistence of contemporary race theory in

Darwin's ethnology. As late as January of 1862, four anthropological theories contravened his humanistic thought: (1) human beings of European extraction were believed to be superior to all other races, an assumption configured as a racial paradigm, with whites at the evolutionary pinnacle of the species and nonwhites on various levels of a downward-descending scale. A cluster of three theories attempted to account for native humanity: extant indigenes were (2) descendants of primitive man, (3) degenerative descendants of a higher extinct civilization, or (4) missing links having more in common with great apes than with Europeans. For many armchair anthropologists, these notions were logical possibilities. For others, they vindicated colonial policies, based on the assumption that native people either were commodities or were impediments to progress.

In the correspondence of Darwin and Charles Kingsley, this moral dilemma was the main topic of discussion, along with theories justifying inhumane practices. Darwin's moral conflict stemmed from the difficulty he had in accepting his kinship with uncivilized man, which is explicit in the letters. The logical path of inquiry opening up for him was to discover why, in terms of culture and civilization, European and native society differed from each other so significantly; and the corollary question was why each native culture was unique. He made great strides in the direction of liberal ethnology when, in conjunction with the Natural History Section of the British Association for the Advancement of Science, he helped to formulate an 89-point Questionnaire, designed for the use of travelers or settlers who were in contact with natives whose tribes were in danger of ethnic extinction. The aim of the Committee's work was to learn about endangered cultures and to preserve historical information. Though the Questionnaire proved to be of limited practical use, Darwin's contribution shows that he understood the value of insular cultures and that these societies were integral parts of the human family.

Chapter 10, "Natural Selection: The Bio-Ethical Dilemma," looks squarely at the immoral idea of native mankind's expendability, a contradiction to which both Alfred Russel Wallace and Darwin gave much thought. Wallace, notably in an essay of 1864, affirms the humanness of native people, their intelligence as being on par with that of civilized man, and he appreciates their ability to adapt to inhospitable worlds. Nevertheless, he differentiates between nonwhite and "Teutonic" intelligence: the latter allegedly being superior in quality and in potential to the former. Instead of clarifying in this context the crucial distinction between the two mentalities, Wallace left the contrast undefined and ambiguous. His ethical position in this essay is undercut further by the assertion that the moral and intellectual superiority of Europeans renders the displacement of "degraded races" inevitable.

At the center of Darwin's philosophy was the dialectical opposition between the ideas of the native person as an evolutionary creature and, differences notwithstanding, as a fellow human being. He expressed the moral dilemma of native expendability in the 1860s' correspondence with Kingsley; and, judging from his dialogue with Kingsley, he seems to have recognized native extinction to be an invariable consequence of natural selection. The Humboldtian aspect of his ethnology persisted, however, manifesting itself as conscientious distress over colonial policies in South America, in Africa, and in the Pacific. By the early 1870s, to find common ground between savage and civilized humanity, Darwin began working on gesture language and on the natural history of man.

In chapter 11 ("Transportation and Census") and chapter 12 ("*Descent* as Synthesis"), I discuss the ethical and the ethnological content of *Descent*, respectively. In chapter 11, I focus on Darwin's efforts to balance evolutionary zoology and its implications for humanity with a call for social amelioration in the Pacific colonies. The extirpation of natives, dramatized by the decline of the Tasmanians and of others, moved Darwin towards modern ethnology: it evoked not only relativism in regard to native character and culture, but also a humanitarian concern for their plight. Through census data, he proved that these populations were being decimated and would disappear unless ameliorative measures were taken. The use of census data in *Descent* indicates that, in his view, the destruction of indigenous humanity was neither inevitable nor acceptable.

*Descent* is not only a forum for ethical dissent, but, as I demonstrate in chapter 12, it was in its time a unifying, core-text in anthropology. I discuss *Descent*'s contribution to the development, and definition, of anthropology as a scientific discipline. Darwin efficiently grouped, in three zoological areas of concentration, an array of sub-disciplines, hitherto only loosely connected to each other. Thus, under the origin of man are included comparative anatomy, zoology, embryology, botany, geography, and geology; under man's physiological development, variation, modification, and inheritance; and under man's mental development, language, mentality, sociology, and religion. The relation of each discipline to man unifies the text, every aspect of the human character having originated in the processes of evolutionary biology. Impressively, Darwin cites 530 contemporary authorities and assimilates more than one-dozen discrete fields into what can best be described as *evolutionary* anthropology.

The coherence and comprehensiveness of Darwin's work on man in *Descent* appears to have contributed to the debate over what constitutes anthropology. His work satisfied the need for a coherent exposition of evolutionary anthropology. In this capacity, it can be viewed as a response to the 1866 presidential address to the British Association for the Advancement of Science. In the address, Wallace defined the discipline, inadequately, as an amalgamation of natural and of social sciences.

# Abbreviations

BD ......... Charles Darwin's *Beagle Diary*

CDC ........ *Correspondence of Charles Darwin*

CDN ........ *Charles Darwin's Notebooks*
  A: ........ Notebook A (1837–1839)
  B: ........ Notebook B (1837–1838)
  C: ........ Notebook C (1838)
  D: ........ Notebook D (1838)
  E: ........ Notebook E (1838–1839)
  GR: ...... Glen Roy Notebook (1838)
  M: ....... Notebook M (1838)
  MAC: ..... Abstract of Macculloch (1838)
  N: ........ Notebook N (1838–1839)
  OUN: ..... Old and Useless Notes (1838–1840)
  QE: ...... Questions and Experiments (1839–1844)
  RN: ...... Red Notebook (1836–1837)
  S: ........ Summer 1842
  T: ........ Torn Apart Notebook (1839–1841)
  ZEd: ...... Zoology Notes, Edinburgh Notebook (1837–1839)

DCP ........ *Darwin Correspondence Project*

DM ......... *The Descent of Man*

EHD ........ *English Historical Documents*

1803 ........ *Malthus ... 1803 Edition*

IT .......... *Wallace, Infinite Tropics*

JR (1839) .... *Journal and Remarks. The narrative of the Surveying voyages .... (1839)*, Volume III

*JR (1845)* .... *Journal of Researches. (1845)*

*L&L (1887)* ... *Life & Letters of Charles Darwin (1887)*

*L&L (1913)* ... *Life & Letters of Charles Darwin (1913)*

*L&R* ........ *Wallace, Letters and Reminiscences*

*Narr. 1* ....... *King, The Narrative of the Surveying Voyages...,* Volume I (1839)

*Narr. 2* ...... *FitzRoy, Narrative of the Surveying Voyages...,* Volume II (1839)

*OED* ........ *Oxford English Dictionary*

*OS* ......... *On the Origin of Species*

*PN* ........ *Humboldt. Personal Narrative*

*1798* ........ *Malthus. An Essay on the Principles of Population: 1798 Edition*

# Part I.
# Precursors and Analogues

## 1. Humboldt's Critical Ethnology

To have some understanding of the quality of Darwin's reaction to native people and of the moral and intellectual conflicts he at times experienced, I will begin the discussion with a review of Alexander von Humboldt's (1769–1859) anthropological opinions. A humanist and opponent of slavery, Humboldt's naturalistic writings had a profound effect on Darwin's thought; in fact, as Aaron Sachs has remarked, "The closest readers of Darwin realized that large parts of his theories were in fact derived directly from Humboldt, for evolution was essentially ecological" (240–41). Phillip S. Sloan is certainly correct in saying that, as a whole, "the *Diary* entries and stray comments in other materials reflect an abiding, Humboldtian concern with the place of human beings in nature" (34–5).

Precisely how the anthropological ideas of Humboldt and Darwin compare to one another is our present concern. Darwin's reflections on native mankind in the early 1830s, which appeared primarily in private writings, probably were not directly influenced by Humboldt's descriptions of mankind in his *Narrative*. However, considering the fact that for decades Darwin held Humboldt in the highest esteem, and since their humanistic feelings are similar to one another, understanding Humboldt's ethnological perspective will help us, comparatively, to appreciate the complexity of Darwin's thinking on man.

Darwin had access to a substantial library on board the *Beagle*. Of the one-hundred and twenty books in the collection, forty percent were travel narratives or works on voyages of discovery (Appendix IV, *CDC* I, 553–66). He read selectively, only six volumes showing evidence of use. Of the six, five were contemporary travelogues on South America, one related to Chile and two to Brazil. The Chilean text was Juan Ignacio Molina's (1740–1829) two-volume *Compendio de la historia geografica, natural y civil del reyno de Chile* (editions of 1794 and 1795), which Darwin read on board and, after 1836, consulted on several occasions. The book is mentioned on the inside cover of the *Red Notebook* (*CDN* 21) and refers to dogs in Tierra del Fuego (*C42e, CDN,* 251), to a book-list on species (*C27, CDN,* 318), and to fish near the Island of Juan Fernandez (*ZEd, CDN,* 481). A second book receiving Darwin's attention was the 1824 edition of Johann and Carl Friedrich Spix's, *Travels in Brazil in the years 1817–1820,* the second volume of which bears an inscription of Darwin's name, the approximate date (October 1832), and the immediate location (Buenos Aires) (*CDC* I 564). While Darwin was in Montevideo, Erasmus Darwin mailed him a copy of a third useful text, Christian Leopold von Buch's (1774–1853) *Travels in Norway and Lapland, during the years 1806, 1807, and 1808* (1813) (*CDC* I, 258). The influence of von Buch's *Travels* extends to the *Notebooks* and touches mainly on geological and botanical subjects (i.e., on Norwegian mountain ranges [*A97e, CDN,* 115], on stunted spruce-fir in the Lapland Alps [*C178, CDN,* 294–95], and on Norwegian gorse [*E153, CDN,* 442]).

Of these influential writings, Friedrich Wilhelm von Humboldt's *Personal Narrative of Travels to the Equinoctial Regions of America during the Years 1799–1804* is arguably the most important for Darwin, especially in terms of how native people and their cultures were treated. Darwin wrote in his *Autobiography* that during his last year at Cambridge University he had read Humboldt's *Narrative* with great care and that it, along with Sir John F. W. Herschel's *A Preliminary Discourse on the Study of Natural Philosophy* (1830), was immensely valuable (67–8).

Darwin greatly appreciated the vividness of Humboldt's naturalistic prose. In fact, while at Cambridge University, he found passages written on Tenerife so aesthetically impressive that he transcribed them, brought them along on a field excursion, and recited them to mineralogy professor John Stevens Henslow, to the Fellow and tutor Marmeduke Ramsay, and to Vicar Richard Dawes. In a letter to his father (dated 8 February–1 March 1832), written while in Brazil, Darwin recommended for study Humboldt's tropical descriptions of Tenerife (*CDC* I 204); and, in a correspondence of 18 May 1832, he reports to Henslow of his great admiration for Humboldt (*CDC* I 237).

Decades later, Darwin expressed enthusiasm for Humboldt's writings on native people. In *Descent* (1871), for instance, he alluded intermittently to the latter's views on the languages of lost tribes, on the cosmetic arts of savages, on the exaggeration of natural characters by man, and on the body painting of American Indians (189, 595, and 604–5, respectively). Humboldt's travels in the West Indian archipelago and in the northern regions of South and of Central America brought him into contact with slave states. His writings on this subject might have been influential in the development of Darwin's moral and geographical thought. If we read the *Narrative* patiently, we will discover, interspersed among naturalistic description and miscellaneous data, that Humboldt was sensitive to human suffering, held human beings of all races in high regard, and was able to balance this humane and moral perspective on native society with an analytical one that, without prejudgment, took into account the material and cultural traditions, as well as the ethnic character, of indigenes.

In the Introduction to the *Personal Narrative,* Humboldt remarks how challenging it had been for him to describe civilizations in the New World, for "the stupendous display of wild and gigantic nature" virtually overshadowed human activity. He was surprised to find that the vast northern regions of South America were so sparsely populated. Because of this low density, he surmises that the native inhabitants of the New World probably are a surviving remnant of "indigenous hordes" and, consequently, only partially civilized (*PN* 1.9 263–64).

Although the region has few ancient monuments and little of archeological interest, Humboldt was not discouraged. He prefers studying the physical constitution of the people and, in an ethnological spirit, decides to use "the analogy of language" as a means of categorizing tribes, of tracing "their distant migrations," and, most important, of communicating with native people. He believes, moreover, that the primordial unity of mankind could be revealed if one observes primitive societies closely, and especially "those family features by which the ancient unity of our species is manifested" (*PN* 1.9 264). Thus, Humboldt began his ethnological journey, not with artificial classifications of human groups emphasizing their diversity and separateness but, rather, with the conviction that the native inhabitants of the equinoctial region of America were simply a remote variety of mankind, having discernible heritages and physical characteristics.

The ways of the native, however, had been overshadowed by those of the European colonists. The "uniformity of manners and institutions" Humboldt finds among native tribes is of European origin and native traditions have been obscured. It was clear to him that the popular travel literature on the South Sea Islands, even in books by great explorers, such as Cook, Forster, and Banks, to varying degrees misrepresented native lifestyles. In the South Pacific, especially, popular works portray a kind of "half-civilization"—a world misleadingly believed to be "a striking mixture of perversity and meekness," in which native people are given a peculiar, idealized charm. To Humboldt, this was a distortion, and, in the light of his experiences in South America, he hoped to convey a more realistic image of how native people lived and of how centuries of European contact had affected them. Since many different tribes occupied the Americas eastward of the Andean Cordilleras, he decided to visit, and to comment on, those who had long held dominion over their neighbors. Established societies, he reasoned, would have greater resources of information and their traditions would be more readily accessible. Humboldt's aim was to identify natives in their own terms and to learn of their origins and migratory histories (*PN* 3.26 63–4).

Of initial interest to Humboldt were the natives' features and characters and specifically how the missions influenced their behavior. The Chaymas nation, more than fifteen thousand of whom inhabited the missions in the provinces of New Andalusia and of Barcelona, was the initial focus of attention (*PN* 1.9 269). Inhabitants of the Caripe Mountains, the Chaymas belonged to one of three principal tribes in the region, the others being the Caribs of the southern savannahs of New Barcelona, and the Cumanagotos who lived in the Mission of Piritu (*PN* 1.9 266). Despite their obvious affinities, each of the three tribes was a distinct nation (*PN* 1.9 267). Humboldt emphasized the uniqueness of each tribe, as well as their ethnic relatedness, so as to counteract the tendency in ecclesiastical and in secular histories to confuse them with each other, notably through the arbitrary ascription of geographical or of personal names to ethnic groups. A European historian might name a tribe after a chief or after a nearby river or mountain. This practice not only multiplied names but also obfuscated identities and cultures. As an ethno-historian, Humboldt had quite the opposite aim.

To differentiate one tribe from another, and then to identify common traits and customs, Humboldt began with physical features. Focusing on the Chaymas, he describes them as generally short in stature, thick-set in build, as having broad shoulders, flat chests, well-rounded limbs, and "dull brown ... tawny" skin color, their tone being unlike the coppery hue typical of natives in equinoctial America (*PN* 1 269–70). Their facial expressions were also recorded. Many of them look either "sedate or gloomy." Their foreheads were generally small; their eyes, black and deep-set, with the corners raised towards the temples, and very elongated, but, unlike the Mongol races, neither oblique nor small; the eyebrows were dark brown, thin, and slightly arched, the eyelids, edged with long lashes, were habitually cast downward, as if from lassitude. Though the Chaymas and most other South American natives resembled the Mongols in the form of the eyes, high cheek-bones, straight smooth hair, and absence of facial hair in men, Chaymas noses tended to be long, to have broad nostrils, and to have downwardly directed nasal openings, similar to those of Caucasians. Chaymas mouths were wide; the jaws were strong and broad, but the chins, short and round; and their teeth, blackened with juices and herbs, were originally white (*PN* 1 270).

Humboldt noticed how closely the Chaymas resembled one another. What he calls the Chaymas' "family look" makes it difficult to distinguish father from son, and it is easy to "confound one generation with another" (*PN* 1 271). He attributes this similarity either to the local situation of the tribes or to "their inferior degree of intellectual culture." To explain the first theory, he posits that, because there existed in the region a virtual "infinity of tribes," and because of tribal enmity, intermarriages between communities, even if the languages were similar, was uncommon; and this held true even if different tribes lived in close proximity to each other. In areas where there were fewer tribes, more inter-marriages occurred between the same families. Over time, this practice tended "to fix a certain similarity of conformation, an organic type, which may be called national" (*PN* 1 271). Under the mission system, this "organic type" has been preserved: that is, since each mission is formed by "a single horde," marriages are contracted "only between the inhabitants of the same hamlet" (*PN* 1 271). Blood ties uniting a whole nation were indicated in the language of a tribe, in those born in the mission, or in those who have been reduced and taught Spanish (*PN* 1 271).

Humboldt also spent time among the Carib Indians, whom he encountered while traveling northward on the Orinoco River. He knew that the Caribs had suffered greatly at the hands of the Europeans and had been nearly exterminated in regions stretching from the West Indians Islands to the coasts of Darien (*PN* 3 65). The Caribs along the Orinoco River presented a unique picture. Paddling in a group of canoes, they were entirely naked, armed with bows and arrows, and painted with a red plant pigment called *onoto*. Everything, from the boats to the furniture on board the canoes, was painted red. Despite the infernal veneer, Humboldt was able to describe their physique and stature and attempted to compare the Caribs to other natives. Overall, they appeared both gloomy and animated. Humboldt highlighted several distinguishing features. One was their rounded foreheads which, he recalled, were dissimilar from West Indian Carib skulls that he had seen in European collections. As far as their habits were concerned, they lacked personal hygiene. Even more disturbing was their bizarre practice of tying ligatures on the extremities of their children, binding them to the point of restricting circulation. One disturbing example of the importance they attach to certain bodily disfigurations is how mothers re-shaped their children's leg calves in this manner, as dictated by "the fashion of the country." Failure to do so would have made the mother appear culpably indifferent to her children (*PN* 2 147).

Overall, Humboldt's experiences with Indians along the Orinoco River raised doubts about the theory that savage society reflected the primitive beginnings of modern civilization and that the natives were noble savages. He could see neither the rudiments of modern civilization nor the earliest expressions of modern intelligence, in natives who appeared "dull" and "inanimate" (*PN* 2 166). Nor did "Human nature," in this region, manifest "those features of artless simplicity," depicted in popular literature. Humboldt occasionally uses strong language: for example, the savage of the Orinoco, like that of the Mississippi, is "hideous." But, more important than his language was his belief that natives such as these were neither degenerates of a higher civilization nor "the feeble remains of nations who, after having been long dispersed in the forests, were re-plunged into barbarism" (*PN* 2 166). Baseless assumptions such as these neither accounted for their present state of mind and body nor illuminated their migratory history.

Humboldt's purpose in writing about native people was not only to debunk popular theories, but also to elucidate the intellectual pre-conditions for a viable civilization. Under colonial rule, he understood that civilization came with a price: a native would have to have surrendered his original independence and part of his "natural rights" to be part of a Spanish or Portuguese community. If he willingly complies, but is not "compensated by the benefits of civilization," the savage invariably regresses to life in the wilderness. This regression subverted missionary work along the Orinoco River. Because the natives did not enjoy the fruit of their labor fully, Christian establishments on the Orinoco never thrived; but the Indians who left missionary settlements for the wilderness lost the opportunity of a Western education and the chance to develop their intellectual faculties (*PN* 2 175–76). Even more important, in his judgment, was moral formation. Since "The human understanding" can not be annihilated, savages could genuinely benefit from moral education, an influence far superior in its ameliorative effects than constraint or coercion (*PN* 2 176). Regression to an uncivilized lifestyle was, obviously, a sad event.

Warfare and cannibalism, two of the most disagreeable activities of the natives, occurred because they had an insular view of the human species, one through which only the immediate family and tribe were seen as kindred, whereas all others were seen as antagonists or as victims. What they lacked, therefore, was a deeper understanding of the kinship of human beings. Without this deeper understanding, they would not be able to appreciate the duties of "humanity." Only civilization, in Humboldt's judgment, can make man "feel the unity of the human race," the ties of "consanguinity" linking one human being to another, despite differences in language and in manners (*PN*

2 336). Ironically, most of the Europeans who made inroads into indigenous society, Humboldt believed, did not abide by this noble truth.

Humboldt was also interested in human geography. At the beginning of the Spanish and Portuguese conquests of the New World in the sixteenth century, native societies were consolidated primarily on the ridge of the Cordilleras of the Andes, on the Western coast of the continent, while wandering hordes inhabited the forests, the plains, and the eastwardly extending savannahs. To describe the diffusion of tribes, and to account for their differences of language, of manners, and of geography, he evokes the image of a maritime disaster, the tribes of the region having been "scattered like the remnants of a vast wreck" (*PN* 1–9 263). After journeying to Cumaná and to New Barcelona, he emphasized that, despite the diffusion of tribes in the New Continent, every effort should be made to preserve the cultural heritages of indigenous people. To this end, he compiled demographic and ethnological data on several indigenous tribes, comprising nearly 60,000 people, the members of which lived independently in the region or in the missionary provinces (*PN* 1.9 264).

Along with this appreciation for human geography, Humboldt also tried to banish misconceptions about indigenous people, and he began by redefining stereotypical terms. He regrets, for instance, having to use the term "savage" to distinguish between "free" natives who lived independently of the missions and "reduced" Indians, those living in missionary communities. The misconception is that the "free" Indians are uncultured primitives. This, however, was a simplification and, in some cases, completely erroneous. Some forest tribes, he observed, were peacefully united in villages and bore allegiance to chiefs. Societies such as these did not necessarily live as hunters and gatherers but were members of agricultural communities, incipient perhaps, but self-subsistent. They produced plantain-trees, cassava, and cotton on extensive tracts of ground, and wove cotton hammocks (*PN* 1.9 264–65). These resourceful communities were hardly more barbarous than the Indians who inhabited the missions. The problem was that Europeans erroneously believed that "free" natives, those not yet reduced to subjugation, were by definition unstable and nomadic. In truth, long before the arrival of the Europeans, agriculture and fishing had been practiced on the continent. One historian points out that, "before 5000 B.C. people began to form more settled communities along the coasts of Chile and Peru, where ... they won a good living from the produce of the sea" (Hawkes 45). Between the Orinoco and Amazon Rivers, where missionaries had never set foot, forest lands had long been cleared for agriculture. So Humboldt's opinion on the matter had a firm historical basis.

It would be inaccurate to consider independent Indians, by virtue of their lifestyle, as being necessarily pagan and savage (*PN* 1.9 265). In reality, "reduced" Indians were not necessarily devout Christians, nor were the independent natives necessarily idolatrous. What they had in common, however, was a preoccupation with the wants of the moment. In fact, both groups "betray a marked indifference for religious sentiments, and a secret tendency to the worship of nature and her powers," a form of worship, Humboldt points out, that prevails in the "infancy of nations," and that recognizes grottoes, valleys, and woods as sacred places (*PN* 1.9 265).

Another fallacy Humboldt rectified was that the arrival of Europeans inevitably diminished native populations. This was not absolutely true. In both North and South America, more than six-million natives lived. And even though many tribes and languages had become extinct while others had merged together, since the time of Columbus, wherever Europeans have penetrated the New World, indigenous populations had increased in number, a surprising conclusion, indeed. To support his point about population, he points to the flourishing populations of two Carib Indian villages in the mission provinces of Piritu and of Carony, which contained more families than four or five villages along the Orinoco. Unlike North American Indians, such as those along the Missouri River who required vast stretches of country for hunting, the savages of the torrid zone, such as those of Spanish Guiana, cultivated plantain and cassava and therefore needed much less ground to supply themselves with food (*PN* 1.9 265). In addition, unlike the North America natives, those of South America did not dread the approach of the whites. The reason why North American tribes feared white incursion is because they were being driven "behind the Allegheny mountains, the Ohio, and the Mississippi" (*PN* 1.9 266), that is, away from their hunting grounds and from their means of subsistence. For this very reason, European colonialism was having an immediate and damaging effect on native tribes in Mexico and in the United States.

For those who criticized the missions as an oppressive force, Humboldt offered an interesting historical explanation, imputing blame mainly to secular rather than to ecclesiastical interests. In South America, since the religious orders had established their missions between the settlements of the colonists and the territory of the Indians, they became, in effect, intermediate states. Although the missionaries encroached on the territory and liberty of the natives, their work and the communities that they founded actually tended to increase indigenous populations and to improve the quality of life. The inexorable pressure of European culture and of civilization, however, eventually disrupted Indian life, both in independent communities and under the governance of the Church; once the missionaries established themselves among the natives, secular European interests followed, invading these settlements. As a result, a protracted struggle between Church and State ensued. Nations vied with one another for colonial territory. Secular powers removed *reduced* Indians from the missions to use as laborers and slaves. The missions eventually were transformed into Spanish villages, and indigenous languages disappeared. From the eastern coast to the interior of the continent, therefore, the "progress of civilization" moved forward slowly and at the expense of indigenous cultures (*PN* 1.9 266).

A fourth misconception Humboldt addressed was that indigenes could be cloaked in civilization and be changed inexorably from savages into urbane citizens. This idea was naïve, he reasoned, for the character and traditions of a people, though suppressible, were not easily eradicated. Most of the Indian tribes of the Orinoco region, for example, exhibit the "strangest contrasts" in manners and behavior. To exemplify this uniqueness, Humboldt referred specifically to a relatively stable Indian society under the auspices of a Spanish mission. No longer subject to the wilderness, they cultivated the ground, made pottery, and wove hammocks and cotton cloth. But some of them practiced an "inhuman" custom. As cannibals, they preyed on newly arrived tribes, murdering some, dismembering bodies, and storing the parts for food. Humboldt expressed horror at this paradox in native behavior (*PN* 2.23 338–39). Although he recognized that barbaric practices and customs were sometimes difficult to expunge, he had reason to believe that practices such as cannibalism could be proscribed eventually; their persistence he blamed on tribal despotism and on foreign conquest (*PN* 3.27 102–03).

Although Humboldt believed that the missions benefited the natives considerably, he was deeply disturbed by the failure of the Church to curtail slavery. On the journey from Santa Cruz to Orotava, he is dismayed over the contradiction that Christianity, which professes the liberty of mankind, "served afterwards as a pretext to the cupidity of Europeans" (*PN* 1 120). The allusion is to the mandate that a person not baptized could justifiably be enslaved. In New Andalusia, the trade in all of its inhumanity was being inflicted on Indians, as well as on Africans. A perverted commercial system had arisen, pitting one tribe against another. Because of slavery, wars broke out frequently between native tribes who profited from the slave market, capturing prisoners and selling them as slaves to the European colonials. Whereas a general "improvement of manners" should have been the natural consequence of the Enlightenment — what Humboldt eloquently calls a "noble awakening of the mind" (*PN* 1 187) — in distant colonies the European powers, driven by cupidity and power, had actually established centers of barbaric civilization. The cycle of inhumanity that was set into motion had begun with Spanish colonial enslavement. Not only had enslavement bred rebellion, and rebellion, greater repression, but the system was often justified in racist terms. In the aftermath of an unsuccessful independence movement in Caracas, Venezuela, one that agitated slave populations in nearby villages, a missionary insisted that the slave trade was clearly justified, that blacks were innately wicked, and that, with the possibility of salvation in sight, they actually benefited from "their state of slavery among the Christians" (*PN* 1 254).

In Guatemala, in upper Peru, and in Venezuela, slave laborers were needed in great numbers for the cultivation of sugar, indigo, and cotton. But the consequences of this policy had proven "fatal to the old and the new world" (*PN* 3 101). The system dehumanized both the victim and the victimizer. In countries where slavery exists, the mind becomes familiarized with suffering, and "that instinct of pity which characterizes and ennobles our nature is blunted" (*PN* 3 182). To rationalize the practice, advocates of plantation commerce often compared slave cultures in different countries to one another, arguing that some plantations offered blacks a better lifestyle than what they had known in Africa. Humboldt was saddened to hear Christian nations debating the merits of the system in terms of which country, over the last three centuries, had caused the fewest blacks to perish.

Although not much could be said in defense of slavery in the American South, Humboldt acknowledged that some plantation systems were worse than others and that, in these establishments and communities, there were levels of human suffering. In other words, a slave who has a hut and a family, and who is not being worked to death, is better off than one who was being "purchased as if he formed part of a flock" (*PN* 3 200). More a businessman than a moralist, the slave owner considers the preservation of families in captivity as economically and socially beneficial: "The greater the number of slaves established with their families in dwellings which they believe to be their own property, the more rapidly will their numbers increase" (*PN* 3 200). Ironically, making life *less* arduous on plantations actually increased the labor force and diminished slave importation (*PN* 3 201).

Although Humboldt superficially distinguished between forms of slave culture, he neither questioned its overall moral indefensibility nor endorsed the arguments of its defenders; rather, he criticizes writers who try to "veil barbarous institutions" in ingenious language, and who invent preposterous expressions, such as "Negro peasants of the West Indies, black vassalage, and patriarchal protection," to assuage moral indignation. Humboldt saw through their rhetorical attempts to mask the truth. The apologists, in his estimation, are culpable in their use of illusory comparisons and of "captious sophisms" to exculpate the suffering of the slaves. The great abolitionist Thomas Clarkson made this very same point incisively in his 1789 dissertation, *An Essay on the Slavery and Commerce of the Human Species*. It was unconscionable, he asserts, to compare the state of colonial slavery to European peasantry; as two dissimilar lifestyles, each presented unique hardships, but the peasant was better off than the slave. The peasant, unlike the slave, lived in his own country and had not been torn from his homeland, away from family and friends. Unlike the black slave, the white peasant, though materially poor, was free, as were his children. Moreover, white peasants were not sold like beasts of burden, as were slaves, nor was a peasant as fearful of corporeal punishment as was the slave at the hands of an enslaver. The African, in short, possessed none of the advantages of the peasantry, and the defenders of slavery refused to acknowledge this truth (Part III ix).

To a degree, Humboldt's assessment of slavery as "the greatest evil that afflicts human nature" is compatible with his socio-historical observation that, in this vast system, there are degrees of suffering and levels of inhumanity, the plight of a sugar plantation slave, for example, being worse than that of one who worked for a rich family in Havana or in Kingston (*PN* 3 224). Though not all slave societies were the same, the focus of an abolitionist's attention, he cautioned, should not be blurred by subtle distinctions. The moral depravity of slavery could not be rationalized away. The abolition of the trade, especially in the archipelago of the West Indies, had to begin with a moral awakening — with the prohibition of activities that treated human beings as livestock; two of the most egregious practices were to separate infants from their parents and to sell them to the highest bidder and to brand slaves with hot irons or to clip ears so as to render "these human cattle" easily recognizable (*PN* 3 226).

A moral reawakening, in Humboldt's terms, meant that blacks and Indians had to be recognized as human beings, possessing inalienable rights. On the basis of this moral truism, laws could be enacted, such as one granting liberty to a slave who had served for fifteen years and to every black woman who had reared four or five children; setting slaves free on the condition that they work a specific number of days for the profit of the plantation; giving the slaves a portion of the net produce, and allocating a budget of the public funds to ransom slaves and to improve their condition (*PN* 3 326).

Humboldt's attitude towards the natives he encountered during his exploration of South America was not completely free of European ideas about the inherent primitivism and inferiority of indigenous people. But he did not let received opinions inhibit his humanitarianism, which manifested itself in different ways. One obvious manifestation of his humanitarianism was that he neither dehumanized nor depersonalized aborigines. Without a sketchbook, he graphically rendered their physiques and features in clear language and did so without distortion. He passed no judgment on their way of life, recording what he saw, to the best of his ability. Observations of social life, though sketchy, were always intended to find commonality between tribes and to learn something about local history. No sentimentalist, he expressed distaste for certain native customs and behaviors but tried to be objective in his commentary. His relativism in regard to life in the missions is a case in point: on the one hand, indigenes benefited from the modicum of civilization they received, but they did so, in the long run, at the expense of language, of culture, and of tradition. The mission's good works were compromised by national interests that led to the exploitation of pacified tribes and to the founding of slave-driven agriculture. Two strong feelings inform Humboldt's ethnography: one was compassion for the natives victimized by colonialism; the other was trenchant criticism of secular interests that, in civilizing regions like the Orinoco, hypocritically betrayed their own moral and religious codes.

Although Darwin's direct indebtedness to Humboldt's ethnology is difficult to establish with any certainty, we know that Darwin read the *Personal Narrative* carefully and appreciated its analytical style and panoramic scope. We shall find that Humboldt's attitude towards indigenous people, unlike Darwin's, was not conditioned by pseudo-scientific assumptions, nor did he describe native people disdainfully. Instead, in the *Personal Narrative*, Humboldt was a patient and meticulous observer who did not judge the value of foreign cultures against European standards and, most importantly, who did not seek to categorize the physical characteristics and behavior of natives according to extrinsic standards. To develop a similar ethnological method, Darwin had first to dispense with pre-conceptions, with pre-judgments, and with artificial standards about humanity.

# 2. Malthus' Theological Demography

On the questions of originality, of ethics, and of influence, Malthus' *Essay on the Principle of Population* (1798, 1803) is a comparative resource for the understanding of Darwin's ethnology and for Wallace's evolutionary thought. The works of Malthus and Darwin relate to each other on these bases, and I would like to consider each of them successively.

Neither Malthus nor Darwin was the originator of the respective theory for which each is best known. The ideas of a struggle for existence and of checks on population growth antedated Malthus' work by centuries, and variants of these ideas can be found in the writings of Hobbes, of Herder, of de Candolle, and others, although, as Ernst Mayr points out, no one stressed the intensity of these ideas more than Malthus (192). Three precursors illustrate the population-subsistence ratio's long history. In *On the Social Contract* (1762), Rousseau states it simply: "the ratio is ... that the land [must] suffice to maintain the inhabitants, and there are many inhabitants as the land can feed" (114). Godwin, in the 1793 *Enquiry*, suspects that "the number of inhabitants in a country will perhaps never be found to increase beyond the facility of subsistence" (VIII 768). And, in 1776, Adam Smith, whom Malthus acknowledged to be a direct source for his theorizing (*1798* 69), pointed to the harsh effects, felt especially by the destitute, of an imbalance between population and resources: "Every species of animals naturally multiplies in proportion to the means of subsistence, and no species can ever multiply beyond it. But in civilized society it is only among the inferior ranks of people that the scantiness of subsistence can set limits to the further multiplication of the human species; and it can do so in no other way than by destroying a great part of the children which their fruitful marriages produce" (*Wealth of Nations* 182).

The theory of natural selection owed a debt to pre–Darwinian contributors, and the question of Darwin's priority in this regard has been debated

(Ghiselin 46–48; Mayr 498–501). Two immediate precursors, the British physician, William Charles Wells (1757–1817) and the Scottish botanist, Patrick Matthew (1790–1874), are often overlooked for their groundbreaking work on selection — although Darwin acknowledged his indebtedness to them and, on several occasions (e.g., on 12 May 1871), corresponded with Matthew (*DCP* Letter 7576). Darwin admitted, in a letter to Charles Lyell of 10 April 1860, that Matthew had adumbrated the theory but that the latter's understanding of it, in Darwin's opinion, was undeveloped (*DCP* Letter 2754). Wells had published a relevant essay, in 1818, which includes commentary on variations of human pigment and on how this phenomenon reflects variants of a species adapt to local climate (Mayr 498). Matthew, who wrote about the concept in his book, *On Naval Timber and Arboriculture* (1831) and in an 1860 essay in the *Gardiner's Chronicle*, anticipated Darwin's idea (Eiseley 125–26; Mayr 498–500).

Both Darwin and Malthus were engaged in an ethical debate and struggled to reconcile two opposing principles. For Malthus, the conflict involved demography and theology: to avoid extinction, human populations are periodically reduced, by the workings of natural laws, if numbers surpassed the level of subsistence. This proposition, however, conflicted with the orthodox tenet that God, Who is benevolent and omnipotent, had established natural mechanisms to maintain the viability of the human race; but this dogma did not extend to isolated minorities who succumbed to war, disease, famine, and natural catastrophe — or to what he called "positive checks." In Darwin's case, the conflict involved ethics and biology: human beings are inherently dignified and possess inviolable, natural rights; but they compete with and dominate one another in the struggle for existence, resulting in the exploitation of fellow men and the extirpation of human groups.

On the development of evolutionary thought, both Darwin and Wallace ascribed to Malthusian theory a catalyzing influence, although the exact nature of this influence is not perfectly clear. Darwin records how impressed he was by Malthus' notion that population doubles very twenty-five years and progresses geometrically (*1803* 8; *D*135, *CDN*, 375; and Mayr 478). Other Malthusian ideas from which Darwin profited were how disease, vice, and moral restraint affected population (*N*10–11, *OUN* 29, *CDN*, 565–66, 609, respectively).

Wallace cites *The Essay* as the first work that he had ever read dealing with the problems of "philosophical biology," its main principles providing him with "the long-sought clue to the effective agent in the evolution of organic species" (*My Life*, 123–24). While on the Island of Gilolo (February 1858), he recalled having read the 1826 edition (its content substantially unchanged from 1803), fourteen years earlier while he was at the Leicester Library (*My Life*, 189). Malthus' explanation of population checks, such as disease, accident, war, and famine, in Wallace's view, appeared to account for the lower populations commonly found in uncivilized regions. Since factors responsible for depopulation affected animals and human beings alike, Wallace realized that most animal species bred faster than did human beings, but that, under the best conditions, few animal offspring reached maturity, and that the mortality rate among animals was exceptionally high, especially if a population exceeded resources.

Wallace also learned from Malthus that population checks, however amoral and brutal, were necessary to the viability of a species; otherwise, unchecked overpopulation could lead to extinction. Wallace posed a fundamental question: "Why do some die and some live?" He deduced that, "on the whole the *best fitted live*." If logically extended, this argument means that only the healthiest resisted disease, only the strongest, swiftest, or stealthiest evaded predators or succeeded as such; or, given prevailing conditions, it was more advantageous to be small than large, and so on. And, if the best adapted survived, the unavoidable conclusion was that, "this self-acting process [i.e., natural selection] would necessarily improve the race because in every generation the inferior would inevitably be killed off and the superior would remain — that is, the fittest would survive" (*My Life* 190).

At a 1908 meeting of the Linnaean Society, Wallace recalled that both he and Darwin had compiled personal observations and reflections relating to the survival of the fittest, and they were enlightened by Malthus' idea of "positive checks," the operations of natural laws to reduce population drastically (*My Life* 190). The progeny of the rugged survivors, they both realized, would propagate and pass on heritable traits conferring biological advantages. Darwin reflected on this insight in well-known notebook entries of 28 September 1838 (*D*134–135, *CDN*, 374–75). Wallace was particularly impressed by Malthus' suggestion that positive checks, disease, accident, war, and famine, were directly responsible for suppressing the population of "savage races" to a much lower level than what is found among civilized peoples (*My Life* 190).

It is not surprising to find that the Rev. Malthus' demography was developed within a theological framework and that, from the 1798 to the 1803 editions, the emphasis shifted from natural to moral theology. Even though, like Darwin, he was concerned with biological ideas, such as survival, competition, adaptation, and procreation, his standpoint was essentially theological.

In the first edition of the *Essay* (1798), Malthus postulated that the two laws of human nature — the necessity of food and the sexual drive — were constant, a proposition with which few would argue. But when he stated that an immediate act of Divine power could suspend them, it becomes clear that *1798* is essentially a theological treatise: God as the First Cause arranged the universe, and the laws of nature that He had established, "for the advantage of his creatures," were fixed and unchanging (*1798* 70–1). One of these laws holds that "the power of population is indefinitely greater than the power in the earth to produce subsistence for man" (*1798* 71). The rate of popular increase, he calculated as being in a geometrical ratio, whereas subsistence increased only in an arithmetical ratio.

Disaster was certain if the slowly increasing capacity of subsistence and the faster rate of procreation were not in relative equilibrium (*1798* 71). Processes built into the natural laws of population, as a consequence of circumstances or by necessity, inevitably adjusted the ratio back into equilibrium; but, for disadvantaged, pre-agricultural communities, the cost in human suffering incurred by the adjustment could be considerable.

The theological problem implicit in *1798*, then, was that the "checks" reputedly balancing population and subsistence, and perennially devastating uncivilized people, were the divinely instituted consequences of fixed laws. For native populations, therefore, the divine order appeared to be deterministic and exclusionary. Malthus had to find a way out of this moral dilemma because it impugned the divine character: native humanity appeared expendable. And since the natural order was a reflection of God's Will, then the conclusion was that a segment of the human race had, for some historical, geographical, or biological reason, been selected, not for redemption, but for unceasing toil.

To solve this theological problem, Malthus invoked the doctrine of the free will. He had already proposed, in *1798*, that conscientious decisions on reproduction, involving social, familial, and economic factors, and the exercise of moral restraint precluding the effects of vice, could influence population growth and maintain safe levels of subsistence (*1798* 79). So the cause of human misery in uncivilized regions was largely an inability to apply the conscience to everyday life. Among uncivilized people, checks such as famine, war, disease, and unusual customs, caused widespread loss of life, scattered settlements, and left itinerants dependent on local resources; hence, hunting, gathering, and scavenging were for many the norm. This recurrent instability, as a kind of self-regulative process, in undeveloped locales had the ironic, dual effect of reducing the population to the level of subsistence and of ensuring the survival of indigenous societies.

Other factors made uncivilized life miserable. Competition between human groups threatened survival, as tribes enslaved or exterminated each other, as colonists invaded native lands, and as environmental factors intensified the uncertainties of life. The perpetual struggle for food and for territory, necessitated by population growth, historically had resulted in "the prodigious waste of human life," especially in savage countries (*1798* 84). As Malthus formulated it, however, the strife experienced by aboriginal societies was imputed to man and not to God.

In the concluding chapters of *1798*, Malthus reiterates the theological problem at hand. Human suffering, due to overpopulation, is consistent "with the various phenomena of observable nature" and, at the same time, "consonant to our ideas of the power, goodness, and foreknowledge of the Deity" (*1798* 200). Malthus' alternative was to approach demography as a natural theologian. He proposed that, in order to discern the work of God in nature, one must reason "from nature up to nature's God and not presume to reason from God to nature" (*1798* 200–01). The "ways of Providence" can only be known in this way, for the "book of nature" reveals "God as he is." To the discerning naturalist, animate life amounts to "a constant succession of sentient beings, rising apparently from so many specks of matter, going through a long and sometimes painful process in this world, but many of them attaining, ere the termination of it, such high qualities and powers as seem to indicate their *fitness* for some superior state" (*1798* 201; italics added).

Malthus conjectures that God may have deemed organic evolution necessary, in order "to form beings with those exalted qualities of mind which will *fit* them for his high purposes" (italics added). If we were to apply this logic to people in undeveloped regions in their unremitting struggles, then their disadvantages and vulnerability could be seen as part of God's foreordained plan. And if the rigors that nature imposes on man were divinely preordained for his spiritual and material formation, those who were unfit had no place in the design, unless they were civilized and converted to Christianity.

For Malthus, the relationship between subsistence and dutiful labor was a supernatural mandate: "The Supreme Being has ordained that the earth shall not produce good[s] in great quantities till much preparatory labor and ingenuity has been exercised upon its surface." Ascribing germination directly to God, since no better explanation of how the plant or tree arose from the seed was then available (*1798* 204), he asserts that, for the Supreme Creator, it was not necessary for life to have growth stages, for the plant to begin as a seed, or for the land to be tilled. Nor did God rely on man to plow, to clear ground, and to sow, as He could, through fiat, produce the harvest without human mediation. These labors, however, are required of mankind and are "necessary to the enjoyment of the blessings of life, in order to rouse man into action, and form his mind to reason" (*1798* 204). Thus, man's cooperation with God's Will, as discernible in nature, will contribute to its fulfillment and to realization of the Providential design: to cultivate the earth and to fulfill the ordinance that "population should increase much faster than food" (*1798* 205). Hunger induced labor, stimulated the intelligence, promoted invention, and established husbandry, so, in this way, man could maintain himself and supply the needs of a growing population.

According to Malthus, God has the power to create by fiat. But had He chosen to manifest Himself in such extraordinary or inconstant ways, this would have stunted human intelligence because man would not have been driven to work for his bread. A "fatal torpor" would undoubtedly have ensued, a malaise that would have threatened the species with extinction. Malthus has no doubt that man's achievements are the results of divine intervention: "The constancy of the laws of nature is the foundation of the industry and foresight of the husbandman, the indefatigable ingenuity of the artificer, the skillful researches of the physician and anatomist, and the watchful observation and patient investigation of the natural philosopher." To the constancy of God's laws in material and human nature, therefore, is owed "all the greatest and noblest efforts of the intellect," and in "the immortal mind of a Newton," we find its greatest achievement (*1798* 205).

Although the population-subsistence ratio was of divine origin and operated for the betterment of man, not every society benefited from it equally, as Malthus knew full well. Historically, pre-agricultural societies, with the exception perhaps of certain Polynesian communities, were thwarted from applying their intelligence to the acquisition of natural resources; so they suffered acutely if population exceeded the means of subsistence (*1798* 206). On the other hand, in civilized or more advantaged nations, even if war, disease, or natural calamity were to thin out a population drastically, replenishment was more likely (*1798* 206). In Malthus' historical view, the same outcome was not guaranteed for insular communities in remote corners of the world. He had no remedy for their predicament, beyond the extraordinary exercise of the free will as a way of extricating themselves from the forces of nature and of man.

I find no evidence that Darwin had read *1798*, but, had he done so, it is likely he would have agreed with the proposition that nature's diversity and operations provide a "wide and extensive ... field for investigation and research," and with Malthus' recognition that man's limited intelligence cannot hope to grasp "the mighty incomprehensible power of the Creator" (*1798* 212). The naturalist, in Malthus' opinion, should begin with the understanding, stated as a doctrine of faith in natural theology, that an imperfect Creation is the medium of revelation, inasmuch as both reason and experience reveal that all aspects of nature are "adapted to further the high purpose of creation and to produce the greatest possible quantity of good" (*1798* 212). Man will never cease to inquire into "the nature and structure of the mind," into "the affections and essences of all substances," and into "the mode in which the Supreme Being operates in the works of the creation, and the whole plan and scheme of the Universe" (*1798* 213). In this sense, scientific research and revelation were, for Malthus, compatible with one another. Unlike Darwin who would write about the difficulties he experienced in trying to accept the literal truth of certain Scriptural passages (*Autobiography* 85–6), Malthus, in *1798*, had "never considered the doubts and difficulties that involve some parts of the sacred writings as any argument against their divine original" (*1798* 213).

In 1803, when Malthus incorporated social sciences more heavily into the *1798* theodicy, the character of the *Essay* changed in several notable ways. Moral theology, ethics, demography, economy, sociology, and political science were, in the second edition, accorded equal emphasis, while the theological principles of *1798* became implicit. A rigid design argument, it seems, could not adequately address the complexities of population dynamics and of human behavior. Malthus needed quantitative evidence to ground his theology, so in 1799 he collected information on populations, as he traveled from Hamburg and Sweden, to Norway, Finland, and Russia. In 1802, he took advantage of the Peace of Amiens to visit France and Switzerland, and, equipped with quantitative information, he revised *1798*. In June 1803, the new edition appeared (Flew, Intro., *1798* 12).

*1803* went through four editions (1806, 1807, 1817, and 1826), and there were no major redactions over this period. The differences between 1798 and 1803, however, were substantial: *1798* was an octavo volume of 396 pages or 55,000 words, whereas *1803* became a quarto of 610 pages or 200,000 (Flew, Intro., *1798* 13). In *1803*, Malthus sought a more perspicuous balance between demography and theology, as he emphasized the idea, initially broached in *1798*, that moral culpability rested with man in the enactment of "preventive checks,."

The dangers of overpopulation cannot be underestimated. Malthus reiterates the theory, in *1803*, that a number of causes (e.g., slavery, famine, disease, war, and other factors) checked population overgrowth. If naturally unchecked, however, population doubled every twenty-five years, increasing in geometrical ratio (i.e., 1, 2, 4, 8, 16, 32, 64, 128, 256, and so on) (*1803* 8): thus, "considering the present average state of the earth, the means of subsistence, under circumstances the most favorable to human industry, could not possibly be made to increase faster than in an arithmetical ratio [i.e., 1, 2, 3, 4, 5, 6, 7, 8, 9]." According to these figures, by the ninth year of unchecked population growth, a disastrous food shortage exceeding 28% would generally be expected. Malthus also restates that the "ultimate check to population appears to be a want of food, arising necessarily from the different ratios according to which population and food increase" (*1803* 12). Without the kind of checks described above, in just fifty years a population could expect disaster and a lessening of its numbers (*1803* 10–11).

Two kinds of checks to population — the preventive and the positive, respectively — are at work in every society, reducing population numbers to "the level of the means of subsistence" (*1803* 12). Preventive checks were enacted by rational thought and conscience. As for the positive checks to population, Malthus attributes some of them exclusively to "the laws of nature," identifying occurrences such as famine and disease as sources of extreme distress; some positive checks, such as war, were attributable essentially to human behavior (*1803* 14). Population levels, he was convinced, could be managed through "moral restraint, vice, and misery."

The moral question, initially broached in *1798*, resurfaces at this juncture in *1803*: in light of the effects these checks and balances have on vulnerable societies, how can a benevolent God be responsible for, or tolerant of, the necessary evils of war, pestilence, famine and geographical disaster? Why, in other words, would God make man prolific but threaten him with starvation for being so? Malthus understood that one of the principal reasons preventing acceptance of the idea of population's tendency to increase beyond the means of subsistence, was the difficulty in accepting the contradiction that God would, through natural laws, bring human beings into existence, yet by the very same laws expose them to starvation (*1803* 160).

The solution, in *1803* (as it was in *1798*), was to transfer moral culpability from God to mankind: man is supernaturally endowed with the procreative impulse, as well as with the potential for self-conscious, rational self-control. To overpopulate, therefore, is to violate divinely established law; therefore, one cannot impute the effects of overpopulation to God, for that would mischaracterize Him as being morally flawed or inconsistent.

Moral restraint, strict obedience to which was called for by "the light of nature and reason" and sanctioned by revelation, was the God-given means to avoid the checks and balances of nature. In other words, man had the capacity to regulate the geometrical increase of population. The right exercise of the free will avoids disaster and permits man to cooperate with, and to share in, God's plenitude (*1803* 160). Not to constrain one's passions "within the bounds of reason" ultimately leads to "misery"— a truism resonating throughout Scriptures, and, in Malthus' lexicon, a word connoting everything from epidemics to war. According to his religious demography, no one has the right to breach "the justice of the Deity," because His general laws make the virtue of conscientious self-restraint necessary; and the punishments resulting from vice, warranted.

Ultimately, the "Creator" wishes to deter human beings from the commission of vice through painful lessons and to lead mankind to virtuous living by the happiness it brings; and this objective is "worthy of a benevolent Creator" (*1803* 167). Thus, the God who works through nature is described as a kind but "severe instructor," admonishing man for his errors, sometimes severely, through "some physical or moral evil" (*1803* 181). To know the laws of nature, he proverbially states, is to know the laws of God (*1803* 202). Moral theology becomes, for Malthus, the only way for savage man to free himself from servitude to natural law.

Until the state of emancipation is achieved, and its envisaged prosperity realized, aboriginal people, as hunters and gatherers, will have barely sufficient resources. Among Native American tribes, both North and South, a state of equilibrium generally prevails: ironically, poorly nourished hunters survive in small, mobile bands because they are depopulated by war, famine, disease, and custom: "in spite of all the powerful causes of destruction ... the average population of the American nations is, with few exceptions, on a level with the average quantity of food which in the present state of their industry they can obtain" (*1803* 43). But at the lowest stages of human society, this equilibrium could have the gravest effects. Among the aborigines of New South Wales, for example, although smaller populations have a sufficient supply of food, there is no reserve; hence, "every little deficiency from unfavorable weather or other causes occasions distress," and starvation was not uncommon (*1803* 25).

If overpopulation initiates destructive natural processes, and if the sought-for balance between human numbers and available resources is, for indigenes, equally as precarious, then the solution is for native society either to cultivate its own food, to inhibit population growth conscientiously, or to do both. In Malthus' view, unless primitive people worldwide took the initiative, they would be enslaved by the material world that God had originally designed to sustain him.

Darwin would struggle with a similar contradiction, but in zoological rather theological terms. The enslavement, displacement, and extirpation of aboriginal tribes by colonials were morally reprehensible acts; however, in *biological* terms, these practices were consonant with natural laws: human beings, like any other creatures, struggle with each and the fittest survive and dominate. The reclamation of primitive people, in Malthus' theoretical view, was unlikely as they were unable, because of their rigorous way of life, to develop, and to apply to everyday challenges, the moral faculties necessary to the realization of preventive checks.

# 3. King and FitzRoy in
# Tierra del Fuego

The manuscript of Philip Parker King's (1793–1856) narrative of the *Beagle*'s first voyage, 1826–1830, published in 1839, was in the ship's library when Darwin came onboard in 1832, but, from what can be gathered, it appears that he had not read it at that time. Even though one cannot cite it as a direct influence on Darwin's thinking from 1832 to 1836, King's book deserves our attention because it is an indispensable preface to Darwin's ethnology. Despite the organizational shortcomings of King's narrative, this text remains an important contribution both to Magellanic and to British maritime literature.

King and contributors give us important behavioral insights into native people, especially in the archipelago of Tierra del Fuego. We also learn something of British maritime policy towards indigenous people and even more about the logistical problems and dangers met during the expedition. One of the most important factors in this regard was the explorers' limited ability to communicate with the natives. Miscommunication between the explorers and the natives contributed significantly to the *Beagle*'s difficulties on the voyage of 1826–1830, and their intimate relationship with Fuegian natives would have an unforeseen impact on Darwin's ethnological thinking on the ensuing voyage.

A naval officer and hydrographer, Captain King commanded the H.M.S. *Adventure* and the H.M.S. *Beagle* on her first surveying voyage to South America and to the South Pacific, 1825 to 1830. He wrote three papers in that period, copies of which were included in the *Beagle*'s weighty collection of 400 volumes (*CDC* I, Appendix IV, 564). There is evidence that Darwin read King's descriptions of Cirrhipedia, Conchifera, and Mollusca, specimens of which he had collected during the voyage, and his findings were later to appear in the *Zoological Journal*. A comment Darwin made in a 1 April 1838 letter to Susan Darwin suggests that, although he had not read King's narrative earlier in manuscript, he read it in 1839, when it was published as volume I of the three-volume *Proceedings*.

Even though Darwin got along well with the King family, he did not refrain from expressing reservations privately about Philip King's narrative, but he had to temper his criticism of the book when he learned that, in 1831, the Captain's eldest son, Philip Gidley King, was to be his shipmate on board the *Beagle*. Diplomatically, Darwin saved his opinion of King's style for a letter (*Biographical Register, BD* 452; Keynes, Intro., *BD* xix–xx).

Despite the inadequacies of the text, King, FitzRoy, and Darwin were destined to collaborate with one another. In a letter of 30 December 1836 to Darwin, FitzRoy expressed excitement about a joint project: the publication in three volumes of the principal narratives: King's, on the 1826–1830 expedition, as the abovementioned volume I; FitzRoy's and Darwin's, volumes II and III, respectively, on the 1832–1836 expedition. Professionally interested in Darwin's collection of shells, William John Broderip (1789–1859), who was Magistrate, naturalist, and founder, in 1826, of the Zoological Society, recommended the joint venture and suggested that the profits be split three ways between the principal authors (*CDC* I 515).

The three-volume *Beagle* history was not the first major work to appear on the exploration of the southernmost regions of South America. The earliest eighteenth-century account of a Fuegian tribe, Joapchin d'Arquistade's narrative of the customs and material culture of the Yahgan tribe, was based on personal observations concentrated over a single-day's visit, in 1715, to natives at Orange Bay (Cooper 67). Commodore John Byron, in his 1741 narrative, included important cultural information on the Chonoan people (76), one of several major tribes in the region, and John Bulkeley and John Cummins, in *A voyage to the South-Seas, by His Majesty's ship Wager* (1743), contributed material on both the Chonos and Alacaluf, met in 1741 in the area of Wager Island (75). Although relying on published narratives and manuscripts, Pedro Lozano, S.J., in 1754–1755, described the earliest Missions to the Chilotans and Chonos, which were established from 1609 to 1614. Another important source of Chonoan culture is the 1766–67 diary of José García Martí (91). All of this fragmentary information is referenced, synoptically, in Charles de Brosses' survey of Magellanic exploration, from 1569 to the mid-eighteenth century (75). In 1768, Louis Antoine de Bougainville recounted his meeting with the Alacaluf, whom he encountered at Port Gallant (71). Captain James Cook's journal of the first voyage, 1768–1771, refers to the Onas, a native culture of northeastern Tierra del Fuego and of southwestern Chile, encountered in January 1769, while in Good Success Bay (79). His narrative of the second voyage, in 1772, contains additional information on natives inhabiting Christmas Sound (80). A significant extant resource for Alacalufan culture, in the region of Port Famine and Port Gallant, is José de Vargas y Ponce's account of 1786 and the 1798 Appendix to the main text (132). Of note among the eighteenth-century texts is Father Gonzalez de Agueros' 1791 history of Chiloé and of the activities and manufacture of the Chilean Chonos (93). James Burney's five-volume, *A chronological history of the voyages and discoveries in the South Sea or Pacific Ocean* (1803–1817), is considered to be the most comprehensive survey of Magellanic exploration of its time (76). And lastly, in the *Narrative of a voyage to Patagonia and Tierra del Fuego through the Straits of Magellan in H.M.S. Adventure and Beagle in 1826 and 1827,* John Macdouall, shipmate of King and Fitzroy, observed native culture firsthand, but his writing is sketchy (108).

Cook's first-voyage narrative, a landmark text Darwin knew well, has an important bearing on what was known at that time about *Fuegian* culture, a term encompassing more than three principal tribes. His first expedition on H.M.S. *Endeavour* had an astronomical purpose: to proceed via Cape Horn to King George's Island, Tahiti, in order to observe the transit of Venus in June 1769. Secret instructions directed him to explore the Pacific, "that vast unknown tract, about the latitude 40'," to find out if a great continent existed to the south of Tahiti, and whether New Zealand was part of this hypothetical landmass (Price, ed., *Explorations* 17–18).

Along with these scientific and oceanographic aims, Cook was "to observe the Genius, Temper, Disposition and Number of the Natives, if there be any" (*Explorations*, 19). Beyond observation, the explorers were to interact with them amicably, cultivating "a Friendship and Alliance with them, making them presents of such Trifles as they may Value." While extending every kind of civility, the crew had always to be on guard, never allowing the natives or any "Accident" to surprise them. With the natives' consent, they were ordered "to take possession of Convenient Situations in the Name of the King of Great Britain." Uninhabited lands could simply be claimed (19).

On 11 January 1769, the *Endeavour* entered Good Success Bay. While Cook began charting his course, naturalists went ashore to get samples of plants and flowers foreign to European collections (*Explorations* 21). On Monday, 16 January, Cook recounts his first encounter with the Onas, a pedestrian rather than canoe-using Indian tribe. Although ethnically akin to the northern Patagonians, who are Pampas Indians of Argentina, the Onas are grouped with the Fuegians for geographical reasons (Cooper 48). The Portuguese mariner Pedro Sarmiento, in 1580, was the first European to meet the Onas, and Bartolomé and Gonzalo García del Nodal, Spanish explorers, wrote the first account of these people in January 1619 (114). Subsequent narratives up to 1775, including those of Cook's expeditions in 1769 and in 1774, provide limited details on Onan material culture and physical appearance (62–3).

Despite the limitations of Cook's narrative, the text gives us an exciting early appreciation of Onan behavior and material culture. When Cook landed, a group of fifty or sixty individuals, of all ages and genders, approached the shore party. They were more curious than hostile, inasmuch as women and children never stood at the forefront of a war party (*Explorations* 22). Upon first impression, the males appeared rather formidable. Of medium stature, they had long black hair, dark-copper skin color, were partially clothed in animal skins, and had painted their bodies with red and black streaks (*Explorations* 21). Cook was very observant and intuited the cultural significance of native accoutrements and attire. For example, he noted that they displayed an aesthetic sense and were craftsmen, prizing red cloth and objects, from which they had made necklaces, beaded with small shells and bones. Their homes, however, were quite ramshackle. The only shelters they had were nothing more than flimsy huts resembling bee hives: that is, they were domed structures, open on one side, and had a fire going on at the opening, fueled with sticks, long grass, and tree branches.

Though Cook called the natives a "miserable set of People," he was nonetheless sympathetic to their hard way of life. He realized that they were making the most of what they had and seemed to be a hardy race, judging from the bad weather and difficult terrain with which they had to deal (*Explorations* 21–2). The native bows and arrows Cook found to be both technically impressive and culturally meaningful, and it was clear that they were quite capable of defending themselves and of hunting large game. Not only were these weapons functional, but, upon close examination, were ornamented with glass, flint, rings, buttons, cloth and canvas, material gotten most likely during their northerly travels to places Europeans visited more frequently.

The Onas knew what firearms were, and they even requested that the crew kill seals or birds for consumption and for skins. Cook astutely noticed that the Onas had no boats, an assumption substantiated by twentieth-century investigators (Cooper 195). Other than flimsy baskets for gathering mussels, they conspicuously lacked utensils. Cook did not draw ethnological inferences from what he saw; for details in this regard, the journal of the naturalist Joseph Banks (1743–1820) is more frequently referenced (Cooper 68; Heawood 228). Nevertheless, Captain Cook's incisive record of Onan life exhibits an intuitive understanding of their culture.

Captain King's contribution to the Magellanic corpus contains extracts from related texts by Captains Pringle Stokes and Robert FitzRoy and by prominent crew members, along with detached memoranda. Entitled the *Proceedings of the first expedition, 1826–1830* or *Narrative* 1 of the three volume set, it was published in 1839. Like Cook's narratives, Narrative 1 is an important resource for our understanding of native cultures in the southernmost parts of South America. Most of the observations gathered in this text describe the main tribes of Tierra del Fuego, known collectively (though imprecisely) as Fuegians. The generic term *Fuegian*, though efficient, is quite misleading. Because it was used to describe discrete ethnic groups inhabiting a vast geographical location — an area of some 50,000 square miles, consisting of a multitude of islands, channels, sounds, inlets, and straits — and because the Archipelago's individual cultures were subsumed under the term, unique tribal histories, languages, achievements, and cultures were obscured. This fact poses a challenge for the reader who wishes to distinguish one tribe from another, especially since three or more principal tribes occupied the Archipelago. So it is important to identify the aboriginal people of the region.

The *Yahgan*, who lived primarily in the southernmost district, in the vicinity of Murray Narrows, were named by the Rev. Thomas Bridges after the region just mentioned. Bridges applied the native name *Yaghan* to them, but this might have been a misidentification. The natives were actually *Yamana*, a word in their language meaning "alive," "living," or "man" (Cooper 2). The *Alacaluf*, the second principal tribe, lived in the western district of the islands and were canoe users (Cooper 5). The third ethnic group, the *Onas*, inhabited the Island of Tierra del Fuego. Related to the Patagonians of the central plains of Argentina, they lived in the northeastern districts, were called *Oens* men by FitzRoy, and were notorious for raiding Yaghan villages on Navarino Island (Cooper 48–49). Each of the tribes mentioned here, it is important to point out, had a lexically distinct language. The Yahgan and the Alacaluf were more closely related to each other than either was to the Onas. Two distinct, smaller tribes — the Aush or Haush and the Western Patagonian canoe Indians — also lived in the Archipelago (E. L. Bridges 61; Montagu 90–1).

King's narrative describes the Alacaluf whom the *Beagle* visited intermittently from January 1827 to June 1830, while surveying the Archipelago. Even though King's text includes large extracts from the journals and reports by other members of the expedition (and, for that reason, seems disjointed), the reader profits from having multiple points of view. All of the narrators, perhaps influenced by Cook, Banks, and others, carefully noted the physical characteristics and habits of native people.

One encounter was exemplary. When native canoes came alongside the ships, King describes one or two of the women as being "young" and "well-featured" yet filthy and disagreeable, since their skins were covered with large quantities of seal-oil and blubber, a practice both unsightly and odorous (Narr. 1 53); as to whether the oil had any purpose, such as an emollient, insect repellant, or cosmetic, he ventured no opinion. Although the children of both sexes and the young men were "well-formed," the elderly had "hideous figures" (53). Despite these subjective comments, King contributes several acute observations, one of which is that the canoe people and the more northern Patagonians shared "a great resemblance," though the former were considerably more diminutive than the latter. King had a point: the southwestern Alacaluf were indeed related to a Patagonian tribe, namely the Puelche (Montagu 90–1).

The captain of the *Beagle* from 1826 to 1828, Captain Pringle Stokes found the Alacaluf to be constitutionally weak, a condition he attributes to "the unkindly climate in which they dwell" (Narr. 1 74). On average they stood five-feet five inches, were deficient in musculature; and their limbs "badly turned." Their black hair was straight and coarse, and the men pluck their beards, whiskers, and eyebrows (Narr. 1 75). Their foreheads were low, noses prominent, and nostrils dilated. Of moderate size, their eyes were dark; their mouths large, their lips thick, and their teeth small, regular but of "bad" color; and their skin is described as being the color of "dirty copper." As for their faces, they appeared listless and expressionless (Narr. 1 75). Another extract conveys an observer's surprise at finding "wretched creatures" who are "shivering at every breeze," when, having spied well-lit camps in the distance, he had expected to find "hardy savages" (Narr. 1 76); apparently, these Indians seemed to have been unprepared for the cold (Narr, 1 76).

A major contributor to King's text was Robert FitzRoy (1805–1865). A naval officer, hydrographer, meteorologist, and Darwin's host on the subsequent voyage, FitzRoy was given command of the *Beagle* from 1830 to 1836, for the duration of both circumnavigations. He gained command of the *Beagle* after Captain Pringle Stokes committed suicide in August 1828. FitzRoy, who was officially promoted to the rank of Captain in 1835, (*BD*, 450), would also write Narrative 2. Published in 1839, it was a full-scale history of the 1832–1836 surveying voyages of the H.M.S. *Adventure* and H.M.S. *Beagle*.

On both voyages, FitzRoy recorded ethnologically perceptive remarks. One of his contributions to Narrative 1 contrasts with King's description. While encountering Indians off-shore, for example, FitzRoy tried to derive behavioral characteristics from their anatomical features. In a canoe alongside the ship were an old woman, her daughter, and a child, and on shore were two men (Narr. 1 216). All of the natives reminded FitzRoy of drawings he had seen of Eskimos: below middle size, clothed in "rough skins," their hair hung down like "old thatch," and, smeared with oil and caked with dirt, their skin was reddish brown. The observer considers their facial features, at first glance, to be "bad" and "peculiar." FitzRoy reads their behavior and emotional state in their faces: they exude "cunning, indolence, passive fortitude, deficient intellect, and want of energy" (Narr. 1 216). Their facial anatomy, moreover, struck him as being quite primitive and atavistic: their foreheads were small and "ill-shaped"; the nose, long and narrow between the eyes, is wide at the point; along with a long, protruding upper lip, the chins are small and recessive; each has high cheek bones, rotten teeth, an "oblique nasal angle," coarse hair, and wide "ill-formed mouth," and the upper lip does not move in laughing; moreover, the head, at the top and in the back, was small (Narr. 1 216). In contrast, another passage, quoted at this point, describes an encounter with another regional tribe. Their features differ markedly from those of the Fuegians previously described, "in being better formed, and having less artful expressions" (Narr. 1 227); thus, FitzRoy and others had reason to believe that facial features reflected ethnic identity, but they also used these observations to make unsubstantiated behavioral and intellectual assumptions about natives.

In Narrative 2, FitzRoy tried his hand at ethnic classification, but his efforts, especially his choice of tribal names, were inconsistent. It made sense for him to borrow the native appellation *Yacana cunnee* (meaning "foot" Indians), from Father Thomas Falkner's *A description of Patagonia and the adjoining parts of South America* (1747), to describe the inhabitants of southeastern Patagonia who, in skin color, stature and clothing, resembled indigenous, equestrian natives (Cooper 86, 48). Believing rightly that the northeasterners were easily distinguishable from those living in the southeast, he identified the former with a new name, *Tekeenica* or *Teke Uneka*. But, at this point, confusion arises. In the Yaghan language *TekeUneka* (phonetically: *Tekeenica*) literally means, "not seen before, strange" (Narr. 2 137). It seems that FitzRoy had learned the word *Tekeenica* from an Alacaluf on board but was ignorant of its literal translation. In actuality, FitzRoy's *Tekeenica* were *Yamana*. R. D. Keynes notes that the canoe-users of the Beagle Channel called themselves *Yamana* (meaning "People"). Those living on the shores of the Murray Narrow, on the other hand, were actually *Yagashagalumoala* (meaning "People from Mountain Valley Channel"); Thomas Bridges understandably abbreviated the polysyllabic name to *Yaghans* (*BD* 135n.).

It is interesting, and somewhat amusing, to learn how FitzRoy picked up the phrase *Teke Uneka* (phonetically in English, *Tekeenica*) and used it incorrectly as a synonym for *Yamana*. Neither a tribal nor geographical name, *Tekeenica* was simply one native's bewildered reply to a navigational question about two nearby islands (i.e., Bay and Hoste, respectively). The native guide responded that the islands in question were *unknown* to him; however, thinking that the guide was actually *naming* the place and its inhabitants, Fitzroy ludicrously dubbed the Bay and Hoste Islanders *Tekeenica*, meaning "strange" or unknown (Narr. 2 136) — hence, the Unknown Islands. The inability to communicate clearly with native people would lead to more serious problems for the expedition. Even though FitzRoy used language rather loosely, this is not to say that he failed to recognize its vital importance to the missions. Evidence of this realization is the inclusion, as an Appendix to Narrative 2, of basic Alacalufan words (see "Fragment of a Vocabulary of the Alikhoolip [*sic*.] and the Tekeenica [!] Languages," Appendix 18, Narr. 2 15–42).

Once ashore, FitzRoy recorded valuable observations. The Yahgans struck the Captain as being diminutive and unhealthy: squat, "ill-looking, and badly proportioned." Their heights ranged from four-feet ten to five-feet six inches, yet the overall body mass appeared to be equal that of a six-foot man; this being the case, they typically look squat, "clumsy and ill-proportioned" (Narr. 2 138). Their hands and feet, though disproportionate to their torsos, were proportional to small limbs and joints. Their skin color, resembling "old mahogany" (137), was dark copper and bronze in hue. For the large trunk of the body being disproportionate to "their cramped and rather crooked limbs," he blamed their occupying low wigwams and canoes; consequently, they stooped, their legs being "injured in shape" because of squatting upon their heels. Though they ambulated with bent knees, they were nimble and strong (Narr. 2 138). Although their hair was "rough, coarse, and extremely dirty," they were scrupulous about hair-growth on other parts of the body: they used crude knives, broken shells, and singeing to remove eyebrows and facial tufts (Narr. 2 138). FitzRoy's general feeling, however, is that they had "a villainous expression" and "savage features" (Narr. 2 137); and he uses the derogatory euphemism "satires upon mankind" to describe them (138).

In contrast to the Yamana were the Alacaluf (a name also having multiple forms, e.g. Alikhoolip [Cooper 5]). This tribe inhabited the Strait of Magellan and the Patagonian Channels. FitzRoy calls them "the stoutest and hardiest" of all natives whom they have met, and whose women were "the least ill-looking of the Fuegians" (Narr. 2 139). The so-called *Huemul* Indians, whom FitzRoy disparagingly named after the animal skins they wore, were canoe-using relatives of the Alacaluf (Cooper 5). Possibly a branch of the Yacana tribe, they may have been a "mixed breed" (Narr. 2 142). Finally, he finds the Chonos (FitzRoy's appellation), inhabitants of the western shores and the islands of Patagonia, to be not as "savage" as the "Fuegians," presumably as either Alacaluf or Yahgan. Referring to the Chonos, FitzRoy observes that their relationship with Spanish colonialists had tended "to improve their character" (Narr. 2 142).

FitzRoy and company were greatly impressed by the statuesque Patagonians, inhabitants of a vast region of more than 300,000 square miles, from southern Argentina, south of the Río Colorado and east of the Andes, and including southeastern Chile and northern Tierra del Fuego. Of the original inhabitants of this vast area, the Tehuelches were the most well-known, notably for their exceptional height. The Onas or Oens men and southern Patagonians, whom FitzRoy attempted to describe, were also related to one another (Cooper 52–6). The Captain held tenuous cultural and behavioral assumptions about the Patagonians, using physiological characteristics as outward manifestations of emotional and mental states. The skulls of the typical Patagonian, as far as he could determine from his casual meetings with them, were broad but not high; and the foreheads, in most cases, small and low. The hair was black, for the most part, coarse and dirty; the brows, prominent; and the eyes, "small, black, and ever restless" (Narr. 2 144).

FitzRoy interpolated physical descriptions into his narrative, and these are of great interest. Preposterous as it might seem, he made a practice of deriving behavioral patterns from the anatomy of the skull: thus, he writes that, "a mixture of simplicity and shrewdness, daring and timidity, with that singular wild look which is never seen in civilized man, is very conspicuous in the Patagonians." For him, these Indians are living contradictions, at once, unassuming yet shrewd, daring yet timid; in essence, they are deceptive in mind and incongruent in body. Echoing Cook's precautionary instructions of 1769, he states that heterogeneous qualities such as these warrant vigilance, especially "while within reach" of these natives. FitzRoy generalizes from the historical record: of all savage nations, the Patagonians "are least inclined to attack or deceive strangers" (Narr. 2 144).

The female Patagonians resembled the males so closely in stature, in physiognomy, and in attire that, at first glance, their genders were indistinguishable. The women whom FitzRoy observed, had round faces, high cheekbones, depressed noses, narrow bridges, but broad, fleshy, and large nostrils. The mouths were "large and coarsely formed"; and the lips rather large, as well. The teeth, though often in good condition, were also rather large, and the flattened front teeth, though appearing solid, "show an inner substance" (Narr. 2 144). The Patagonian chin, unlike the more recessive one of the Alacaluf previously described, was usually "broad and prominent." The latter Indians, "compared with other savages," had "open and honest" expressions, and exuded an "intrepid" and "content look." FitzRoy was especially impressed by the confidence and composure these Indians displayed as they boarded the

*Beagle* unarmed and even undertook local travel with their "white acquaintances" (Narr. 2 145).

It seems probable, in view of the physical similarities noticed by earlier explorers, that the natives who inhabited the northern side of the Strait of Magellan were descendants of the northwestern Patagonians, an inference FitzRoy drew on the basis of stature. A passage from Falkner's *A Description of Patagonia and the adjoining parts of South America* (1774) is quoted at this point to support the claim of extraordinary height, Falkner describing a chief who allegedly stood more than seven feet tall, which contrasts sharply with the diminutive and gnarled Alacaluf (Narr. 2 145).

On the basis of visual differences, the crew was able to differentiate one tribe from another, and they gradually realized that there were significant ethnic differences between members of neighboring communities. In *Narrative* 2 (1839), for instance, Captain FitzRoy added an extract from the journal of the ship's surgeon Benjamin Bynoe (1804–1865), written during the second expedition. Bynoe recalled that, while surveying in the vicinity of the Gulf of Trinidad, the ships were approached by oar-drawn, plank-canoes, "full of fine stout Indians." Their appearance was striking. Far superior to the "Fuegians," they were members of a taller race, more upright, and better proportioned; their limbs were better formed, more muscular, rounder, and fuller than those of natives from the Strait of Magellan or from Barbara Channel. Nor were their backs as disproportionately elongated as those of the Fuegians. On the basis of these observations, Bynoe and his shipmates "pronounced these people to belong to a finer race" than any they had met previously, though they remained unidentified (Narr. 2 197–98).

The theory that the structure of the skull was a valid index to the mental faculties and character of individuals and of races is a pseudo-science called *phrenology*. Two cranial methodologies, which need to be differentiated from each other, were in practice during the nineteenth century: phrenology, as mentioned, presumed to ascertain mental and behavioral traits from the shape of a skull, whereas *craniology*, a classificatory science, studied variations in skull size, shape, and proportion. Although FitzRoy, among so many of his contemporaries, took phrenology seriously, studying skull formation did not always lead to de-humanizing conclusions. For example, in one instance, FitzRoy surmised that the cranial features of certain Fuegians *did not* conform to broad assumptions about the atavism and mental inferiority of human beings inhabiting the outskirts of civilization. Furthermore, and much to his credit, he rightly stated that, as far as the physical characteristics of uncivilized humanity were concerned, a great variety of physical differences could be seen, and there was enormous diversity among them. During the South

American voyages, in particular, he found both men and women with curly hair (much like that of Polynesians or Malayans), with high foreheads, with straight or aquiline noses, and with features common, not to Fuegians, but to the Maoris, natives of New Zealand. Empirically, he arrived at the understanding that physical variations were somehow connected with migrations, with environment, and with the commingling of ethnic groups; moreover, he was reasonably certain that geographical isolation, though an important factor, was not the primary determinant of physical variation. The experience in the Galápagos Archipelago and the subsequent evaluation and classification of specimens would, by the 1840s and 1850, confirm for Darwin that physical variation was the effect of natural selection.

The limitations of phrenology and of other physiological modalities, on the other hand, were glaringly evident in FitzRoy's description of the natives whom he and Dr. Wilson had contacted. The heads of two Fuegians under examination were both low and wide, and full from the ears backward; the necks were short and strong; the shoulders, square but high; the chest and body were very large; compared to the limbs and head, the trunk was long; the arms and legs, rounder and less sinewy than those of Europeans. Because of the habit of walking barefoot (or so he presumed), they had developed squared toes as well. Most of the Fuegians he viewed were bow-legged and turned their feet inwards when walking; their thigh muscles were large; but muscles of the leg were undeveloped (see "Remarks on the Structure of the Fuegians," Appendix 16, Narr. 2 142–47).

FitzRoy's description of these natives, which conveys the image of skeletally deformed individuals, was derived from the examinations of Dr. John Wilson, whose essay, "Remarks on the Structure of the Fuegians," was published as Appendix 16 to *Narrative* 2 (142–47) (see also, "Phrenological Remarks on Three Fuegians," Appendix 17, Narrative 2 147–49). Much of what FitzRoy wrote in his narrative came verbatim from Wilson's opening paragraph, which declares that "The general form of the Fuegians is peculiar" (Narr. 2 Appendix 16, 142). An examination of cranial features, likely of the repatriated Fuegians themselves, supposedly corresponded to brain anatomy where specific faculties were thought to be located; thus, examining the skull reputedly revealed behavioral, emotional, and intellectual proclivities that, in turn, were presumed to be characteristic of all members of that society.

Accordingly, Dr. Wilson asserts that certain skull features of the first of two male specimens reveal his "propensities": he was reputed to have been promiscuous, combative, very destructive, and secretive. Cranial anatomy disclosed to the anatomist that this person, like most members of his ethnicity, had the capacity to concentrate on specific tasks but was not constructive, which suggested a deficiency in learning and creativity (Appendix 16, Narr. 2 144). Furthermore, the skull reflected the individual's low self-worth, his savoring of praise, his obstinacy, and his cautiousness. The assessment allegedly depicted a personality lacking benevolence, ideals, hopes, or conscientiousness; moreover, the subject was deficient in the capacity to venerate, that is, to show respect, admiration, or deference to other human beings or to a supernatural entity.

The shape of the first man's skull allegedly had broader ethnic implications. Like most of his kind, he was thought to have limited mental capacity, the skull presumably indicating not only a poor sense of individuality, but also an array of perceptual, of sensory, and of intellectual disabilities, having to do with motor reflexes, timing, and tonality. Along with these disabilities, the subject was thought to be incapable of reasoning and of making critical distinctions pertaining to form, number, causality, and comparativeness. Wilson included craniometrical statistics showing a projecting jaw and a sloping forehead, both of which, if contrasted to the European-white standard, were intended to support the interpretation of primitivism and of limited mental capacity.

Overall, the anatomical features of the individual's skeleton and skull were proclaimed to be valid indices of Fuegian culture, at large. In regard to temperament, the individual being examined (Jemmy, York, or Boat Memory) had "warlike" propensities, the "general view of the head" being neurologically congruent with that of a "barbarian." Except for "cautiousness and firmness," both of which were appropriate to barbaric life, the sentiments were "small." By the same measure, intellectual "organs," reputedly associated with civilized man, were commensurately undeveloped.

A second Fuegian man's skull under examination exhibited features similar to those of the first man. Certain variations notwithstanding, the second male was portrayed as libidinous, tenacious, destructive, cunning, and more covetous than his predecessor. Emotionally, he was allegedly more egoistical than the first subject: the latter reputedly had high self-esteem, desired praise, had the capacity for veneration, and was decisive. On the other hand, like the first, the second personality was abject, without hopes and ideals, and overly cautious, a mixture of sentiments suggesting that the second personality was pragmatic. Dr. Wilson acknowledged that, although the "propensities" and moral sentiments of the second individual were superior to those of the first, the latter, too, was intellectually debilitated. Nonetheless, his destructive, secretive, and cautious personality was environmentally appropriate to "a savage warrior."

Undoubtedly, phrenology obfuscated any genuine understanding of native people because it reinforced biased preconceptions. On the one hand, to describe, to catalogue, and then to compare physical variations to one another, constituted scientifically valid activities. Using this data to make a case for the superiority of one human group over another, on the other hand, was neither valid nor moral. It is not surprising to learn that, for the explorers, the most tangible source of knowledge about native life and behavior would come from direct contact and interaction with indigenous people, and not from pseudo-clinical examinations of living subjects. Of course, face-to-face meetings were often fraught with difficulties, stemming from ignorance, matters of trust, and miscommunication on either side. On the *Beagle*'s initial voyage to Tierra del Fuego, simple interactions between the Fuegians and Captain King's crew showed great promise, but the difficulties just mentioned were seriously evident. An incident at Port Famine is a perfect illustration of how miscommunication nearly caused a disaster.

Having anchored at Port Famine on 13 April 1826, the crew of King's vessel, while awaiting the arrival of H.M.S. *Adelaide*, performed boat repairs on the *Beagle* and, if possible, were to gather meteorological data. On 21 April, nine canoes full of Fuegians arrived and went on shore. King decided against allowing them to encamp too closely to his bivouac because he believed that their presence would "impede" or distract shore-parties that were gathering wood and water. King met the Indians at the watering place under Point St. Anna, near one of their boats on the beach. The crew recognized three of them as notorious troublemakers. Even with this knowledge, King treated the Fuegians amicably; but he had his doubts as to whether a show of good will would be taken as a sign of weakness and as an opportunity for theft and aggression. Seeing that the Indians were well armed, their sling-shots and pebbles at the ready, King ordered them to disarm, and they surprisingly complied. By this time, however, more Indians were arriving. As their numbers swelled to about eighty, they "began to make themselves very familiar" (Narr. 1 316).

Diplomatically trying to check their advances, King directed them, probably through hand gestures, not to remain on the side of the cove where the encampment was, but rather to go around the Point to an adjoining cove. It cannot be determined from the text if the tribe understood what King was saying. They departed, nonetheless, as King and company returned to their ship. But the natives soon returned to the northern side, in the middle of the bay, and there they encamped. So, when King returned to the beach the next day, he found unwanted neighbors (Narr. 1 316).

On that very morning (21 April), other men of the tribe visited King's tents but found it cordoned off by a rope (Narr. 1 317). At noon, after observing the sun's transit, King went to the barrier while the shore party was at dinner, with the intention of amusing the "visitors." The Commander showed them a pocket set of sun-glasses that were being used to make solar calculations. The natives used them roughly and broke the frame (their intention being unclear), which caused King to rebuke them and chase them away. Perhaps realizing that this incident could precipitate a conflict, the Commander approached the native who was responsible for breaking the frame, but, rather than to castigate him, he gave him a set of beads and "restored the peace." Then King ordered the Indians back to the wigwams that they had constructed on the beach as temporary shelters. Along the way, the natives mischievously broke a wooden meridian marker that had been set in the sand, but King quickly repaired it. The natives who had seemed to be baiting the crew congregated around the broken marker, evidently anticipating King's rebuke. He ordered them away and into their canoes. Again, they obeyed, but one person, muttering some angry words, loaded his sling with a pebble, which prompted King to aim his musket in the native's direction. Obviously understanding the musket's power, the sullen native and his companion fled. The Captain backed his words up by firing over the heads of the principal offender and his companion, as they ran along the beach near the water.

In this tense atmosphere, a chain reaction of events ensued that could have been anticipated and prevented if the lines of communication had been open. Lieutenant Mitchell aboard the *Beagle* was expecting a "fracas." When he heard King's warning gunshot, he then saw the hasty retreat of five canoes and the two runners on the beach. Because of the lack of communication between the ship and the shore party, not to mention that between King and the natives, Mitchell assumed that a fight had broken out. In response, he manned a boat and tried to intercept the fleeing canoes. Believing that *they* were under attack, the Fuegians, at first, tried to evade Mitchell's boat, but then they slung stones at it. Discharging a musket over their heads which forced the canoes to stop, Mitchell pulled around the canoes to intercept them, but then allowed them to proceed unharmed, as yet not knowing what had transpired near the camp (Narr. 1 317).

Seeing that Mitchell's boat had fired warning shots and intercepted the canoes, the women at the wigwams hastily gathered their belongings, got into their canoes, and paddled round Point St. Anna with the others. The men, however, landed at the Point and remained on shore. Armed with slings, spears, and bows, they were ready to defend themselves and defied the sailors to land. The crew, mistakenly believing they were rescuing King's party, ignored the Fuegians. After a short time, the Indians retreated to the northern part of the cove. As the two parties had now "openly quarreled," even though the conflict was more a matter of confused reactions, King thought it best to drive them even farther away. So he took two boats to the Indian camp and directed them to Rocky Point, five miles distant.

Presumably to determine the natives' position, King's shore party injudiciously pursued the evacuating tribe. This was a bad course of action. When the British appeared offshore, the women had already set up their wigwams. King's pursuing boats appeared to be intended as an imminent attack on innocent women and children. As soon as the two boats appeared, the hills echoed "with the screams of the women and the shouts of the men." The men, who had furiously rearmed, suddenly descended onto the beach, "stark naked, armed, and daubed with white paint, their heads being stuck full of white feathers" (Narr. 1 318). The beach, which had large rocks, was a good defensive position for the Indians, who could hide behind them and hurl their rocks with dangerous accuracy at anyone approaching them.

King's intention, unbeknownst to the Indians, was to make peace, but his tactics were poorly conceived. Within a few yards of the beach, as the crew and the Indians began to "parley" (the mode of communication at such a distance being unclear), King undiplomatically ordered the Fuegians to go farther northward. The Indians then made it known that King and his men should leave. Realizing that there was no way for them to drive the Indians out without bloodshed, King's boats retreated from the shore. The Fuegians hurled stones at them but with no effect. The crew answered with a shot over their heads, to which the Indians responded with another hurled stone that fell short of a boat. Several shot-for-stone exchanges transpired. Realizing the futility of the standoff, each side receded from one another.

Without the ability to communicate, King's expedition, like the missionaries who followed them, was greatly disadvantaged. The situation remained very precarious. As the *Beagle*'s crew cut wood for essential repairs and gathered water and provisions, for example, the Fuegians again planned an ambush. King pre-empted it with cannot shot above their heads, but this made matters worse. The enraged natives scattered from out of their hiding places and retreated to Rocky Bay, as King had originally suggested, where they encamped on the open beach. In what would seem to be another bad decision, as the customary white flag had no meaning and since there were no native guides on hand to translate, King sent Mitchell to their camp to make peace, using trivial objects as peace-making gifts (Narr. 1 319). Unexpectedly, a few days later, the Indians who had been keeping close to their camp peaceably communicated with the watering party, "as if nothing had happened." A day or two later, the Fuegians broke camp and dispersed.

Despite this experience, King did not acknowledge in the text the dire need to establish direct communication with indigenous people, along with a ship-to-shore system of communication, using flags, torches or any other means. Instead, King concludes, from this string of misunderstandings, that the "wretched Fuegians" are "petulant and quarrelsome," intent upon mischief, and restrained only by the fear of punishment. Though well intended, King seems to have jumped to conclusions about Fuegian temperament on the basis of a series of confused and potentially tragic events; and he amplifies his experience into a maritime advisory: "weakly-manned vessels" passing through the Strait of Magellan should avoid the natives of the region, especially if they are numerous: "for unless they are given what they want, they try to steal it, and any consequent punishment probably brings on a quarrel" (Narr. 1 319).

King's admonition, to be fair, was not completely unfounded. It seems that the Fuegians with whom King quarreled had a maritime reputation for aggressiveness. Although some of the people on the beach appeared servile, timid, and inactive, they had some history of violent boarding and of other unpredictable behavior. Fuegian natives probably had similar opinions of European visitors, whom they could not understand. As far as the Port Famine incident is concerned, had the pursuing boats landed, as King recognized, they probably would not have dislodged the natives and likely would have suffered casualties from stone-throwing, which the Captain considered as dangerous as musket shot (Narr. 1 320). Ironically native confidence was fed in part by small-arms fired over their heads (artillery had a different effect): they considered the weaponry as "uncertain in their effect" (Narr. 1 321); in fact, it was preferable, in King's judgment, to inflict a slight wound as a warning (Narr. 1 321).

On the return voyage to England, the *Beagle* had on board four Fuegians, three young men in their twenties and a nine-year-old girl; three were Alacaluf and one Yaghan (Cooper 87). Theirs is probably the most astonishing episode in Darwin's ethnography. John M. Cooper has justifiably called this text, "One of our most important sources for the culture of the Alacaluf of the Strait and Patagonian Channels" (87). The primary source for this story is Captain Robert FitzRoy's 1839 *Narrative* 2. In this book, FitzRoy recounted the difficulties leading up to the detention of the four Fuegians who were either hostages or guests, of how they went to England to be educated and converted to Christianity, and of how attempts were made to repatriate the three survivors on the return voyage (a male called Boat Memory dying in England).

In a series of letters, reprinted in Narrative 2, and spanning the period from 12 September 1830 to 10 August 1831, FitzRoy narrated the intriguing story of how he met four native companions. In the 12 September letter to Captain King, he identified the four natives who were given random names. Janet Browne rightly comments that these names were "nonhuman in their terms of reference ... [and] more appropriate to dogs than people" (235). They were York Minster, 26; Boat Memory, 20; James "Jemmy" Button, 14; and Fuegia Basket, a nine-year-old girl. Their actual names were Yokcushu (Fuegia), Orundellico (Jemmy), and El'leparu (York) (Browne 235). As we have already seen, the personality traits of, and assumptions about, two of the three males aboard the *Beagle*, written in London in 1830 and published in 1839, appeared as Appendix 17, under the title, "Phrenological Remarks on Three Fuegians" (Appendix 17, Narr. 2 148–49). FitzRoy assumed complete responsibility for their welfare and eventual return to Tierra del Fuego. He wondered if "some public advantage" might come from this unusual situation, and if it would be appropriate to bring them to the Government's attention (Narr. 2 4). At this point, he began to explain how the natives wound up on board in the first place.

In February 1830, as the *Beagle* was moored in Townshend Harbor, southwest of Tierra del Fuego, FitzRoy had sent ship's master Matthew Murray, along with six men, in a whale boat to Cape Desolation, a mountainous island about twelve miles' distance from the *Beagle*'s anchorage. Murray reached the Cape and secured his party and boat in a cove nearby. During the night, some Fuegians, whose presence was unknown to the shore party, "approached with the dexterous cunning peculiar to savages and stole the boat" (Narr. 2 5). This was a terrible calamity since they had lost one of the most capacious craft on the *Beagle* (on the upcoming voyage, the *Beagle* would have three whale-boats), and since Murray's party was now stranded. Nothing is said either of the obvious failure to safeguard the boat upon which their lives depended or of the veracity of the explanation.

There is no doubting the resourcefulness of the stranded party. Using a canvas tent and tree branches, they made a makeshift canoe which permitted three of the seven castaways to return to the *Beagle*. It took the canoe twenty hours to reach Townshend Harbor. FitzRoy responded to the incident as soon as possible, ordering the *Beagle* to pick up Murray's party and then to pursue the stolen boat. The futile chase lasted several days. Along the way, the *Beagle* came across the boat's gear, which was in the possession of women and children, presumably the families of those who had stolen the boat. At Christmas Sound in late February, FitzRoy picked up hostages, apparently to use in exchange for the boat, but, for some inexplicable reason, all the males escaped, leaving three little girls behind. Of the children, two were returned to their own tribe safely, near what had been appropriately named "Whale-boat Sound." Seeing a canoe in Christmas Sound, the crew picked up a man to act as interpreter and guide. From families inhabiting wigwams on an island in the Sound, they took another young man as "guide," but neither of them knew anything about the stolen boat.

The *Beagle* then sailed to Nassau Bay. There, the "captives" informed them that the natives on the eastern coast, likely to have been Onas, were their enemies and spoke a different language. To prevent an altercation, FitzRoy was reluctant to persuade one of the eastern tribe to come on board. But while in a small boat exploring Beagle Channel, FitzRoy met three eastern-tribe canoes and prevailed upon them to put a "stout boy" into his boat to return to the *Beagle*. It is hard to say whether the youth was more captive than guide; in return, FitzRoy gave them beads, buttons (hence, the boy was nonsensically christened "Jimmy [or Jemmy] Buttons"), along with other trifles, and was at a loss to know whether the adults intended for little Orun-dellico to remain with the expedition permanently: astonishingly, they sim-ply paddled away, as if "contented with the singular bargain." FitzRoy's boat went to the shore and was followed by a number of canoes whose occupants endeavored to barter with them (Narr. 2 6). Now, with four "companions"— three males and a girl — FitzRoy decided to leave the Fuegian coast. He recalls that the native guests appeared "cheerful and contented with their situation." No longer hostages, they had become wards of a benevolent, proselytizing nation, for FitzRoy thought "that many good effects might be the conse-quence of their living a short time in England" (Narr. 2 6). Attired as sea-men and being well cared for, they understood "why they were being taken," and looked forward with pleasure "to seeing our country, as well as to return-ing to their own." FitzRoy had a plan: by procuring a suitable education for each of them and, after two or three years of civilizing, he would return them to Tierra del Fuego as the vanguard of a settlement. Equipped with an edu-cation, converted to Christianity, and well provisioned, the natives were to be cultural missionaries of a kind, their envisaged purpose being to improve the condition of their countrymen, "now scarcely superior to the brute cre-ation" (Narr. 2 6).

During the return voyage from Rio de Janeiro to England, beginning in August 1830, FitzRoy recalled spending a considerable amount of time with his four "companions," and becoming acquainted with their abilities and incli-nations, not by poking their scalps, but by interacting with them as human beings (Narr. 2 1). FitzRoy remarks that three of the four were in no way "sav-age," although the fourth, York Minster (named after an island near Cape Horn [Bridges 30]), "was certainly a displeasing specimen of uncivilized human nature" (Narr. 2 2). Nonetheless, the Fuegians on board, FitzRoy sincerely believed, had come from a morally destitute and desperate world.

To define what savagery meant in regard to the Yaghans, Onas, and Alacaluf, Fitzroy alluded to charges that these particular natives practiced cannibalism. His suspicion had dubious origins and was communicated through signs, innuendos and "revolting accounts." One of these was of the reputed murder and consumption of elderly women during times of famine. FitzRoy received this information as a "half-understood story," to which, at first, he paid scant attention because it was so unbelievable. Gradually, as certain Fuegians became fluent in English, they supposedly informed FitzRoy and others, "of this strange and diabolical atrocity." FitzRoy eventually endorsed its veracity, as did the Scottish sea trader and sea captain William Low, who called the charge "the most debasing trait" of the Fuegian character (Cooper 2). But the evidence supporting Yahgan and Onan cannibalism was inconclusive, while that for Alacalufan cannibalism was questionable (Cooper 176). Esteban Lucas Bridges (1874–1949), son of the missionary Thomas Bridges (1842–1898), considered the charge baseless, the result of hearsay, of rumor, and of miscommunication. He speculated that because the young men and the young girl, Fuegia Basket, were barely fluent, they simply answered yes or no to questions about cannibalism, without understanding what was being asked. Esteban Lucas conjectures that FitzRoy's protégés might even have made the story up (33–4).

Confident that the Fuegian "companions" were innocent of this revolting crime, FitzRoy recorded their reactions to new experiences on the voyage to England. Referring to them as his "copper-colored friends," he noted that at the various seaports visited on the way they seemed more interested in animals, ships, and boats than in human beings and buildings. Whenever their interest was aroused by something, instead of becoming animated and curious, "they would appear, at the time, almost stupid and unobservant." On other occasions, they chattered to one another and made sensible remarks afterward about past experiences on the voyage. Only when they saw a steamvessel in Falmouth Harbor did they show outward emotion: they could not figure out if it was a huge fish, a land animal, or the devil, passing at full speed in the dark night near the *Beagle* (Narr. 2 2–3). Although sailors who explained the nature of a steam-powered ship made little headway with the Fuegians, FitzRoy likened the bewilderment and fascination of "these ignorant, though rather intelligent barbarians" to what a European may have experienced upon first witnessing the roaring power and magnificence of a steam-driven train, as it dashed along, "smoking and snorting" (Narr. 2 3).

Captain King, who was Commander of H.M.S. *Adventure* on the second voyage, immediately upon arriving in England in early October, forwarded the letter containing FitzRoy's plan to the Lords Commissioners of the Admiralty, from whom FitzRoy received a positive response in a letter of 19 October 1830. Commissioner John Barrow told FitzRoy that the Admiralty had no objection to his desire to superintend the Indians personally, to his "benevolent intentions" to maintain and educate them in England, and to bring them back home (Narr. 2 7). Upon receiving this communication, FitzRoy was greatly encouraged.

Captain FitzRoy realized that the Fuegians had no immunity to common and sometimes fatal infections prevalent in England. To protect them from contagious disorders, chiefly smallpox, he gave them comfortable lodgings and arranged that they would be immunized against the disease on the very next day. For this purpose, he then transported them a few miles inland to a quiet farm-house, where he hoped "they would enjoy more freedom and fresh air" and be less at risk of contagion than in a populated sea-port town, "where curiosity would be excited" (Narr. 2 7). Unfortunately, on 1 November 1830, Boat Memory became ill with a disorder like that of small-pox, even after receiving four inoculations. To protect the four patients, Dr. Armstrong of the Royal Hospital at Plymouth suggested that they be brought to the hospital, a precaution with which the Admiralty agreed on 10 November: since the natives' vaccinations were incomplete, there was the possibility that they could develop small pox, too (Narr. 2 8–9). FitzRoy was relieved to hear that all four were now in the best hospital in the country; however, Boat Memory died of the disease shortly thereafter. FitzRoy recalls his popularity among all who knew him, his good disposition, notable abilities, and, "though born a savage," his "pleasing, intelligent appearance" (Narr. 2 10). It was presumed that the first three inoculations had failed to take effect, and that the fourth had been administered too late (Narr. 2 9–10). FitzRoy expressed his regret over having unintentionally brought Boat Memory into contact with the disease, but the survivors remained in good health and completed treatment (Narr. 2 10). A further step was taken to strengthen their immunity when, under hospital care, they were exposed to children with active measles infections. Fuegia Basket contracted the disease and recovered thoroughly, thereby gaining immunity (Narr. 2 10).

FitzRoy planned for their education and maintenance, applying to the Church Missionary Society for help. The Rev. William Wilson, of Walthamstow, not only permitted the three Fuegians to join the parish, but he persuaded the master of the Infant School, Mr. Wigram, to take all three into his home "as boarders and pupils" (Narr. 2 10–11). FitzRoy paid their expenses while the school-master and, with the help of Wilson and Wigram, made arrangements to convey the natives to London. They were accompanied by Mr. Murray and Mr. Bennett, both of the *Beagle*, and the party went to Walthamstow by stage-coach. Upon their arrival, the Fuegians were astonished by the sights, such as the lion upon Northumberland House, which York Minster thought to be real (Narr. 2 11). The school-master and his wife were relieved to find their boarders to be well disposed, quiet, and clean and not "fierce and dirty savages" (Narr. 2 11).

The Fuegians lived at Walthamstow from December 1830 to October 1831, and they were treated by all concerned with great kindness. Casual visitors who became interested in them gave them presents. Their instructor taught them English and "the plainer truths of Christianity," along with the use of common tools, and he provided them with basic understanding of husbandry, gardening, and mechanics, Fuegia Basket and Jemmy Button made exceptional progress, but York Minster was "hard to teach," although he showed some interest in carpentry, blacksmithing, and in animals. He disliked learning to read and did not care much for gardening. Gradually, their benefactors collected words of their languages (a Yaghan, Fuegia spoke a different dialect than that of the Alacalufans, York and Jemmy), and some interesting "native habits and ideas" (Narr. 2 12). FitzRoy occasionally took them along with him to visit family and friends who questioned them and gave them serviceable articles for their use when they return to Tierra del Fuego. In the summer of 1831, King William IV and Queen Adelaide invited them to St. James Palace, where the natives were given gifts and money (Narr. 2 12).

FitzRoy supposed that the survey of the southern coasts of South America would be continued, providing an opportunity for bringing the Fuegians back home (Narr. 2 13). But the Lords of the Admiralty decided not to prosecute the survey, so FitzRoy became alarmed about the future of the Fuegians. On 27 June 1831, after two shipping contracts did not work out, FitzRoy was appointed to the *Beagle*, along with his friends and shipmates, Lieutenants Wickham and Sulivan. Mr. Wilson, learning of the impending voyage and departure of the Fuegians, wondered if two instructors could volunteer to accompany them in order to continue their educations. If this were possible, would they be permitted to sail on the *Beagle* and, once in Tierra del Fuego and with the help of FitzRoy, be able to establish friendly relations with the natives? If the plan were realized, would FitzRoy be able to visit their settlement, assist them, and, if needed, remove them "if they should find it impracticable to continue their residence among the natives"? (Narr. 2 14). With these concerns in mind, FitzRoy immediately contacted the Admiralty Office. In a letter of 10 August 1831, the Admiralty consented to all of these requests (Narr. 2 16).

A seven-year-long voyage was planned. One aim was to carry a chain of meridian distances round the world, if the *Beagle* were to return to England across the Pacific and by the Cape of Good Hope. Re-commissioned on 4 July 1831, the *Beagle* was ready for service (Narr. 2 17). On a southerly course from Patagonia, the *Beagle* returned to the coast of Tierra del Fuego on Sunday, 16 December 1832.

# Part II.
# A Voyage to Humanity

## 4. Slavery in South America

In April 1826, while Captain King was on the verge of combat with enraged natives at Point St. Anna in the Archipelago, Darwin was enrolled at Edinburgh University, attending anatomy lectures, prejudging the value of dissection, and becoming unnerved by botched surgeries (*Autobiography* 56–74). In marine biology, however, his experiences were to his liking, as he collected trawled specimens, made several original discoveries with respect to minute marine animals, and even published his findings. He joined professional scientific societies, attended meetings, and heard discussions on natural history and geology. From February to August 1830, while the sailors of the *Beagle* were frantically searching the channels of the Archipelago for a whale-boat and for its thieves, Darwin was passing Cambridge University examinations and soon to undertake an entomological excursion in North Wales. After the examinations for the B.A. degree were passed on 23 January 1831, he associated with learned men at Cambridge, read Herschel and Humboldt, and contemplated a trip to Tenerife. John Stevens Henslow (1796–1861), clergyman, botanist, and mineralogy professor at Cambridge, encouraged him to pursue geological studies and to take a midsummer trip to Shropshire, as well as a tour in Wales. Crossing the mountains to Barmouth, Darwin returned to Shrewsbury at the end of August 1831, not realizing that his life would soon be radically changed.

J. S. Henslow wrote to Darwin, on 24 August 1831, of a promising opportunity that had arisen for a naturalist. George Peacock (1791–1858), a professor of geometry and astronomy at Cambridge, was searching for a qualified naturalist to accompany Captain FitzRoy on a government-funded surveying trip to South America and the Pacific. Though Darwin was not yet an accomplished naturalist, Henslow was confident enough in his ability to recommend him: in his judgment Darwin was qualified to collect specimens, to observing the scenes, and to note important features of natural history (*CDC*

I 28–29). In a 26 August 1831 letter, Peacock offered the job to Darwin. The *Beagle* was to set sail in September, bound for the southern coast of Tierra del Fuego, afterwards to visit the South Sea Islands, and to return to England via the "Indian Archipelago" (*CDC* I 130). After Darwin had discussed the opportunity with his father and with Josiah Wedgwood II, he officially accepted it on 1 September, in a letter addressed to Francis Beaufort (1774–1857), naval officer and liaison (*CDC* I 135). Intended primarily for scientific work in natural history, the expedition had the secondary purpose of returning to their homeland the three surviving natives whom Fitzroy had educated at his own expense in England.

Darwin's record of his experiences among the slaves of Chile and Brazil four months later is a study in contrasts. While exploring the interior of St. Jago (Santiago), Chile, on 20 January 1832, Darwin, accompanied by ship's surgeon Robert McCormick (1800–1890), encountered two black men on the road. Darwin and McCormick purchased some goat's milk from them, and the blacks were more than generous. Not only were these "simple hearted men" good humored, but they were also quite intelligent; in fact, Darwin reflects that he "never saw anything more intelligent than Negroes, especially the Negro or Mulatto children." He was struck, particularly, by their insatiable curiosity: they immediately were intrigued by percussion guns, examined supplies "with the liveliest attention," and pulled objects out of their pockets, including Darwin's silver pencil case, not to pilfer as had Fuegians but to examine them, and they returned the objects to their owners. Along with their generosity and intelligence, the children were genuinely concerned about the explorers' well-being. When Darwin caught a stinging insect, for example, the children pinched themselves so as to show that it could sting (*BD* 26).

While touring the town of Ribera Grande, on 26 January 1832, Darwin and McCormick were accompanied by jovial blacks: "every thing we said or did was followed by their hearty laughter" (*BD* 30). But, at this point, they were reminded that this was a slave culture and that blacks were always at risk. Reminding them of this reality, the Spanish interpreter who was about to leave Darwin made an ambiguous and unsettling remark. Mounting his donkey, he loaded "a formidable pistol with slugs," and referring to the gun quietly remarked "this very good for black man," perhaps meaning that the noise of blank rounds was enough to get the slaves' attention — or perhaps he meant something else (*BD* 30).

The hospitality Darwin received in St. Jago did not obfuscate for long the repression of the slaves. Up to this point, he had had only fleeting glimpses of the inequities they were enduring. Difficult living conditions were evident in small towns. On a riding excursion to St. Domingo, begun at daybreak on 2 February 1832, Darwin, George Rowlett (1797–1834) (the purser of the *Beagle*), and the surgeon Benjamin Bynoe (1804–1865), took the wrong road and wound up in the village of Fuentes. Fuentes was "pretty" and prosperous looking, except for a glaring discrepancy: "The black children, perfectly naked & looking very wretched, were carrying bundles of fire wood half as big as their own bodies.—The men & women badly clothed looked much overworked" (*BD* 32).

As they approached St. Domingo, Darwin and his companions were met by a hospitable Portuguese man who invited them to "a most substantial dinner of meat cooked with various sorts of herbs & spices, & Orange Tart." Their host, a principal owner of the plantation, apparently lived luxuriously. After dinner they visited a nearby lake and were amazed to find on either shore, "flourishing Bananas, Sugar Cane, Coffee, Guavas, Cocoa Nuts, & numberless wild flowers" (*BD* 33). After admiring the natural beauty of the valley, they headed towards the village of Praya. In this village, a multitude of people were present since it was a feast day. On the way, they overtook twenty young black girls, who, dressed "in most excellent taste," wore brightly colored turbans and large shawls. When they saw the travelers, "they suddenly all turned round & covered the path with their shawls." As they performed this well-rehearsed gesture, they sang a wild song "with great energy" and beat time with their hands upon the legs. Darwin showed his appreciation to the singers who responded with "screams of laughter" (*BD* 33).

While recuperating from a knee injury on board the *Beagle*, Darwin recalls a visit by Charles Henry "Cap" Paget (b. 1806), naval officer and Commander of H.M.S. *Samarang*. Paget dispelled the air of plantation joy and hospitality, exposing the facts on slavery in the region. After hearing Paget's disturbing account, Darwin reflected that, if these facts were revealed in England, they would have been dismissed as anti-slavery propaganda. The moral insensitivity of British advocates of the trade and of those indifferent to its enormities genuinely perplexed him: "The extent to which the trade is carried on," he points out, along with "the ferocity with which it is defended" and the number of "respectable [!]" people profiting from it in England, cannot be exaggerated (*BD* 44). Darwin rejected the viewpoint of those who amorally dismissed popular indignation against slavery, and who justified its continuance on economic grounds. But, at the same time, he did not align himself with abolitionists who were often ignorant of the social and economic difficulties that the slave trade entailed. Instead, he formulated an objective understanding of slave civilization. On the one hand, he observes that colonial enslavement did not necessarily mean squalid living conditions: "the actual state of by far the greater part of the slave population was far happier than one would be previously inclined to believe"; in thinking this, Darwin was not borrowing a page from pro-slavery apologetics (*BD* 45). He recognized that colonial benevolence and adequate living conditions could not alter the fact that human beings had been transported into forced-labor colonies. However considerate the proprietor, for whom productivity outweighed moral compunction, it was untrue that the slaves did not wish to return to their countries. One of these people is reputed to have said to Darwin "'If I could but see my father & my two sisters once again, I should be happy. I can never forget them.'" The dejection conveyed by these words angered Darwin. His obloquy is directed at "the polished savages in England" who rank as "hardly their brethren, even in God's eyes" (*BD* 45). In this context, the state of savagery is determined by moral hypocrisy and not by race or the level of material civilization. Despite the sophistries and meaningless distinctions that the advocates of slavery employ, those who defend it were "blindly & obstinately prejudiced," while opponents continued with the struggle (*BD* 45).

Darwin came into contact with other black slaves in his sojourn through Bahía Blanca. While in a tavern, on 16 March 1832, they were surrounded by excited men, women, and children. The crowd was astonished by the paraphernalia in Darwin's pockets, especially his fly net, small pistol, and compass. The excellent manners of the residents delighted Darwin's party. At the Venda, after giving his native friends some wine and bidding them farewell, he departed with the firm belief that, "no Dutchess with three tails could have given such court[-]like & dignified bows," as the salutes with which the black women of Bahía gave to him (*BD* 46). In the evening of 17 March, while on a farewell stroll with Captain King, Darwin muses that Brazil was a natural paradise of sorts: "If to what Nature has granted the Brazils, man added his just & proper efforts, of what a country might the inhabitants boast." Indeed, Brazilian natural resources provided a foundation for a thriving civilization. However, because large parts of the country are "in a state of slavery," and because this anomalous system is stifling education, "the mainspring of human actions," civilization has been established at the expense of national character (*BD* 46).

The issue of slavery, especially in Brazil, was a source of great debate between Darwin and FitzRoy, but our understanding of this debate needs clarification. To this end, I will provide some historical background on the British slave trade and on its opponents. The political struggle to emancipate the slaves in the British West Indies began in May 1807, with the efforts of abolitionists like Granville Sharp (1735–1813) and Thomas Clarkson (1760–1846). Sharp wrote philological, legal, political, and theological pamphlets and is best known for his writings in defense of African slaves. In a famous case, he defended the slave James Somerset, securing the greater judgment, in 1772, that a slave becomes free upon reaching British soil. Sharp's plan for a colony for freed slaves in Sierra Leone was realized in 1787 (*Chambers* 1166). In his "Short Sketch of Temporary Regulations ... for the Intended Settlement of the Grain Coast of Africa, Near Sierra Leone," Sharp spoke of a "community of free Africa," of a society grounded economically on an indenture system that would lead to free labor and economic autonomy. Anticipating the arguments of emancipationists of the 1830s, Sharp called for gradual manumission, facilitated through a program of moral and of religious education. As a liberal evangelical, he outlined an egalitarian constitution for the settlement. As a member of the Established Church, Sharp advocated freedom of private worship, provided that the religion in question was *consistent* with the religious Establishment, meaning the Church of England. Its citizens, therefore,

> Must be careful ... *not to establish* any *Religion* that is *inconsistent* with the *religious Establishment of England,* though, as individuals, they are certainly entitled to a *perfect liberty of conscience,* and to a *free exercise* of their several modes of worship in *private* assemblies; but not as *public,* or equal establishments. For the *Common Law* of England, and the *established Religion* of England, are really more closely connected together than is either generally conceived by the good people of England at large, or than is ordinarily apprehended even by the learned professors themselves, of the two excellent establishments... [iv–v; italics in text].

The philanthropist Thomas Clarkson, at the age of twenty-five, was awarded a prize for a 1785 Latin essay. It was translated and well received, in 1786, under the provocative title, "Is it right to make slaves of others against their will?" After the 1807 passage of the Abolition Bill, Clarkson who was a tireless opponent of slavery wrote his magisterial, two-volume *A History of the Abolition of the African Slave-trade* (1808). He became a leading member of the Anti-Slavery Society, which was founded in 1823 for the abolition of slavery in the West Indies (*Chambers* 282).

The efforts of Sharp, of Clarkson, and of others were realized in "An Act for the Abolition of the Slave Trade." On 24 June 1806, both Houses of Parliament resolved to outlaw the trade, as of 1 May 1807, and to proscribe all of its activities, whether directly or indirectly carried on anywhere in or on the coast of Africa, on the passage from Africa to the West Indies, or anywhere else in the overseas dominion of the King (*EHD.* vol. XI, 803). The Statute contained severe penalties: the forfeiture of a vessel, substantial fines per slave on board, and the freedom of slaves on board foreign slave vessels captured in war was to be conferred after fourteen years of military service (804). However, despite the steep fines for violations of the Act, the trade persisted illegally (803–04).

In the post-abolition period, emancipationists, such as William Wilberforce (1759–1833) and Thomas Fowell Buxton (1786–1845), committed themselves to the struggle of freeing slaves who were still living in the colonies. A philanthropist and close friend of William Pitt, Wilberforce in 1788 had joined with Clarkson and the Quakers in the abolition struggle. In 1823, Wilberforce's pamphlet, "Appeal ... in behalf of the Negro Slaves in the West Indies" expresses consternation that Christian nations tolerated slavery and that its continuance, for two centuries, was destroying the moral character of the nation: "That such a system should so long have been suffered to exist in any part of the British Empire will appear, to our posterity, almost incredible" (25).

Buxton was a social reformer, a brewer by trade, and an M. for Weymouth (1818–1837). A reformer of criminal law, the penal system, and advocate of slaves, he succeeded Wilberforce, in 1824, as leader of the Anti-Slavery Party (Chambers 205). Evangelical and secular opponents of slavery worked together against the powerful sugar commerce of the West Indies, but their efforts were obstinately resisted (Mathieson 111–14, 215–16). Eventually, the increasing danger of social unrest and the growing economic liability of the system contributed to the 1833 manumission of the slaves.

Darwin and FitzRoy had a misunderstanding while aboard the *Beagle* that was connected indirectly with slavery in Brazil and with manumission of the slaves in British colonies, which at the time was a source of heated public contention. We must remember, to begin with, that Darwin held the Captain in high regard. In his *Autobiography*, he wrote approvingly of FitzRoy's devotion to duty, generosity, bold determination, indomitable energy, ardent friendship, and helpfulness (72). But Darwin also found him to be temperamental. The disagreement arose from a simple conversation. Darwin alleged that, while at Bahía Blanca, FitzRoy visited a slave owner who had assembled many slaves and asked them whether they were happy and wished to be free. All then answered, yes and then no, respectively (74). After hearing Fitzroy relate this experience, Darwin recalls having said the following: "I then asked him, perhaps with a sneer, whether he thought that the answers of slaves in the presence of their master [are] worth anything. This made him excessively angry, and he said as I doubted his word, we could no longer live together" (*Autobiography* 73–74).

To assume on the basis of this exchange that FitzRoy held a pro-slavery position does not take all the information we have into account. Politically, we know, they were on opposite sides of the aisle: FitzRoy a Tory and Darwin a Whig. Darwin observes, in an 18 May 1832 correspondence to J. S. Henslow, that Fitzroy was hospitable and got along well with him, but he was glad the Captain had not made him an apostate to Whig ideas. He could never become a Tory because of their callousness about slavery (*CDC* I 238). It is reasonable to infer from this passage that they had political discussions and that FitzRoy was sympathetic to Tory politics. That the conversation explicitly involved slavery, however, cannot directly be inferred. It is clear that Darwin found the Tory stance on slavery irksome, but there is no evidence that FitzRoy upheld it.

More could be learned about FitzRoy's understanding of slavery as a political, historical, economic, and moral anomaly by reviewing his writings on the subject in 1839, and if his reactions to the enslaved themselves are taken into account. In the 1839 *Narrative*, FitzRoy maintains, as had Darwin in 1832, that even though some Brazilian plantation owners treat the slaves humanely (probably out of economically self-serving motives), it is improbable that this benevolence "will eradicate feelings excited by the situation of those human beings" (Narr. 2 61). FitzRoy made the evocative assertion that, despite the material opulence slavery created, the system was self-destructive, and its presence was having adverse, national implications. The colonial system, in its need for slave labor, was endangering its own welfare, thought FitzRoy, in that the danger of violent upheaval was increasing in direct proportion to the growing slave population. The "immense extent and increase of the slave population," he predicts, will override factors long believed to have stood in the way of a general black revolt. Brazilian slavers, then, could no longer feel confident that the pervasive ignorance, mutual distrust between slaves, and differences in language would suffice to keep the blacks disunited (Narr. 2 61). The Brazilians had been experiencing the lamentable consequences of slavery: white colonists have been demoralized by "extreme indolence" (Darwin agreed) and had sunken into "gross sensuality"; and the "growing hordes of enemies" (their identities not specified) were a cause of dread and perplexity throughout the country (Narr. 2 61). FitzRoy articulates a pragmatic and moral argument: to ameliorate this situation would require the Brazilians to condemn the excesses of the slave economy with one voice, for "the selfish conduct of individuals" was destabilizing the country (Narr. 2 61).

One sure way of ending the system would have been to stem the supply of forced labor and to emancipate the slaves, as the introduction of new ones was prevented. If these conditions were met, FitzRoy is reasonably certain that Brazil "would commence a career of prosperity, and her population would increase in an unlimited degree." The chief reason for the Brazilian slave trade, as he sees it, is the "want of population" needed "to clear away primeval forests, and render the soil fit for culture" (Narr. 2 61). An industrious work-force was required to labor long hours in the heat to cultivate sugar cane, cotton, and other tropical crops. Because of the labor necessity, "selfish, unprincipled owners of immense territories" imported thousands of "unhappy wretches" who, once arriving in Brazil, have become "the helpless instruments of immense gain to their owners" (Narr. 2 61).

In FitzRoy's judgment, the trade could be effectively suppressed by external methods, such as blockades and "the cause of so abominable a traffic" eventually eliminated. If the black population were freed, he counsels, they could be encouraged to work for their own benefit, receiving remuneration from their employers (former slave-owners); under such circumstances, they would have "a prospect of future comfort for themselves and their offspring." Under these conditions, the agricultural economy would continue to prosper, and the demand for labor would considerably diminish (Narr. 2 62). The first step towards achieving this satisfactory result, then, would be for the government of a slave-importing country to designate the trade piratical. A juridical declaration of this kind would rest on a firm, ethical foundation: the government can then proclaim "every human being free, bound to no one," and free to do anything "not contrary to religion, or law," in its sovereign territory or on its ships. This plan would assuredly cause "individuals" (that is, slave owners) to suffer economically for a time, "but the mass of society would be beneficiaries." Furthermore, the danger of a bloody uprising would be diminished (Narr. 2 62).

The Captain's reflections on the abolition of slavery and on the manumission of those in colonial bondage in Brazil were timely and motivated by ethical conviction. For decades, politicians had wrangled over the issue. The hypocrisy of the trade resonated throughout the proceedings of both Houses. William Pitt the Younger, at the time a Whig, condemned slavery in an impassioned and well-reasoned address to the Commons in April 1792. As early as 1787, he had worked closely with Wilberforce to enlist the government in the campaign (Jarrett 123–25). Its iniquity, Pitt avers, is the direct result of laissez-faire economic policy: "I know of no evil that has ever existed ... worse than the tearing of seventy or eighty thousand persons annually from their native land, by a combination of the most civilized nations inhabiting the most enlightened parts of the globe." Most appalling was that the laws of these nations, which call themselves free, were perpetrating this crime (Pitt 28). Unfortunately, the abolitionists' cause was inhibited by political delays for fifteen years, that is, up to 1807, the year of Pitt's death. Socio-historical realities called for caution, however. In the colonies, Dissenting ministers, who had preached natural-rights doctrine to the slaves, were accused of being rabble-rousers, directly responsible for serious uprisings in Demerara (August 1823), in Jamaica (June 1824), and in Montego Bay (1832) (Mathieson 211). The danger of revolution in the West Indies was a subject of fervent debate.

Though natural-rights enthusiasts framed their rhetoric in a revolutionary context, it would be incorrect to assume that revolutionary France, in 1789, was an anti-slavery bastion. On the contrary, although the French Revolution abolished slavery, and rather belatedly at that, anti-abolitionists were well organized, amply funded, and actually controlled the National Assembly. A restored slavery system lasted in the French colonies until 1848, but it was never re-instituted in Saint-Dominique (which, on 1 January 1894, became the Republic of Haiti) (Doyle 412–13).

Another factor that affected FitzRoy's opinion of slavery was the slaves' rehearsed responses and behavior. Darwin realized that the owner ordered the slaves to choreograph a welcome dance or celebration when visitors arrived. When the slaves were asked if they were content with their lives or wanted to go back to Africa, they responded yes to the first question and no to the second. They complied in this way because public disobedience would invariably have incurred grave punishment. When FitzRoy visited the Bahía plantation, for which Darwin criticized him, the "great slave-owner" gave him the royal treatment: the assembled slaves loved where they were and would not think of repatriation. Their resounding affirmation confirmed FitzRoy's idea that, with careful planning, slavery could be gradually transformed into a contractual system, but it masked the human suffering slavery was causing.

Another factor involved in the disagreement between Darwin and FitzRoy was miscommunication and bad form on Darwin's part. Although FitzRoy was naively taken in by the slaves' performance, Darwin was not. His mistake was to ask the ship's Captain and host, "*perhaps with a sneer*," if he thought "that the answers of slaves in the presence of their master [were] worth anything." FitzRoy had been insulted by a guest, an act of insubordination. The Captain's anger was not necessarily precipitated by the debate over the pros and cons of slavery, because FitzRoy did not need to be convinced of slavery's moral turpitude or whether or not it destroyed a nation internally. It was the sneer and Darwin's impertinent questioning of the Captain's word that caused his temporary eviction. The affront to the Captain was obvious: Darwin had implied that he was a fool. The Captain eventually apologized to Darwin for having dislodged him from his cabin. The important point is that the argument, according to Darwin's version of events, seems to have been ignited more by a perceived insult than by ideological differences between the two men. In light of what FitzRoy had to say about slavery in 1839, and judging from his humane behavior to native people throughout both voyages, I see no evidence supporting the charge that he was a pro-slavery opponent of Darwin's.

As we return to the *Diary*, we find Darwin and company exploring inland regions, more acutely aware of the living conditions of black people. In Rio de Janeiro, on 8 April 1832, he visited the small village of Ithacaia, situated on a plain, on the outskirts of which were the huts of black slaves. The configuration and positioning of these huts reminded him of drawings he had seen of Hottentot habitations in South Africa (*BD* 53). In a *Field Notebook*, he records that the huts resembled those built by Hottentots, and they were probably designed this way because "poor blacks" were trying to persuade themselves "that they are in the land of their Fathers" (*BD* 53n.). The creation of facsimile villages certainly evidenced nostalgic longings.

Anecdotes accumulating in the *Diary* exposed slave civilization for what it was. At a campsite outside the same village, Darwin comes across a notorious location, "a long time ... residence of some run-away slaves who by cultivating a little ground near the top contrived to eke out a [means of] subsistence" (*BD* 53). Slavers pursued them diligently. A deleted passage reads: "At length some soldiers were sent & secured them all, excepting one old woman, who sooner than be again taken, dashed herself to pieces from the very summit.—I suppose in a Roman matron this would be called noble patriotism, in a [black woman] it is called brutal obstinacy!" (*BD* 54). Interpolated into the *Journal* (1839), this note bore the unequivocal message that heroic gestures on the part of blacks were meaningless (*JR* [1839], 16).

On 13 April 1832, while visiting a Portuguese farm in the region of Socêgo, an estate in Rio de Janeiro, Darwin described the topography of the coffee plantation and the architecture of the buildings, admiring their simple efficiency. Outside the main buildings were huts, housing one hundred and ten blacks whom the proprietor Manoel Joaquem da Figuireda, a relation of one of the men in their party, had been managing in a kindly manner. The pasturage boasts an abundance of game, and oranges and bananas flourished, so there was a "profusion of food" (*JR* [1839] 19). Each guest was expected to sample from a diversity of dishes.

But this little world, its material abundance and economic order notwithstanding, was no paradise. Darwin could see through the veneer and glimpsed the tell-tale signs of its moral depravity. During the meal, for instance, "it was the employment of a man to drive out sundry old hounds & dozens of black children which together at every opportunity crawled in."

Darwin seemed to be of two minds in his reaction to Figuireda's world. On the one hand, it exemplified man's ability to harness natural resources and to carve a civilization out of raw jungle, while, on the other hand, its pervasive inhumanity was unnerving. The grouping of children with scrounging dogs angered him; nevertheless, he admired the simple proficiency of the plantation and "its patriarchal style of living" (*JR* [1839] 19). The alluring aspects of da Figuireda's establishment, the application of European ingenuity to the jungle, intrigued him, but, at the same time, he realized that this was a fallen paradise, its efficiency and material abundance having been bought at the expense of human dignity. In the midst of the jungle, the *Fazenda* appeared to be "a place of perfect retirement & independence [from] the rest of the world" (at least for the Portuguese). But, despite the ordered landscaping, at every turn Darwin was disturbed by the lifestyle of the blacks, the tranquility of which he thought to be illusive. He had difficulty rationalizing the moral anomaly, and the contradictions, of da Figuireda's plantation: slaves sang religious hymns as they engaged in forced labor, yet they seemed to pass "contented & happy lives" (as far as material needs were concerned), and the proprietor (according to Darwin's view) was "intelligent & enterprising" (*BD* 57).

Of course, Darwin had not yet interviewed the slaves. Even if he had done so, their opinions could not have been taken at face value, for, at his departure, they would have been held responsible for what they had said. Darwin's impression, on the basis of what he saw and heard, was that the slaves had adapted themselves to captivity. In the *Diary*, he explained why da Figuireda's farm did not fit the image of a squalid, forced-labor camp. The blacks of Socêgo were indeed slaves, he wrote on 14 April 1832, but they had a degree of economic freedom. On Saturdays and Sundays, they worked for themselves and lived off the produce they gathered, which was sufficient to feed a man and a family for a week (*BD* 58). By 1839, Darwin would revise this judgment considerably.

The efficiency and order Darwin perceived in da Figuireda's plantation obscured the moral depravity of the system that sustained it. On 15 April 1832, at another and quite different estate, this one on the Río Macae, the deprivation was worse and more obvious. On the way to the estate of Patrick Lennon, an Irish merchant, Darwin views slaves at a farm who appear "miserably overworked & badly clothed" (*BD* 58). The system in place there was quite different from that which Manoel da Figuireda employed: instead of giving slaves Saturday and Sunday off, during which to work for themselves, and instead of allowing them to store their harvest to support their families for a week's time, these slaves were arduously at work long after dark. Even greater abuses were glaringly evident. At Lennon's estate, Darwin overhears "a most violent & disagreeable quarrel between Mr. Lennon and his agent" over a lawsuit. In retaliation, Lennon threatens to sell at public auction "an illegitimate mulatto child to whom Mr. Cowper [the agent] was much attached." Lennon threatened to take all of the women and children from their husbands, to sell them separately at the market in Rio de Janeiro, and, in effect, to separate family members from one another (*BD* 58). In the *Journal*, Darwin observed that, for financial not moral reasons, Lennon reneged on his threat (*JR* [1839] 20).

Darwin's indignation over this scene brings to mind August Ludwig von Schlozer's "A New Year's Letter from Jamaica," written at Kingston on 17 December 1778. Schlozer describes a horrible scene. On the morning of 7 December, he had heard a black man walking through the streets with a bell, advertising the sale of African slaves, five-hundred fifty in all, who had been captured on the coast of Guinea. Schlozer remarks that the slaves are being advertised, as if they are "oysters and dried cod." At the "market," Schlozer is shocked to find a mass of black men, women, and children, "all stark naked," and each having a numbered card hung around the neck. He compared the spectacle to the selling of geese and pigs. Potential buyers walked about, examining the blacks. Prices ranged from 200 to 600 Reichsthaler, the elderly and children being the cheapest. One sugar planter purchased for 150 R. a twelve-year-old girl who was separated forever from her family (von Schlozer 688–89).

Lennon's behavior stirred Darwin to ask: "Can two more horrible & flagrant instances be imagined?" He was particularly astonished by Lennon's moral duplicity: European visitors were treated with elegance while blacks were dehumanized. Darwin can not fathom how Lennon, a supposed paragon of "humanity & good feeling" whose character seems "above the common run of men," has absolutely no compunction about selling human beings and about settling litigation through the dispersal of thirty families "who had lived together for many years" (*JR* [1839] 21).

Lennon's character flaw could have been the result of conditioning, another point that FitzRoy considered in regard to the mentality of slaveholders. Darwin also thought that people like Lennon could become so inured to the slavery system that they had no sympathy for their victims; thus, for slave merchants, blacks were units of merchandise, not human beings. Astounded at how the system had warped Lennon's outlook and eroded his conscience (although Lennon's background and mental health were unknown), Darwin profoundly states, "How strange & inexplicable is the effect of habit & interest." Subtle arguments maintaining slavery to be a "tolerable evil," he asserts, dissipate before the moral enormity of the system and before the depravity of its purveyors (*JR* [1839] 21).

Darwin's choice of anecdotes was judicious and effective. In 1839, for example, he interpolated into the *Journal* a disturbing recollection of a black man whom he had encountered on a ferry. In an effort to make his meaning plain to the man, Darwin spoke loudly, made signs, and inadvertently waved his hands near the man's face; at this gesture, the man abruptly shut his eyes and cringed, as if expecting a blow to the face. Darwin writes that he will never forget "his feelings of surprise, disgust, and shame at seeing a great powerful man afraid even to ward off a blow" (*JR* [1839] 21). It was obvious from this disagreeable experience that the man had been degraded (*JR* [1839] 21). Clearly, the system destroyed the dignity of the enslaved, adversely affecting both mind and body.

On 30 May 1832, while ascending the Corcovado Mountain to measure its altitude and to take barometric readings (*BD* 68), Darwin alludes to its notorious history as a hideout for "Maroon or run-away slaves." On an earlier ascent, he and his companions had the misfortune of meeting three "villainous looking ruffians, armed up to the teeth," whom he identifies as "Maticans or slave-hunters" (*BD* 69). The hunters received payment for escaped slaves they either returned or killed. As proof of having killed an escapee, they "bring down the ears." One slave, in particular, who escaped Lennon's estate on the Macae, survived in a cave for two and one-half years. He was able to support himself, possibly by finding work in the lowlands. This story of perseverance contradicts the anti-abolitionist argument that a freed slave will not work. If slaves will work when they are in hiding, thought Darwin, then surely they will work if emancipated. He, no doubt, was thinking of the hard-working slaves of da Figuireda who, though captives, had great incentive to work hard on weekends, since they kept the produce they harvested. Blacks freed from slave-ships by British naval vessels had been hired out to different tradesmen for seven-year apprenticeships and could support themselves thereafter. Despite these facts, anti-abolitionists and slavers, motivated by self-interest and blind prejudice, obstinately defended the system (*BD* 69).

In the entry of 3 July 1832, Darwin broadly described the Brazilian colonialists as being morally and legally corrupt (*BD* 79–80). As far as he could judge, the Brazilians "possess but a small share of those qualities which give dignity to mankind." They appeared to be ignorant, cowardly, and indolent, and his description of them was quite demeaning. With his interest in expressions and in how physiognomy reflected one's thoughts and personality, he derided the monks, whose faces were plainly stamped with the look of cunning, sensuality, and pride, one old man reminding him of a woodcut depiction of Judas Iscariot. One obvious reason for Darwin's hostility was the pervasive brutality of the Brazilians, the clergy included, towards black slaves; but to generalize in this manner about an entire ethnic group was comparable to reading skulls.

Anecdotal experiences continued to fuel Darwin's indignation. Augustus Earle (1793–1838), official artist on the *Beagle*, for example, claims to have seen "the stump of the joint, which was wrenched off in the thumb-screw," a device often found in the homes of slavers (*BD* 79). Mr. Earle's experience led Darwin to consider the subject of slave ethnology and demographics. The enormous slave population, he noted, was a matter of interest to everyone who visits Brazil (*BD* 79). As one walked through the streets, one spied a variety of African tribes, identified by the various ornaments cut in the skin, and by their expressions and mannerisms. In his view, the mixing of so many people and languages hindered the unification of the slaves, lessening the chance of uprising. All were taught Portuguese and had to communicate in that language, although one wonders at the wisdom of that practice, as a common language facilitated cooperation between slaves and fostered dissent. Darwin foresaw the blacks ruling Brazil, given their large population, their physical superiority to the colonialists, their underrated intellects, and their efficiency in all the necessary trades. He predicted an imminent revolution, presumably after general emancipation, if freed blacks increased in number, as they inevitably would, and became discontented at not being equal to white men (*BD* 80). In the ambiguous statement, "the slaves are happier than what they ... expected to be or than people in England think they are," Darwin seems to be saying that life on a reformed plantation, such as on the Socêgo model, no doubt, was better than the ordeal of the Atlantic passage, than the humiliation of being examined while naked and sold as livestock (as per von Schlozer's *Letter*), or than the tyranny of a Patrick Lennon (*BD* 80). This admission aligned him with FitzRoy: slave societies were not homogeneous in character.

Unquestionably, then, Darwin respected and sympathized with the blacks in Brazilian captivity. "The leading feature in their character," he writes, "appears to be wonderful spirits & cheerfulness, good nature, & a 'stout' heart mingled with a good deal of obstinacy." He hopes that, when they eventually assert their rights against the slavery system, they will have "forget[ten] to avenge their wrong" (*BD* 80).

Between 1833 and 1845, Darwin wrote about slavery in his correspondence, in his notebooks, and in the 1845 *Journal of Researches*. Though discontinuous and fragmentary, these writings reveal the consistency of his thinking on the subject. To his sister Catherine, he writes, on 22 May 1833, of how happy he was to learn that the anti-slavery sentiment in England was increasing, and he expresses his pride that England will be the first European country to emancipate the slaves. Of his ideas on slave culture and personality, the most prominent in his mind was the stalwartness of blacks, their dignity overshadowing the small and murderous Portuguese. So moved was he by the experiences in places like Fuentes and Socêgo that he intemperately wished for Brazil what had happened in Haiti (i.e., independence from France through violent struggle in the 1790s). This, however, was a dangerous utterance for a naturalist and guest on board a British vessel to make. It naively ignored the horrific violence that could take place in a race war. On a more sanguine note, Darwin extolled the Whig campaign for manumission in a letter of 2 June 1833, to J. M. Herbert; and he praises Whigs who were soon to attack colonial slavery, which was a national disgrace (*CDC* I 320).

Darwin's Brazilian experience stimulated his interest in race and inheritance. Meditations on race in Notebook-*B* passages, entered from July 1837 to February 1838, have to do with inheritance and speciation. He read widely on the subject. Among the contemporary sources on his list was the work of the zoologist and diplomat William Sharp MacLeay (1792–1865). MacLeay's insect treatise, *Horae Entomologicae* (1819–21), in particular, stimulated Darwin to compose nearly two-dozen notebook entries on entomology (*CDN* 678) and one-dozen reflections on MacLeay's 1829–1830 botanical research, chiefly on the dichotomous system. Of relevance to our discussion are the botanist's speculations on the human species and, specifically, on the transmission of genetic traits, such as skin color.

MacLeay's interest in inheritable traits was directly relevant to his training as a botanist, and he explored these ideas in relation to human beings and to race. In Note *B*179, according to Darwin, MacLeay postulates that the offspring of black and white parents will revert invariably to the "native stock"—the implication being that all races had originated from white forebears and had subsequently degenerated into races having dark skin. When MacLeay suggests that the offspring of black and white parents will often be whiter than white parents, he seems to have been advocating a monogenetic view of human origins, a theory of human origins Thomas Huxley identified as Adamite Monogenetics. Those espousing this doctrine held that the "native stock" or original race of human beings was white ("Ethnology" 85).

In animal husbandry, Darwin was aware of reversion occurring if species or hybrids are crossed artificially: "When species cross & hybrids breed, their offspring show [a] tendency to return to one parent," a less strongly marked tendency being true for varieties of the same species (*B*203, *CDN*, 222).

MacLeay's system implied that miscegenation was not a mixing of *races* but of different *species*, in Darwin's view, an unacceptable assertion. A hereditary mechanism, the botanist further implied, resists the intercrossing of white with nonwhite human beings; hence, the offspring reverted to white on the grounds that this was purportedly the original skin color of the human race (according to the Adamites' biblical reading of human origins and of racial descent).

MacLeay's concepts of race and of human descent were outgrowths of his *Quinary* system of taxonomy. A numerical and diagrammatic model designed to show the intrinsic harmony of nature, the Quinary format was incompatible with the theory of evolution because it schematically classified organisms with circular model (Ghiselin 104). MacLeay arranged all taxa or zoological classes into circles, five in each; adjacent circles representing distinct taxonomic categories were placed in circumferential contact with larger circles or categories (Mayr 202–03).

To refute MacLeay's racist notions, in *B*179 Darwin consulted the work of zoologist and army surgeon Andrew Smith, in particular, the latter's *Report of the expedition for exploring Central Africa, from the Cape of Good Hope*, 23 June 1834 (published in 1836). Smith's explanation of skin-color variation was more plausible than that of MacLeay: Smith learned from mulattos whom he had met on his journey that this lightening of skin color through several generations was attributable, quite simply, to subsequent intermarriages between mulattos and whites. The actual mechanism of heredity, of recessive and dominant genes and the propagation of traits, was not known at the time. Gregor Johan Mendel (1822–1884) had begun experimenting with peas in his garden, in 1857, culminating in his discovery of the laws of heredity in 1860 and the publication of his genetic theories in 1865.

The suffering of Brazilian slaves at the hands of plantation owners became a powerful emotive force that inspired Darwin to define the idea of humanness and to dismiss artificial models such as MacLeay's. As far as Africans were concerned, Darwin realized that being human had nothing to do with race. FitzRoy agreed with this truth. Accordingly, on his second trip to Tierra del Fuego, he would differentiate the savage anomaly (i.e., human beings in a rude or uncivilized state) from the anomalous savage (i.e., natives being inherently subhuman), and he would do so despite his occasional references to monogenetic paradigms and to his endorsement of the Mosaic account of human migrations. This humanistic revelation was ethically, biologically, and psychologically meaningful for Darwin as well. The Chilean-Brazilian experience with slavery taught him a clear lesson on adaptation and gave him valuable insights into natural selection: the adversities of Brazilian slavery, rather than reducing blacks to incivility, made them stronger and more inventive.

Darwin also recognized that those who were inhumane degraded themselves. In several notations of the period, he expressed an intuitive understanding of slavery's adverse effects on human beings. He realizes, for example, that slave-owners and their supporters soothed their consciences with perverse interpretations about the humanity of black people: "We do not like to consider animals whom we have enslaved to be our equals. Do not slave holders wish to make the black man [an]other kind" (*B*231, *CDN*, 228). In essence, the enslavers' practice of degrading blacks and of depersonalizing them numbed their consciences and damaged the moral character: "Has not the white Man, who has debased his Nature & violates every best instinctive feeling by making [a] slave of his fellow black, often wished to consider him as other animal — it is the way of mankind" (*C*154, *CDN*, 286).

The private discourse also suggests that Darwin subscribed to a kind of secular humanism vis-à-vis Africans, differentiating his abolitionist view from that of religious figures in the movement. Since his humanitarianism was secular and naturalistic, he distanced himself from religious abolitionists on the grounds that, in his opinion, they exhibited the sin of pride in thinking that man was specially created or elected. Even though abolitionists of this kind advocated the Africans' cause and "justly" exalted the dignity of mankind, they unjustifiably assumed humanity to be "godlike" and the Bible to be the inerrant source of this revelation (*C*154–155, *CDN*, 286). The "natural arrangement," countered Darwin, was otherwise: the origin, development, and variations of man, though monogenetic in the sense of the singular origin of the species, must be understood as a "descent," the races of man differing from each other, not as one species to another, but in terms of physical differences, such as size, skin color, and outward features. Rhetorical features of the note — parentheses, a question mark, and jumbled syntax — suggest that Darwin was reluctant to engage with this issue too closely or could not develop his argument fully within its limits. He briefly raised the question of intelligence and race: if, as he believes, the races of man differ chiefly in terms of physical attributes, is there a fundamental difference in mentality between different human groups: "*(hence intellect?) & what kinds of intellect*" (*C*204, *CDN*, 303; italics added)?

Darwin's afterthoughts on Brazilian slavery were added to the revised 1845 edition of the *Journal*. Leaving Brazil on 19 August 1832 was a relief, and he hoped never again to visit "a slave-country" (*JR* [1845] 499). The experiences, though brief, were unforgettable: "To this day, if I hear a distant scream, it recalls with painful vividness my feelings, when passing a house near Pernambuco, [where] I heard the most pitiable moans, and could not but suspect that some poor slave was being tortured, yet knew that I was as powerless as a child even to remonstrate" (*JR* [1845] 499). He recounts how, near Rio de Janeiro, he had lived opposite to an old lady who used thumb screws to crush the fingers of female slaves; and he remembers being in a house where he helplessly witnessed the daily mistreatment of a young mulatto, who was "reviled, beaten, and persecuted enough to break the spirit of the lowest animal." With his own eyes, he witnessed a Spanish slave-holder horse-whip a six- or seven-year-old black child, all because the child had handed Darwin an unclean glass, and while the child's father trembled at a glance from his cruel master (*JR* [1845] 499). As these anecdotes suggest, the idea that slavery was a tolerable evil was a fallacy, but few people had a true and comprehensive understanding of its ugliness. Travelers tended to meet slaves briefly and under arranged circumstances.

Darwin even rethought the argument that there were different levels of enslavement, some better than others. It is difficult to refute the notion that da Figuireda was not Lennon, but more general assertions and comparisons usually were questionable. One contention was that slaves could, under certain circumstances, be better off than poor whites. Darwin rejected this anti-abolitionist claim outright: poor whites have never been placed in perpetual servitude, to be "sold like beasts to the first bidder." What perplexed Darwin the most was that those who enslaved, those who justified slavery, and those who rationalized its continuance, professed "to love their neighbors as themselves" (*JR* [1845] 499).

# 5. FitzRoy and Darwin
## in Tierra del Fuego

In the *Diary* entry of 17 December 1832, Darwin records his enthusiasm upon entering Good Success Bay and at anchoring "in so wild a country as Tierra del F[uego]," as "the very name of the harbor ... recalls the idea of a voyage of discovery" (121). Tierra del Fuego or "Land of Fire" was Ferdinand Magellan's metaphor. When he had arrived there on 21 October 1520, at first sight no natives were visible, but the inhabitants' signal fires illuminated the coastline, inspiring him to name the place accordingly (Cooper 108). Excitement and apprehension were mixed, as Darwin and company entered this mysterious and foreboding region. This was dangerous territory. He recalled a tragic incident during Cook's 1769 voyage when Sir Joseph Banks and Dr. Solander, while mountain climbing at Good Success Bay on 16–17 January, were caught in a snowstorm and lost two members of their party (*BD* 121, 122n.).

On Sunday 16 December 1832, any question about the presence of natives was answered when, like Magellan and company, the crew of the *Beagle* glimpsed "the usual signal fires"; but, unlike the Spanish navigator, they spotted natives who were, in turn, watching the ship intently. Darwin was unsure about the purpose of the fires: were they lit to communicate with other Indians, with the *Beagle,* or with both? In the afternoon of the 17th, while doubling the northern entrance of the Bay, they saw Fuegians "perched on a wild peak overhanging the sea & surrounded by wood" (*BD* 121). As the ship passed by, they sprang up, waved cloaks, and shouted sonorously, following the ship up the harbor. Just before dark, their cry could once again be heard, as they lit a fire at the entrance of a newly assembled wigwam.

FitzRoy's account of their arrival was similar to Darwin's. Perhaps recalling his first encounter with the Fuegians, the Captain reflects that, to one who had never seen "man in his savage state," even a very distant view of these people was of great interest. In this statement, the Captain was making a significant distinction: savagery is a *state* or condition in which some men exist, rather than a state inherent in certain men. FitzRoy uses an oxymoron to highlight a moral dilemma experienced by numerous European explorers: "To those who had never seen man in his savage state — one of the most *painfully interesting* sights to his civilized brother — even this distant glimpse of the aborigines was deeply engaging" (Narr. 2 119; italics added). Seeing the aborigines for the first time was, at once, deeply shocking yet irresistibly interesting. The shock was due, of course, to the sight of frenzied, half-naked, body-painted natives, armed with spears and clubs, and speaking an unknown language.

Once the initial surprise had subsided, the explorer could view the natives in one of two ways: as degraded anomalies or simply as unfamiliar human beings. What distinguished FitzRoy's account of the initial meeting was his humanity. He uses the phrase "civilized brother" to communicate the fraternal bond he sincerely felt between explorer and natives, between human beings separated from one another by environmental, historical, and cultural circumstances (Narr. 2 119). In saying this, FitzRoy had also taken the first step towards the formulation of a critical ethnology: he not only recognized the native people as fellow human beings, but also that their present condition was a mysterious consequence of their unique social, cultural, and natural history.

The Alacalufan guests on board, York Minster and Jemmy Button, however, reviled the natives on shore, not because of their obviously uncivilized condition, but because the former recognized them as belonging to a tribe traditionally hostile to their own; that is why they were quoted as having called them "bad men." According to FitzRoy, the notorious *Oens* men (or rather *Onas*), inhabitants of a mountain range on the northeastern side of Beagle Channel, were fierce raiders who often attacked, not only the Alacaluf, but also the weaker Yamana and Yaghan tribes in the south, carrying off women and children, killing male prisoners, and looting villages. In April and May 1833, Oens raiders, numbering fifty to one hundred, would seize the canoes of a peaceful tribe, cross over to Navarino Island, and drive captives before them. Jemmy spoke of hard battles in the past and of an acrimonious history between the Oens, the Alacaluf, and other weak tribes (Narr. 2 204). Though they were face-to-face with traditional enemies, the Fuegians onboard were nonetheless happy about being so close to their homeland, and Jemmy spoke of how glad his friends would be to see him and of how well they would treat the crew for their kindness to him.

Seeking anchorage, the *Beagle* sailed deeper into the Bay. The Onas or

Oens became so excited at the prospect of the landing that they continued to shout, to wave their skins, and to set additional fires. On the 18th, FitzRoy, Darwin, and midshipman Robert Nicholas Hamond (1809–1833), who, in 1832, had accompanied Darwin on long excursions in Montevideo, met the natives for the first time, face-to-face (Narr. 2 120). This was a turning point in Darwin's ethnological thinking. Since 1580 Europeans had visited the Onas, but since the literature of these visits lacked detail, little was really known about them. So this was a groundbreaking moment. FitzRoy, however, was emotionally removed from the scene. More interested in the reactions of Darwin and Hamond to the natives than to the Onas' behavior towards them, the Captain writes of how he hoped to witness "the effect caused in their [the British] minds by this first meeting with man in such a totally savage state" (Narr. 2 119–20).

The moment had arrived. Five or six stout confident-looking men, standing six feet tall, half-clothed in guanaco skins, stood before FitzRoy, Darwin, and Hamond. Except for skin color and facial features, according to FitzRoy, they resembled the Patagonians more than the Fuegians, such as the Alacaluf, whom King had described in his book. Hamond, greatly impressed, remarks how pitiful it is that, "'such fine fellows should be left in such a barbarous state'" (Narr. 2 20). FitzRoy appreciated the genuineness of Hamond's sympathy: his expression of "natural emotion" should not be taken either as "individual caprice" or as "erroneous enthusiasm." The Captain experienced a revelation of his own. The sympathy and benevolence Hamond feels for "these ignorant, though by no means contemptible human beings" recalls feelings he had had on the previous voyage: a sense of fraternity and of moral responsibility, motivating him to care for the Fuegians, whom he had brought to England, and whom he was returning to their homeland (Narr. 2 121).

Any hope of understanding the Onas, Fitzroy reflected, could only be fulfilled if the visitors suppressed unpleasant feelings or preconceptions they might have had about savage humanity. The "mental contemplation of a savage," he acknowledges, is disagreeable and painful, given their appearance and behavior. An even more unmanageable emotion was denial: the explorer had to acknowledge his natural affinity to them. For this reason, some Europeans are unwilling to consider themselves "even remotely descended from human beings in such a state," while others, proudly and disdainfully, maintained savagery to be intrinsic to certain nonwhite races. Early ethnographers who felt this way constructed racial and social paradigms to distance themselves from the savage state, from which they themselves had emerged in the distant past. FitzRoy's perspective was more historical in scope: to stress the Fuegians' humanness, the Captain alludes to Caesar's astonishment at finding the Britons "painted and clothed in skins, like these Fuegians" (Narr. 2 121). In 54 B.C., Caesar describes the Britons in these terms: "All Britons stain themselves with woad [an herb], which makes them blue and more terrifying to confront in battle. Their hair they wear long, but they shave all the rest of their bodies except the head and upper lip" (*Gallic War* 102).

The Onas were somewhat like the ancient Britons in behavior and appearance, and their physical demeanor also had cultural meaning. Despite FitzRoy's perceptiveness, an air of condescension lingers in his allusion to the Onas' "childish ignorance of matters familiar to civilized man." Yet ignorance did not degrade them, in his opinion: though uncivilized by modern European standards, from what can be gathered they have achieved a "healthy, independent state of existence" (Narr. 2 121). Unlike the natives who employed narrow canoes in the network of waterways coursing through the regions, these natives were neither cramped, stooped, nor misshapen. Instead, they stood erect; some were stouter than others, but generally they were well proportioned. Most striking was their gregarious behavior. They express "satisfaction or good-will" tactilely, patting and rubbing their bodies and those of the visitors, and are pleased by the antics of crewmen who danced and mimicked. Although they looked rather frightening with their elaborate body paint, some having white circles around the eyes, red ochre and oil daubed on the upper lips, and full-body black paint, they were good-humored, danced, talked, and played with the shore party. Although these people did not act aggressively, York and Jemmy mocked them, nonetheless, and refused to acknowledge them as countrymen or neighbors. But, apparently, York understood some of what the Onas' were saying, which suggested their shared heritage (Narr. 2 121–22). In this sense, the repatriates' reaction was ironic: in their contempt for the Onas, they seemed to be repudiating their common history and a culture very similar to their own. The passage is doubly ironic in that the British Captain, and not the repatriated natives, exhibited great openness and objectivity towards the unexpectedly friendly Onas. On the 22nd, the *Beagle* sailed away from Good Success Bay.

FitzRoy's appreciation of the Onas belied the assumption that British explorers of the period were invariably insensitive to, and condescending towards, native cultures. The Captain not only differentiated the savage *human* being from the savage condition, but also did not dehumanize them in light of their deprivations; in fact, FitzRoy and Hamond regarded indigenous Fuegians of any tribe, not as inhuman, but rather as primitive human beings in a remediable condition. No doubt, they had come to this understanding through their personal relationships with the Fuegian guests. Even though a language barrier separated the two parties, the British and the Fuegian guests were able to overcome the breach in communication through expressions of friendship.

Unfortunately, unlike FitzRoy and Hamond, Darwin did not entirely resist the tendency to dehumanize native inhabitants and to treat them as if they were specimens in the London Zoological Gardens. Correspondence with his second cousin, the Reverend William Darwin Fox, on 23 May 1833 (five months after the encounters described above), exemplifies Darwin's tendency in this regard. The Feugians whom he encountered were wild, wretched, but intriguing (*CDC* I 316). The Onas' frenzied, though innocuous, behavior leads Darwin to reflect on the great difference "between savage & civilized man" (*BD* 122). At this point, the anthropological opinions of FitzRoy and of Darwin diverge considerably from one another. Whereas the Captain recognized the inalienable humanity of the Onas, their savage condition notwithstanding, Darwin offered only an abstruse analogy. The difference between savage and civilized man, he proposes, is "greater than between a wild & domesticated animal, in as much as in man there is greater power of improvement" (*BD* 122) The analogy that wild and domesticated animals were more closely related to each other than was savage to civilized man implied that savagery had degraded their humanity.

Savage mankind, some great minds of the period conjectured, had forfeited their humanity in the eyes of domestic or civilized man. One possible reason behind the dehumanization of aborigines in Darwin's early writings stemmed in part from the thought that they were reluctant or unable to develop their evolutionary advantage, which meant exercising their intelligence to meet the challenges of their world. If a man or tribe of men remained gatherers forever, then they must be intellectually stunted. According to this reasoning, the Fuegian could not be a *human* being in the fullest, European sense of the word, since his evolutionary endowment was barely evident in his material culture, and since he remained subjugated to the wilderness. Whereas FitzRoy saw dignity, perseverance, and strength in the Onas, Darwin could only demonize them: thus, they resemble "Devils on the stage, for instance in *Der Freischultz*" (*BD* 122). Janet Browne, calling this an apt metaphor, provides some interesting background details to the play and to its infernal imagery:

> The theme of Weber's melodramatic opera was a young wanderer in search of magic bullets to win a shooting contest and the love of his future bride. First performed in London in 1824, and seen by Darwin in Edinburgh in the same year, the high point was the scene in the "Wolf's Glen," where the magician's forge was sited. Staged with many novel lighting effects, including green and red smoke, and ghostly props that played to the British audience's fondness

for spectacle, the Glen was a gothic, pre–Wagnerian set piece that had caught Darwin's vivid adolescent imagination. The civilized world of Shrewsbury and country parsonages was indeed far behind him; in his mind, Milton, Humboldt, and Shakespeare were abandoned in favour of the sheer sensationalism of theatre. Weber, not *Paradise Lost*, provided the analogy for the supernatural other-world of his Fuegian experience [241].

Browne is quite correct to say that the spectacle and excitement of the first encounter overwhelmed Darwin emotionally and stifled analysis.

Perhaps because of the emotional excitement, Darwin described Onan language disparagingly, as noises chickens made at feeding, and thus being completely inarticulate. If by inarticulate, Darwin meant speech unintelligible to him, he was correct; however, if he meant speech that, in its own right, was incoherent, unclear, or ineffectively communicated the speaker's ideas or feelings, then he misinterpreted what he heard. To be fair to Darwin, it might be that he was following Captain Cook's example of comparing Fuegian speech patterns to a man clearing his throat, to a hoarse man trying to shout, or a to horse sputtering through the side of its mouth — sounds mixed together with "a few gutturals" (*BD* 124). All of these descriptors approximated their language phonetically. The absence of velar and of palatal sounds, and the preponderance of gutturals, would certainly sound strange to a European ear. But unknown to Darwin at the time, the Onas were indeed speaking a language and a complex one at that. Serious linguistic study of the Onas, however, would begin with the work of Thomas Bridges in 1875. In 1901 Henry Arctowski compiled a lexicon of 139 Onan words, phrases, and sentences, and José Maria Beauvoir wrote a dictionary of 1,876 words, 76 sentences and phrases, 132 proper names and the Lord's Prayer in the Onan language; in 1915, he would publish an important book on the subject; and Antonio Cojazzi authored the first book on Onan linguistics in 1911 (Cooper 67, 69, 78, 142).

It is interesting to note that, in the 1839 *Journal*, Darwin tempered what he had written earlier about the Onan language (*JR* [1839] 177). In 1839, he reiterates the opinion that these natives were not "articulate" — literally, that what they said was meaningless, devoid of a lexicon and of grammar. But he concedes that the Onas could repeat words with "perfect correctness" and even remember these words for some time; thus, they were curious about English words and sounded them out. Beyond parrot-like imitation, in 1839 Darwin concedes that the lack of communication between explorers and natives can be blamed less on the supposed verbal disability of the Onas than on the Europeans' inability to recognize sounds "in a foreign language" — an admission that the Onas' sputtering constituted a mode of verbal expression (*JR* [1839] 177).

By the standards of European civilization, the Onas appeared to have been in a miserable state (*BD* 124). Their diet, consisting of shellfish and mollusks, birds, seals, and guanaco, appeared to Darwin as being nutritionally inadequate. Although lacking property, they seemed nonetheless well equipped to hunt and to fight, possessing as they did bows, arrows, and spears. Since the land was so inhospitable, the Onas are reduced to occupying the beaches, where "these wretched looking beings pick up a livelihood" (*BD* 124–25). These factors lead Darwin to conclude that, "if the world was searched, no lower grade of man could be found.— The [South Sea] Islanders are civilized compared to them, & the [Eskimo] in subterranean huts may enjoy some of the comforts of life" (*BD* 125). This comparative statement suggests that, rather than to identify defining human characteristics in the natives, Darwin was more inclined to position them under the rubric *Fuegian*, and then to fix the entire group in a hierarchy of modern primitives. On a comparative scale, language, subsistence, technology, and habitations were measured against European standards. The hierarchical paradigm of races, to which Darwin resorted, rather than being an original approach to ethnology, was "an accepted part of conventional anthropological wisdom" (Stocking [1968] 113). But this conventional methodology proved to be a major impediment to ethnology, understood today as a "the science which treats of races and peoples, and of their relations to one another, their distinctive and other characteristics" (*OED* IV 314). Unfortunately, Darwin reused this spurious construct as late as 1871 when, in the peroration to *Descent*, he positioned "the Fuegians and other living savages in a chain which ran from ape to European" (Stocking [1968] 113). As Loren Eiseley points out, this method was a rigid and artificial way of looking at human evolution. Though simplistic, it lent coherence to the natural history of man, as native mankind was considered an extant remnant of early modern humanity. Western Europeans of the milieu were therefore as comfortable with the "notion of racial gradation ... leading downward toward the ape" as they were with the idea that indigenous people were "incapable of achieving high culture" (Eiseley 264).

From 21 December 1832 to 15 January 1833, the *Beagle* made its way to Goree Roads, a waterway running diagonally between Lennox and Navarino islands, near the eastern entrance of Beagle Channel (*BD* 132–33). This region was Jemmy's home and the place where FitzRoy had intended to assist the Rev. Richard Matthews (1811–1893), of the Church Missionary Society, to establish a settlement. York Minster decided, at the time, that he would live with Jemmy and Matthews at the new mission. Searching for a suitable coastal area fit for agriculture, they found a seemingly uninhabited inlet. FitzRoy then decided that they would board boats and head eighty-miles west to Ponsonby Sound, in the direction of Jemmy's homeland (*BD* 133).

On the morning of 19 January 1833, three whale-boats and the yawl, twenty-eight men in all, set out for the eastern entrance of the channel. Once in the channel, they entered an island cove on the 20th and began to explore the country (*BD* 134). Unidentified natives spotted them, lit signal fires, ran along the coast to spread the news of their arrival, and five of them suddenly appeared on a nearby cliff. With more than one group of natives in sight, Darwin describes them and conveys his feelings: "I shall never forget how savage & wild one group was ... they were absolutely naked & with long streaming hair; springing from the ground & waving their arms around their heads, they set forth most hideous yells. Their appearance was so strange, that it was scarcely like that of earthly inhabitants"(*BD* 134). In the 1845 *Journal*, Darwin interpolated into the text, at this point, a passage extolling Jemmy's character and intellect, his pride in tribe and country, and his scrupulosity about clothing. Despite Jemmy's foppishness, Darwin marvels at how far removed in manners he was from his race, and that Jemmy had once been a "miserable, degraded" savage, like the people whom they had met that day (*JR* [1845] 207–08).

According to the *Diary*, the unidentified natives behaved reasonably well. Understandably suspicious at first, they kept their sling-shots at the ready, but once the explorers gave them sought-after gifts, such as red tape for forehead bands, they were pleased. Discontentedly, they asked for more trifles, using the phrase *yamask-una* (phonetically in English: *yammerschooner*), variously defined as, *come here* or as *do be liberal to me* (Cooper 21; *BD* 134n.). Overall, on that day the natives were "inoffensive," perhaps because they were few in number (*BD* 134). But on the morning of the 21st, a party of "troublesome" natives arrived and threatened to skirmish. Realizing the destructive potential of their slings, Darwin reflects how unfortunate it would have been to have fired "on such naked miserable creatures" (*BD* 134). Ironically, as we have seen in King's narrative, the natives were brazen in the face of firearms, perhaps because Europeans tended to fire over their heads; thus, they may not all have understood the consequences of a bullet, thinking the guns noisemakers (*BD* 135). Twice they scoffed at pistol shots over their heads and at brandished cutlasses. Darwin disliked this tribe intensely, calling them "thieves" and bold cannibals (*BD* 135).

On 22 January 1833, after bivouacking in what appeared to be neutral location between hostile Yaghans and Jemmy's Alacalufan brethren, they set out again in the Channel, arriving at Ponsonby Sound by nightfall. There, they quartered with a Yamana family (*BD* 135n.). Uncharacteristically, on 20

January, FitzRoy had described these people contemptuously: "The Tekeenica [or Yamana], natives of the southeastern portion of Tierra del Fuego, are low in stature, ill-looking, and badly proportioned.... The trunk of the body is large, in proportion to their cramped and rather crooked limbs ... black hair half hides yet heightens a villainous expression of the worst description of savage features ... these satires upon mankind wear a part of the skin of a guanaco or a seal-skin upon their backs ... often there is nothing, either to hide their nakedness or to preserve warmth, excepting a scrap of hide" (Narr. 2 203).

Just as FitzRoy judged these natives harshly on the basis of their physical bearing, he likely misjudged their intentions, as many of them gathered for a celebration on the morning of 23 January, presumably in honor of the British (*BD* 135). They did not arrive in a calm, orderly procession, in their finery and bearing gifts. Instead, their hectic arrival astonished Darwin. Many of them ran so fast that their noses bled and mouths frothed. To make their arrival even more astonishing, they were painted in white, red, and black, making them look "like so many demoniacs who had been fighting" (*BD* 137).

The three boats, accompanied by twelve native canoes, then headed for Jemmy's cove where his family once lived. Once ashore, Jemmy had particular difficulty communicating with his brother, since Jemmy who had acquired a basic command of English astonishingly had forgotten his original tongue completely. His visit to England obviously had had a detrimental effect on his language skills. Darwin finds his predicament both "pitiable" and "laughable." Jemmy learned of his father's death and claimed that he had had a dream foretelling the event. Nothing could be learned about the father's death, however, as it was a custom not to speak of the deceased, but Jemmy refused to eat land-birds since there was reason to believe they fed on the bodies of the unburied dead. The crew believed that the father had been buried in the hills.

FitzRoy was taken aback when the repatriates met their relatives. On the one hand, the now-civilized natives looked down on their native countrymen, not with the historical contempt they held for the Onas, but with a mixture of pride in their current status and shame over their squalid past: "It is interesting to observe the change which three years only had made in their [the repatriates'] ideas, and to notice how completely they had forgotten the appearance and habits of their former [Alacalufan] associates; for it turned out that Jemmy's own tribe was as inferior in every way as the worst of those [i.e., the tribe met on 20 January], whom he and York called 'monkeys — dirty — fools — not men'" (Narr. 2 203). By the same token, the returning natives are not greeted with open arms: "instead of an eager meeting, there was a cautious circumspection which astonished us" (Narr. 2 206–07).

The behavior of Jemmy's family was even more disconcerting to the explorers. In the throes of cultural shock, fear, and resentment, his mother hardly looks at him, his two sisters run away, and his four brothers (and perhaps his uncle) simply stand still, stare at the finely dressed and coifed Jemmy, walk up to, and around him, and do so "without uttering a word" (Narr. 2 206–07). Their behavior mortified him, but, having lost fluency in his native tongue, he could only express his feelings in broken English. FitzRoy remarks, in a Darwinian tenor: "Animals when they meet show far more animation and anxiety than was displayed at this meeting" (Narr. 2 206–07).

Having settled in Woollya or Jemmy's cove (presently called Ushuaia), the settlers, on 23 January 1833, found rich ground for cultivating European crops. Three houses were being built, and two gardens were dug and planted. All of the nearly one-hundred-and-twenty natives were very quiet and peaceful, virtually unconcerned about the construction work. They asked for everything they saw, however, and stole whatever they could get their hands on; yet they danced, sang, and seemed to pose no overt threat to the shore party, as Darwin and others took long excursions into the hills and woods (BD 138).

On 27 January 1833, Alacalufan behavior took an ominous turn. Neither York nor Jemmy understood why the women and children suddenly retreated to the hills, for this behavior "did not promise peace for the establishment" (BD 138). Although Darwin and company could not account for this sudden change, there were several theories in the air: one was that the natives were frightened by target practice; the other more likely one had to do with a quarrel between a sentry and an old man. FitzRoy provided more information: it seems that two or three old men "tried to force themselves into our encampment." One old man, when barred by the sentry, "spit in his face; and went off in a violent passion," muttering, and gesturing at the sentry "who had very quietly, though firmly, prevented his encroachment" (Narr. 2 212–13). FitzRoy took the precaution of breaking camp and then of moving to a more defensible settlement. On the 28th, however, everything seemed to be normal, so FitzRoy sent the yawl and one whale-boat back to the *Beagle*, while Darwin and the remaining crew took the other two boats into Beagle Channel, to explore the western islands. That evening, after having set up camp, Darwin writes disconcertedly that "a party of Fuegians appeared" (probably Alacaluf) (BD 139). He was alarmed because FitzRoy and part of the landing party had already gone, and because they were situated on open ground (BD 139). The Fuegians' general reputation as relentless and unpredictable adversaries was on his mind; indeed, this was a moment of great anxiety.

At FitzRoy's return, the explorers disembarked and found a coastal inlet where they went ashore and set up another camp. On watch until one o'clock in the morning, Darwin reflected on the eerie solemnity of the scene. In the spaciousness of a savage world, he felt trapped. The consciousness of the situation, of being in a remote corner of the globe, "rushes on the mind." The sounds of breathing, the cry of night birds, and the occasional bark of a dog reminded him "that the Fuegians may be prowling, close to the tents, ready for a fatal rush" (*BD* 139). The night, fortunately, was uneventful.

On 6 February 1833, Darwin's contingent returned to the Settlement at Woollya/Ushuaia, only to find that the natives had been mistreating the missionary so badly that Captain FitzRoy advised him to return to the ship (*BD* 141). The harassment had begun on 28 January, shortly after the shore party had departed for the *Beagle*. The natives plundered the supplies, surrounded the Rev. Matthews' house, and threatened the occupants (including York and Jemmy) with stones and stakes. Naively believing the natives wanted only to rob them, Matthews met them with presents; however, Darwin thought that this threatening show meant something far worse, for the natives "showed by signs they would strip [Matthews] & pluck all the hairs out of his face & body" (*BD* 141). For Darwin, the removal of Matthews from this situation came with not a moment to spare. Matthews confided in FitzRoy about what had happened. Three days after the *Beagle* had departed from the fledgling mission, strangers in canoes arrived with the intention of robbing Matthews. One enraged native, demanding property, brandished a large stone. The natives teased the missionary, pulled his beard, and pushed him around. After these threats and the mistreatment, Matthews stated that he did not feel safe among "such a set of utter savages" (Narr. 2 219–23).

After describing Matthews' rescue, Darwin tries to account for native thievery, conjecturing that the "perfect equality of all the inhabitants will for many years prevent their becoming civilized: even a shirt or other article of clothing is immediately torn into pieces" (*BD* 141). Moreover, plunder did not remain with a single family or tribe, as there was a constant succession of canoes from other tribes, intent on pilfering. Jemmy's own family was partly to blame in that they showed strangers what they themselves had stolen and encouraged them to do the same.

The frenzy over material goods would not have happened, Darwin thought, if a chief were present to confiscate and apportion livestock (*BD* 141). Darwin ruminated on Fuegian polity. As far as Jemmy's Alacaluf tribe was concerned, FitzRoy observes that leaders were, in fact, designated. Jemmy's elder brother, for example, is a kind of witch doctor or conjurer who pretends to cure illnesses, and who is held in "high estimation" (Narr. 2 211–12).

The elder of a family or tribe among the Alacaluf is endowed with a kind of "executive authority," while the witch doctor dispenses advice on "domestic affairs" (Narr. 2 211–12). From this experience, FitzRoy logically deduces that, "In all savage nations, I believe there is a person of this description — a pretended prophet, conjuror, and, to a certain degree, doctor" (Narr. 2 211–12). Cooper, however, does not agree entirely with Fitzroy's claim for there being a predominant elder among the Fuegians: "There are no chiefs, hereditary or elective, among any of the Fuegian tribes" (177). The only "fixed authority" is of a man over his family, whereas older men and "wizards" exercise "a certain undefined influence" (178).

The apparent transformation of Jemmy and of the other natives into semi-civilized barbarians, for want of a better phrase, bode well for the missions and for colonial aspirations generally. Darwin had reason to believe that the experiment in acculturation succeeded in changing savages, "as far as habits go, [into] complete and voluntary Europeans" (BD 143). York Minster, for one, though a grown man "with a strong violent mind," will in every respect "live, as far as means go, like an Englishman." Jemmy momentarily preferred returning to England over staying, since he scorns his people: "they were all bad men, no 'sabe' [Spanish: to know] nothing" (it was later learned, Jemmy was mortified to find his own brother stealing from him).

In a moment of profound introspection, however, Darwin faces the possibility that what was learned in England "will not be conducive to their [the natives'] happiness," and he makes the ominous prediction that the male Alacaluf (Jemmy and York) and the female Yahgan (Fuegia Basket), though having been exposed to "the vast superiority of civilized over uncivilized habits," will inevitably regress to uncivilized living (BD 143). This was an interesting turn in Darwin's thinking. Two questions surface here: did he predict the repatriates' backsliding as the consequence of their ethnicity? Or did he envisage their backsliding as a consequence of living under the inhospitable conditions of Tierra del Fuego? If asked these questions, FitzRoy probably would have thought the second possibility as likely. Judging from his ethnological opinions in the early 1830s, Darwin would likely have endorsed the first.

As the Beagle prepared to set sail, FitzRoy visited the repatriates. He returned with an account that eased Darwin's misgivings: not only were the natives peaceful, but very few of the things belonging to Jemmy, York, and Fuegia had been stolen. Moreover, he was optimistic about the garden, the produce of which would doubtless improve native diets, becoming the basis for a stable, agricultural society.

On 15 February 1833, the Beagle left Woollya/Ushuaia, on her way to survey the southernmost area of South America. Via the Goree Roads, they steered due south for about thirty miles, to explore the Wollaston Island group and False Cape Horn (*BD* 142). Once in the Falkland Islands, Darwin addressed a 30 March 1833 letter to his sister Caroline, recounting his experiences among the aborigines of Tierra del Fuego (*CDC* I, 302–03). Instead of trying to account for the unpredictability of Alacalufan behavior, he derided them, undoubtedly because they had mistreated the good-natured Rev. Matthews and wrecked the mission. The native Fuegians, initially encountered on 18 December 1832, are "untamed" savages and displayed unusual characteristics. He reiterated the analogy between domesticated and wild animals, on the one hand, and savage and civilized man, on the other, to suggest how nonhuman the natives were.

The Fuegian experience, by the early spring of 1833, reinforced Darwin's suspicion that the natives were either lethargic or mentally debilitated. Despite the repatriates' progress, the natives remained in Darwin's mind distantly removed in reason and behavior from the European. Hence, recognizing one's kinship to "the naked barbarian" whose body is painted, and who gesticulates wildly and unintelligibly, continued to be difficult for him (*CDC* I 303). No drawing or description, however, could account for the great interest the first sight of these savages had evoked (*CDC* I 303). He also related the failed endeavor to settle the Rev. Matthews at Ushuaia and the return of the three Fuegians. He told of how, while the crew surveyed the region in two boats, the natives had taken the opportunity to plunder and destroy the settlement, and to terrorize the missionary who, on the advice of Captain FitzRoy, abandoned the project (*CDC* I 303).

The most compelling reason of all for Darwin's resentment of the Fuegians and for his pessimism about their social advancement was the rumor of cannibalism. Darwin tells his sister that he dwelled among savages whose cannibalism was unprecedented in recorded history (*CDC* I 304). One source of this information was Jemmy himself who allegedly informed Captain FitzRoy that in the winter the Alacaluf sometimes ate the old women (Darwin observed that there were few women in the tribe). The crew did not accept the story at first, until a Sealing Captain related that another Fuegian boy had purportedly uttered the words: "'woman good for nothing'— man very hungry'"; the informant claimed that women were being smothered and consumed. Darwin, it appears, was persuaded by circumstantial evidence, by anecdotes, and by hearsay based on misunderstood conversations. Finding it difficult to discount the boys' explicit stories, he expressed moral outrage over these charges (*CDC* I 304). Along with the unprovoked mistreatment of the Rev. Matthews, the idea of women being enslaved and eaten erased any sympathy he might have had for the Fuegians. By 1871, however, he would upgrade their status somewhat from savages to barbarians, although he qualified this classification with a list of pejoratives: they were hideous, indecent, antisocial, and the artless practitioners of torture, of human sacrifice, of infanticide, and of superstition — but their reputed cannibalism is unmentioned in this passage (*DM* 642–43).

In a letter written to J. S. Henslow of 11 April 1833, written while bound from the Falkland Islands to the Río Colorado and eventually to Montevideo, Darwin repeats the opinion that the natives of the region are in the depths of barbarism (*CDC* I 306). He is amazed to see that in a country wracked by storms and extremes of temperature, the natives are naked and built flimsy, ramshackle wigwams (*CDC* I 306). To Darwin, seeing primitive human beings for the first time was like meeting troubled spirits (*CDC* I 307). It seems that Tierra del Fuego was fallow ground for civilization, for although the repatriates were schooled in European habits and offered a better life, their people were uncooperative. And although the crew built houses for them and planted gardens, Darwin did not hold out much hope that, upon their return, much would be found intact (*CDC* I 307).

When the *Beagle* returned to Tierra del Fuego on 24 February 1834, anchoring at Wollaston Island, Darwin decided to survey inland. While headed to shore, they pulled alongside a canoe in which were six Fuegians, possibly Alacaluf— the people whom Darwin had called miserable creatures. Not only were they naked, but they were bedaubed with red and white paint, had filthy and greasy skins, and their faces were altogether ugly. With their tangled hair, discordant voices and wild gesticulations, made all the more revolting since women and babies were in this state, Darwin had difficulty acknowledging the humanity he and the canoeists undeniably shared: "Viewing such men, one can hardly make oneself believe that they are fellow creatures placed in the same world" (*BD* 222). The spectacle of the Fuegians was nevertheless captivating. But his use of the equine adjective in the phrase "unbroken savages" suggests, for him, that the Fuegians occupied an intermediate state between man and beast (*BD* 223). This assumption is clearly evident in the language he uses: they are "gifted animals," whose "pleasure in life" was indeterminable (*BD* 223).

By 1834, Darwin became more inclined to speculate on why the Fuegians lived under these dreadful conditions. Degrading characterizations and efficient classifications of the Fuegians in relation to Africans, to Eskimos, and to others, could not answer broader biological and geographical questions. So, along with the dehumanizing rhetoric, which might have been Darwin's exasperated reaction to the Alacalufs' failure to meet environmental challenges, were descriptions of their impoverished material culture — that is, of their flimsy wigwams being nothing more than little depressions in the soil, over which rotten trees and tufts of grass were placed; of huts which housed five or six naked human beings, "coiled up like animals," exposing them to the wind, rain, and snow; and of the everyday scrounging for limpets, mollusks, berries and fungi (*BD* 223).

Darwin simply could not comprehend how they survived inter-tribal conflict, famine, and inhospitable climate and geography. In this world, natives who were canoeists moved from spot to spot. Although the Alacaluf had canoes suited to rivers and inlets, they had no sense of a stable home because "the habitable land" along the coast could not support a community; as a consequence, "domestic affection" was unknown. Probably because of these factors, the mental faculties are stunted: imagination had nothing "to paint"; the reason, nothing "to compare"; and the judgment, nothing on which to decide. Moreover, their meager skills in knocking limpets from rocks required no mental effort, and their most ingenious work, by which he might be implying their canoes, wigwams, and bows and arrows, had not progressed technologically for three centuries. So, unarguably, their intellects in no way resembled those of civilized human beings. Thus, when he exclaims, "What a scale of improvement is comprehended between the faculties of a Fuegian savage & a Sir Isaac Newton," he is underscoring the reality that, in intellect and achievement, an unbridgeable gap separated these two antipodes of the species from each other. Darwin suggests, however briefly, that our understanding of how and why the Fuegians lived below human potential required the careful study of biological and of geographical factors. That he described habitations, rudimentary technology, and material culture, indicates that he was thinking ethnologically and, at least in this passage, had been growing dissatisfied with stereotypes and with prefabricated taxonomies. Interestingly, he had already begun exploring demographic ideas — e.g., the population-subsistence ratio and warfare as a check on population — six years *before* reading the 1826 edition of Malthus' *Essay*.

Even though Darwin used zoological terms, in early 1832, to describe the Fuegians, he sincerely tried to account for their marginal condition. To understand them better, he articulated five ethnological questions. These questions possibly foreshadowed the 1839 Questionnaire, drawn up by committee, at a meeting of the British Association for the Advancement of Science, to which Darwin was a major contributor. The questions he devised in the *Diary*, four in all, were concerned with matters of origin, of migration, of social development, and of adaptation. He asked the questions, where have they come from? Have they remained in their present condition since "the creation of the world"? What led forerunners to leave the North to travel down the mountainous backbone of South America to this southernmost archipelago? And why did they come to "one of the most inhospitable countries of the world"? (*BD* 223).

Unlike the commentary of 1832–1833, which was impressionistic and stereotypical, the writings of 1834 indicate Darwin's desire to learn *how* and *why*, historically, the Fuegians arrived at their present state. His ethnology, at this point, had entered a Humboldtian phase. As early as 25 February 1834, he also began to question the veracity of earlier assertions about the Fuegians. One assumption was that their population was steadily decreasing. On the contrary, he maintains, their population had not been declining (it is unclear as to whether Darwin had access to valid demographic data), and they obviously enjoy "a sufficient share of happiness (whatever its kind may be) to render life worth having" (*BD* 223–24). The implication is that the Fuegians had survived by virtue of their intelligence, though barely so. Their tenacity, in a broad sense, exemplified man's extraordinary ability to persist in the face of adversity, notwithstanding their failure to adapt natural resources to their needs.

For Darwin, however, their primitive ingenuity should rightfully be accorded, not to innovation, perseverance or talent, but rather to the effects of natural law: "by making habit omnipotent, [Nature] has fitted the Fuegian to the climate & productions of his country" (*BD* 224). According to Darwin's thinking, therefore, the Fuegians persisted in spite of their limitations, but not through day-to-day planning, innovation, or initiative. Their crude way of life, apparently, was sufficient enough for them to avoid extinction. Possessing the means to kindle fire, according to Darwin's reductive view, they unselfconsciously scraped together food, shelter, and habiliments from the surface of shore and landscape.

The sense that the Fuegians owed their survival to unconscious, natural processes, which had forced them to adapt, however incompletely, to their difficult environment, unavoidably reinforced Darwin's idea that they were cognitively debilitated. This attitude, of course, would be modified gradually as ethnologists visited these tribes over prolonged periods of time, and after they studied their unique cultures. According to John M. Cooper, they would learn that the Yahgans, for instance, had a complex language, a belief in the supernatural, practiced magic and medicine, and observed a rudimentary creation myth. Marriage practices, for Onas and Yahgans, were loosely defined, though incest was reviled and conjugal fidelity strongly upheld; the aged were respected, the children reputedly well treated (despite claims to the contrary), but abortion was common. As far as personal morality was concerned, later scholars appear to have rejected Darwin's contradictory assessment of the Fuegians as being impulsive. On the contrary, all Fuegian tribes were respectful courageous, brave, and able to endure hardship (Cooper 177).

The *Beagle*'s return to Tierra del Fuego rekindled Darwin's thinking about human adaptation. Upon entering Ponsonby Sound, on 5 March 1834, seven canoes approached the ship (*BD* 226). The crew was uneasy, since there was no sign of Jemmy and of the other repatriates, and since the Indians in the canoes were armed. Then, to the explorers' surprise, a canoe bearing Jemmy appeared, but he was barely recognizable. Darwin writes of how painful it was to have seen him, for he was "thin, pale, & without a remnant of clothes, excepting a bit of blanket round his waist"; and his hair hung over his shoulders (*BD* 226). Even though Jemmy had obviously lost his European garb, he was still very self-conscious about it; in fact, he was "so ashamed of himself, he turned his back to the ship as the canoe approached" (*BD* 226). To Darwin, Jemmy's physical degradation was startling — a "complete and grievous change." Nor did FitzRoy recognize him in the canoe until he saluted, a sudden movement of his hand to his head telling him it was Jemmy — "but how altered!" (Narr. 2 323–25). The Captain worked quickly on Jemmy's behalf:

> I could hardly restrain my feelings, and I was not, by any means, the only one touched by his squalid, miserable appearance, he was naked, like his companions, except a bit of skin about his loins; his hair was long and matted, just like theirs; he was wretchedly thin.... We hurried him below, clothed him immediately, and in half an hour he was sitting with me at dinner in my cabin, using his knife and fork properly, and in every way behaving correctly [Narr. 2 323–25].

Equally shocked, Darwin, like FitzRoy, did not jump to any conclusions about Jemmy's state of mind. On the contrary, once Jemmy was aboard and clothed, he gradually explained that life among his people was not as degrading as it had appeared; rather, there was plenty to eat, and he was not cold; moreover, he had friends, had married, and had been teaching his friends some English; additionally, he was beginning to speak the local language, although he had some difficulty doing so. Above all, he had no desire to return to England. Clearly established among his people, he brought otter skins and spearheads as gifts. Darwin learned, however, that York Minster, who had planned to return to his own country with his wife, had actually robbed Jemmy's belongings (*BD* 227). On 6 March 1834, Jemmy told the Captain that the tribe had left their old wigwams and crossed the water to be out of the reach of the Oens men, the foot Patagonians of the east coast who regularly raided southern villages.

Eventually, Jemmy had to return to his people, and it was a sad farewell for all who were involved (*BD* 227). Darwin, cautiously optimistic about the repatriates' homecoming, expresses renewed enthusiasm about Jemmy's future: "I hope & have little doubt he will be as happy as if he had never left his country; which is much more than I formerly thought" (*BD* 227). In an important letter of 30 March 1834 to Edward Lumb, British merchant in Buenos Aires, Darwin resignedly writes of his return to Cape Horn. At Ushuaia, he was stunned to see Jemmy standing naked in a canoe with a rag around his waist but nonetheless content. Contrary to what Darwin recorded in the *Diary*, Jemmy had forgotten his English and had married a squaw (*CDC* I 378). Implicit in this comment was the hope that their final meeting with Jemmy might encourage the people of Ushuaia to treat British missionaries more amicably, but this would not be the case for some time. Darwin retold the story of the final meeting with Jemmy in a letter to Catherine, dated 6 April 1834, written on East Falkland Island. They hardly recognized Jemmy, who was naked, debased, and thin. More details came to light about Fuegia and Jemmy, subsequent to York's betrayal. Unexpectedly, York *and* Fuegia had moved away together some months prior, after York had stolen Jemmy's clothes, and this might have accounted for the latter's animal-skin attire.

Understandably, Jemmy was glad to see his British friends and brought presents. Captain FitzRoy offered to bring him back to England, but Jemmy declined the offer, as he and his wife paddled away in a canoe loaded with provisions. Jemmy had indeed taught his people some English (*CDC* I 380). Both Caroline and Emily Catherine Darwin (1810–1866), Charles' sisters, were glad to learn that Jemmy was becoming re-acclimated to Ushuaia (30 September [from Caroline] and 29 October 1834 [from Catherine], Letters to Charles; *CDC* I 409, 412–13). Fitzroy agrees: "It was generally remarked that [Jemmy's] family was become considerably more humanized than any savage seen in Tierra del Fuego: that they put confidence in us; were pleased by our return; that they were ready to do what we could explain to be for their interest; and ... that the first step towards civilization — that of obtaining their confidence — had undoubtedly made been made" (Narr. 2 325). As it turned out, FitzRoy's confidence was not to be rewarded.

# 6. The "Barbarians" of Argentina

When the *Beagle* arrived on the Argentine coast in the summer of 1833, Darwin was about to enter a politically tumultuous world. The redoubtable General Juan Manuel de Rosas (1793–1877), a rich cattle rancher who had begun a political career in 1820, and who was governor of Buenos Aires, from 1829 to 1832 (a title he regained, from 1835 to 1852), had recently defeated political opponents in a bloody struggle (Hopkins 114–27; Desmond and Moore 89–91). After relinquishing the governorship in 1832, de Rosas remained a powerful political boss or *caudillo*. As a federalist leader, his rise to power represented the ascendancy of the *estancias*, the new landed oligarchy whose empires were based on commercial ranching (*estancia*: cattle ranch).

In 1833, certain tribes of indigenous people stood in the way of territorial expansion. With a powerful force of gauchos, of regular army, and of Indian allies, de Rosas began driving the Pampas tribes out in order to claim the vast grazing territory, needed to sustain the ranching empire. Whereas in Brazil the colonial economy depended on imported blacks for forced labor, in Argentina natives were to be driven out for their land. In the midst of a campaign of Indian extermination, and with the primary aim of exploring the geology, the flora, and the fauna of Argentina, Darwin was able to compile a body of writing on the native population, ranging from archeology to ethnology.

When the *Beagle* arrived at Patagonia, a vast 300,000-square-mile region in southern Argentina, south of the Río Colorado and east of the Andes, the plan was to conduct a number of inland expeditions: the first, from Patagonia to Bahía Blanca, would be undertaken from 11 to 17 August 1833, and would involve arduous coastal travel over rivers, mountains and through woods and jungles; the second, a distance of 400 miles from Bahía Blanca to Buenos Aires, would take place from 8 to 20 September, and was equally as difficult a passage. These expeditions would challenge Darwin's physical stamina. Almost as a modern war correspondent, he found himself perilously close to combat. His record of these months in the *Diary* includes descriptive, impressionistic, and historical commentaries elucidating his attitude towards the people whom he met. Some entries contain valuable ethnographic passages, including several pertaining to physiology, sociology, and religious culture. Whereas some passages are saturated with ethnographic description, others lack detail and consist largely of opinion. Once again, we find Darwin struggling to reconcile racial assumptions about indigenous people with their humanity, even though their suffering was blatant. Though modulating the tone of his criticism now and then, Darwin continually expressed indignation over de Rosas' campaign against the Indians.

Brief ethnographic passages describing habitations, diet, and social conditions occur in these entries intermittently. On 6–7 August 1833, Darwin arrived at the town of Patagonia. Of the limited number of inhabitants, most were either pure-blooded Spaniards or Native Americans, with a smaller mixture of the two races than was usually found in these countries. One indigenous community, whose chief was named Leucanee, caught his attention. Incorporated into the Spanish colony, the tribe constructed *toldos* or huts outside the town. Barely self-sufficient, these Indians depended on the government for food, mainly horse meat, and they made horse-rugs and boots for horses' legs. Though they had become a settled community, they had a reputation for promiscuity, but some of the younger men, Darwin remarks, were improving their behavior. Not averse to labor, some who had agreed to go on a sealing voyage behaved rather well. Clearly, this tribe was dependent upon the Spanish and, as a result, was nearly impoverished. Native religion, an important aspect of ethnology, received only a passing reference during the eighty-five-mile journey between the town of Patagones and the Río Colorado.

Along the road, Darwin's party came across a spring and a famous tree that he suspected as being an Indian shrine: the Indians, he writes on 11 August, revered the tree as a god or used it as the altar of the god Walleechu (*BD* 166–67). According to a gaucho in Darwin's party, when natives saw the tree, they customarily "offer their adorations by loud shouts" (*BD* 167). Low to the ground, branched and thorny, the tree stood by itself and had a diameter of three feet. Since it was winter, it was bare but was adorned with threads, from which offerings were suspended. Indians pulled threads out of their ponchos and hung everything from cigars to meat on the branches. They even poured liquor into holes and burnt offerings, the smoke wafting their intentions upwards to appease the god. This was also a place of animal sacrifice, as evidenced by the bleached bones of slaughtered horses surrounding the tree. Believing the god will make their horses tireless and their fortunes abundant, indigenes of all ages and of both genders made their offerings.

The gaucho who was Darwin's source of information at the time admitted that they used to wait for the natives to leave, at which time they stole the devotional gifts from the tree of Walleechu. Although the gauchos thought the tree itself was revered as a nature deity, Darwin believed it was more likely an altar, the focus of cultic worship. The tree also had practical, geographical importance. Travelers passing within sight of the tree used it as a landmark along their journey, and the tree, like a fixed compass, marked the direction of the Sierra de la Ventana, a mountain located due north of their position.

Although Darwin said nothing further on the Walleechu altar either in the *Diary* or in 1839 *Journal,* the tree generally has both a symbolic and a literal place in his biological thought. It is impossible to know whether Darwin was thinking of the Patagonian altar-tree when he developed his own rendition of the Tree of the Knowledge of Good and Evil from *Genesis,* chapter 2, verses 16–17; however, unlike the author(s) of *Genesis,* Darwin employed it as a symbol for evolutionary history, its irregular branching elegantly representing the development of species over time, each of which was represented as a bud (*B*21, *CDN,* 176).

The symbol of the Tree of Life is central to Darwin's thought and was more than an emblem or efficient visual representation of proliferating life. As a symbol, it was part and parcel of the life it reflected: thus, as he suggests, it should perhaps be called "the coral of life," that is, a kind of supercolony of diverse creatures (*B*26, *CDN,* 177). At Kensington Gardens, Darwin recalls how fascinating it had been to look at trees as "great compound animals united ... [in a] wonderful and mysterious manner" (*M*41, *CDN,* 529). The idea of the tree as an ecological niche is a very modern one and might have been evoked in these notational contexts with biological rather than metaphoric intent. Darwin certainly had his uncle Erasmus' 1794 publication, *Zoonomia; or, the laws of organic life* in mind, particularly the passage in which the tree is described as a "congeries of many living buds ... resembl[ing] the branches of coralline, which are a congeries of a multitude of animals" (*M*41 note 1, *CDN,* 529). An analogy of tree to coral is correct since both are aggregations of organisms. A teeming microcosm, the tree is both a product and a symbol of evolution on the macrocosmic level.

In Darwin's symbolic Tree, the bifurcation of phyla into classes appears as ramifying branches: "At what Part of [the] tree of life can orders like birds and animals separate [?]" (*B*263. *CDN,* 235). He actually subsumed geometrical models of natural history (e.g., the linear, the dialectical, and the circular) under the Tree symbol: "We may fancy, according to [the] shortness of life of species that in perfection, the bottom of branches deaden.— so that in Mammalia birds it would only *appear like circles*;—& insects amongst articulata.— but in lower classes, perhaps a more *linear arrangement*" (*B*28, *CDN*, 177; italics added). Using a branch diagram, Darwin illustrated how extinction accounted for gaps in the natural history of species (*B*35–44, *CDN*, 179–81).

Darwin's most elaborate use of the Tree of Life symbol can be found in texts related to and including, *Origin*. He was at work on a document titled, *Natural Selection, Being the Second Part of his Big Species Book Written from 1856 to 1858, the long version of the Origin*. After he had completed the 1844 *Essay*, he expanded this project gradually over the years, using topical portfolios rather than notebooks, and this compositional method eventually became the basis of chapters in the *Big Species Book*, in *Origin*, and in subsequent works (Glick & Kohn, *On Evolution*, 129). In "On the Principle of Divergence," a central topic in *The Big Species Book*, Darwin presents the "relation of all past & present beings" in the imagery of "a few gigantic trees" (*On Evolution*, 148). Buds and twigs higher up represent extant species, while buds and twigs situated beneath their living extremities represent extinct forms. The natural classification of organic beings was depicted as twigs proceeding from smaller branches; these branches, from larger ones; and larger ones, from the unequally sized main limbs feeding from the trunk. Arboreal linkages of every kind, seen as gnarled and leafless branches, corresponded to the evolutionary kinship and divergence of organic forms; thus, forked branches represented the point at which one form produces two distinct organisms. The difficulty one had in finding these connecting links on the tree was emblematic of the fossil record's incompleteness. The death of tree limbs and of twigs symbolized the extinction of organic groups through time, and other features of the tree were used to describe the intricate relations of organic life.

Narrowly focused on natural history, and on evocative images such as the tree, Darwin did not immediately comment about the human predicament he witnessed — about the abject dependency of the Leucanee people or about the overt pilfering that occurred at the tree. He also missed the opportunity to speculate on how the tree was employed as a religious symbol in non–Christian traditions. Edward B. Tylor, in *Primitive Culture*, mentions that many primitive societies attributed souls to trees and plants or believed they housed human and animal souls (vol. 1 475). The Dayaks of Borneo, for example, believe that human souls can enter tree trunks, rendering it "damp and blood-like" (vol. 2 10). Typical of Animism is the belief that a tree is "a conscious personal being, and as such receives adoration and sacrifice"; conversely, a people, like the Mintira of the Malaysian Peninsula, considered a tree inhabited by malign entities that bore human disease. Interestingly, the Walleechu tree had an analogue thousands of miles away in the society of the Tonga or Friendly Islands. The Tonga laid offerings "at the foot of particular trees, with the idea of their being inhabited by spirits" (vol. 2 215).

Darwin's notion of the proliferating diversity of living things in an ecological habitat was efficiently symbolized by the coral or the tree. But often, when he encountered human diversity, he was uncomfortable and wary. He reacted negatively, for example, to the men of mixed blood whom he met at de Rosas' camp. After crossing the Río Colorado, on 13 August 1833, his party reached the encampment, which was situated close to the river (*BD* 169). The settlement was strongly fortified: configured in a square with a 400-yard perimeter, the redoubts enclosing wagons, artillery emplacements, and huts. Nearly all of the soldiers were cavalrymen. Darwin's first impression of them is reminiscent of the disgust he expressed when first meeting Fuegians of various tribes. The soldiers appeared, at first sight, a "villainous Banditti-like army." This negative impression stemmed from the belief that the greater number of the men were of "a mixed race, between Negro, Indian & Spaniard." Darwin did not explain his aversion for mixed ethnicities or why he associated their physiognomies with moral disorder and lawlessness: "I know not the reason, but men of such origin seldom have good expressions" (*BD* 169). On 12 September, he would make similar observations of soldiers at a military post at Bahía Blanca (*BD* 86), four of whom he describes as "strange beings." The first was "a fine young Negro," the second, "half Indian & Negro"; the third and fourth were "nondescripts": a Chilean miner "of the color of mahogany" and a mulatto, respectively. With passports in hand, Darwin and company were graciously received by General de Rosas and were accommodated in the Rancho or hovel (*Rancho*, in its idiomatic sense, means country house).

Because the weather was bad and the surrounding country a swamp, Darwin could not undertake an excursion on August 14th. Despite the restriction, he used his time productively. His "chief amusement" was to watch Indian families, members of tribes allied to de Rosas, as they purchased small articles at the Rancho, a kind of trading post. Darwin had the opportunity to watch them closely and recalled what he saw for the *Diary*. The men were "a tall exceedingly fine race." Their faces, most intriguingly, resembled those of the Fuegians whom he had seen and suggested kinship between the two geographically distanced Indian groups. Three principal tribes lived in the Patagonian region: the Pehuenche (west of Buenos Aires), the Puelche (south of Buenos Aires), and the Tehuelche (farther south, near Santa Cruz). Darwin's observations proved quite accurate. If the Indians he met at the Rancho were indeed of Pehuenchen ancestry, the comparison between them and the Fuegian tribes made sense. The Pehuenche were, in fact, related to the Onas, both tribes having relatives throughout Chile and in northern Paraguay, as well as in northeastern Brazil (Montagu 90–1).

Darwin made the interesting, though controversial, point that the environmental conditions to which the Onas and Pehuenche were subject determined their respective demeanors. Whereas the Pehuenche were a noble and "exceedingly fine race," the Fuegians were "rendered hideous by the cold, want of food & less civilization" (*BD* 169). The implication is that, if the Onas lived in Patagonia, with all of its advantages (including colonial civilization), their lives would be less difficult. It also implies that the missions had the ability to transform uncivilized life. Of greatest value in this context is his observation that ethnographers who separated these two classes of Indians from each other had been wrong in doing so (*BD* 169). Darwin's inexplicable aversion for mixed ethnicities contrasts with his professional interest in and admiration of certain native tribes.

Darwin catalogued the personal adornments, clothing, hair, and behavior of the women. The young women or *Chinas* were beautiful, and he especially admired their coiffure, eye color, elegantly shaped limbs, bracelets, beads, and horsemanship; like the Fuegians, both men and women painted their bodies, but, as far as he could remember, color and design differed between the two tribes. In addition, he reflected that "Nothing could be more interesting than some of the family groups" (*BD* 169). But the image of savage nobility deflated significantly, Darwin described how the women were overworked. This is one of several ethical points in his Argentine narrative: here he takes a decided stand on an important social issue. With respect to gender, labor was divided but unequally so. Women packed and unpacked the horses, made the tents, and "like the wives of all Savages [were] useful slaves." The men, on the other hand, fought, hunted, tended to the horses and riding gear, and were known for their expertise in making bolas, a word having the double meaning in Spanish of *ball* and *hit the mark*. By continually knocking stones together, they rounded stones into balls, two of which were tied together with a rope and then thrown with such accuracy as to entangle a horse's legs or to kill a person (*BD* 170).

On the way to Bahía Blanca (16 August), Darwin's party was hoping to rendezvous with the *Beagle*. Along the way, they passed another Indian village, which he found impressive: the *toldos* or huts, shaped like little ovens and covered with hides, each had a tapering *Chusa* stick in the ground at the entrance. The huts were grouped under the jurisdiction of each chief or *Cacique*, and, within each group, family huts were clustered together. For security, de Rosas had set up a series of small posts, the first of which was built along the Río Colorado. Judging from the fertility of the land in the area, Darwin expected de Rosas's plan for *estancias* to be a success.

Darwin then turned to the Indian inhabitants who had to be overcome before the land could be developed, but, on this moral issue, his rhetoric conveys an ambiguous message: "This war of extermination," Darwin observes, "although carried on with the most shocking barbarity, will certainly produce great benefits; it will at once throw open four or 500 miles in length of fine country for the produce of cattle" (*BD* 172). Darwin's choice of words in this complex sentence, perhaps unintentionally, sends the following message: the brutal extermination of the inhabitants (in the subordinate clause) is of secondary concern to the "*great* benefits" in land development (in the main clause). On the one hand, Darwin was obviously captivated by the geographical grandiosity of the plan: extending from the Atlantic coast to the Andes, the *estancias* would cut through approximately three-hundred miles of steppe and prairie grasslands and one or two-hundred more of rain-green forest, woodland, scrub, and savanna, up to the desert bordering the Andes. In the process, the westward movement of the *estancias*, an Argentine precursor of manifest destiny, a popular notion in 1840s America, would ineluctably remove indigenous people from its path.

The inevitable expansion of Spanish sovereignty was also similar to the global dominion of Anglo-Saxon empire, along with the selective extermination of weaker societies, some thought of as being expendable. This brings us to the inevitable question: in Argentina, did Darwin actually believe that genocide was a reasonable price to pay for nation-building on a grand scale? Since his view of black slavery, a system also justified on economic and imperial grounds, was consistent and unwaveringly humane, it stands to reason that he would sympathize with the Pampas tribes. If indeed Darwin were morally consistent in this regard, then his self-contradictory statements were either meaningless (nothing more than quirks of style in personal prose), or reflect an introspective struggle between the imperative of progressive civilization and a sense of moral responsibility.

The Indian tribes in the Pampas, just like certain Fuegian tribes, threatened travelers. The first *Posta* or outpost, manned by a handful of soldiers, was quite vulnerable, as Darwin points out (*BD* 174). A band of Indians on horseback passed through there in the night and, fortunately for Darwin and company, did not see them. Alarms were sounded by cannon shot whenever Indians were seen (*BD* 174). Darwin's guide had had a close call two months before. On a hunting excursion with two men from the fort, they were attacked by bolas- and spear-wielding Indians, who killed two men; the severely wounded guide escaped back to the fort. From that time on, no one was allowed to leave the post. Darwin, however, was unaware of the Native American tensions when he began the journey to Bahía Blanca: in effect, he was traveling through dangerous territory unawares.

By 23 August, after arriving at Punta Alta, native intentions became absolutely clear. Darwin learned from his fellow traveler James Harris, who had arrived recently from the Río Colorado, that a tribe had massacred everyone at the first *Posta*. The suspicion was that the tribe of the *Cacique* Bernantio was to blame. Ironically, they were considered to be friendly, for that very day they intended (or pretended) to join General de Rosas (*BD* 177). A British trader, sea captain, and hired pilot for the *Beagle*, Harris had been trailing Darwin's party and was in a vulnerable position. Along the way, he ran into Bernantio's men a few miles from the Río Colorado, presumably as they were heading for the *Posta*, but there was no incident. As late as 19 September, his position on the conflict was diplomatically vague, although Darwin's comments might have had ironic intent. He writes that native aggression and mercilessness, leaving "neither man, woman, [n]or cow" immune from their attacks, made enthusiasm for General de Rosas universal; and his campaign against them, the "'most just of all wars because against Barbarians'" (*BD* 190).

Darwin was in the midst of a cycle of hostility and faced with a paradox: he had to be loyal to de Rosas in order to protect himself and others from native raiders, while he realized that he was a relentless despot whose multi-ethnic army looked forward to the campaign. On Sunday, 25 August, the *Beagle* could not send a boat to shore to pick Darwin up because of bad weather, so he had to spend a day on shore in hostile territory. In the evening of 25 August, Commander Miranda, de Rosas' subordinate, arrived with three-hundred men to track down those who murdered the outpost sentries. It was decided that, if Chief Bernantio himself were guilty, then his entire tribe would be slaughtered. If only a few murderers were responsible, Miranda's forces were ordered to track them all the way to Chile, if they had to (*BD* 177).

Darwin recalls, and no doubt was taken aback by, the fact that many of Miranda's soldiers were themselves natives. Their encampment had a striking impact on him. Some of them were reported to have drunk "the warm, steaming blood of the beasts which were slaughtered for supper" (*BD* 177). But this almost ritualistic preparation for battle was anti-climactic, since Bernantio was proven to be guiltless, and, as for the rogue Indians who murdered the soldiers, they had escaped "into the great plains or Pampas" and could not be found (*BD* 177).

In the entry dated 4–7 September 1833, at the safe haven of Punta Alta, Darwin recounted a disturbing anecdote regarding the indigenous people. It seems that a captive chief, presumably of a hostile tribe, had turned informant. He gave de Rosas information on some who had camped at a small Salinas or salt mine, located a few leagues (about 8–10 miles) off the road, between the Río Colorado and Bahía Blanca. On 5 September, one-hundred men were sent against them. The man who had brought the intelligence gave Darwin an account of the last battle at which he was present. To destroy a tribe north of the Río Colorado in that operation, de Rosas had dispatched two-hundred men. The soldiers found encamped natives in a wild mountainous country (between one and two thousand feet in altitude), in full view of the Andes. The tribe consisted of one-hundred and twelve people, men, women, and children, who were all either captured or killed. Darwin sardonically writes in the margin that in the battle, "only one Christian was wounded" (*BD* 179). He seems to be scoffing at the notion that the women and children had put up formidable resistance. This passage is further evidence of Darwin's muted contempt for de Rosas and for his soldiers.

After the Bernantio incident, and by the autumn of 1833, neighboring tribes, it appears, were on the defensive and emigrating westward, but this turned out not to be the complete picture. The migrating tribe was only a remnant trying desperately to outdistance de Rosas' light cavalry. Unknown to those at the Salinas, strategic plans were underway among the Pampas chiefs to consolidate their forces in the Andes for a counterattack. Although captured native ambassadors, whom Darwin called "noble patriots," chose death rather than to reveal the strategy, a *Cacique* "confessed all the plans," identifying a meeting point in the Andes where as many as twelve-hundred aborigines were to amass within the month (*BD* 180). It seems that the ambassadors were to have been sent eastward to the small tribe at the Salinas near Bahía Blanca to apprise them of the plan. Were the migrants to be the bait? Before the plan got underway, other captives betrayed their position, and de Rosas' forces besieged them mercilessly.

The isolated tribe at the Salinas was so terrified of de Rosas' troops "that they offered no resistance in body" (*BD* 179). The informant, whom Darwin surprisingly believed to be a very intelligent man, described the natives as being both cowardly and cunning. Each tried to escape and even abandoned wife and children. Perhaps embittered by the memories of past battles, the soldiers were said to have pursued and sabered every man. Those who fled fought like "wild animals" to the very end, biting, hurling bolas, and, treacherously pretending to surrender, some used hidden knives against the soldiers (*BD* 179–180).

Up to this point, it seems that Darwin was uncritically accepting the war anecdotes of the informant, but his personal thoughts on this particular incident put his actual feelings beyond doubt. The massacre of male combatants was, for Darwin, a "dark picture." But he found shocking beyond all description that women older than twenty were also massacred in cold blood. Darwin condemned these activities; but, once again, judging from his inland position and status as guest, he could only muffle his indignation ("I *ventured to hint*, that this *appeared rather* inhuman" [italics added]). The informant, on the other hand, was blunt: the women had to be killed because "'they breed so'" (*BD* 180). In a sense, de Rosas was being unnaturally selective. Darwin's indignation evoked a more robust statement, as he rejected the colonial rationale that this was a just war waged "against Barbarians." On the contrary, through a rhetorical question, Darwin implied that de Rosas' civilization was the actual seat of barbarism: "Who would believe in this age in a Christian, civilized country that such atrocities were committed?" (*BD* 180). The massacre of combatants and of helpless women was hardly assuaged by the sparing of Indian children — who were destined for sale and slavery.

While adversarial tribes were conducting a grand council in the Andes, de Rosas had to plan his strategy against the main body of Native Americans gathering in the East. His plan was to kill stragglers, such as those at the Salinas, and to drive the rest "to a common point," regardless of the possibility of counterattack. Because the plains were arid, and native travel restricted as a result, Darwin believed that the summer was the time for a pincer attack against them: the Argentines would strike from West to East; and the Chileans, from East to West. To divide and conquer the indigenous nations, de Rosas astutely made a treaty with the Tehuelches whose task it would be to prevent adversarial tribes from escaping to the south of the Río Negro, an unknown country that could have provided a safe haven (*BD* 180–81). The Tehuelches' chief opponents were likely the Pehuenche and other tribes near the Cordillera or mountain range (*BD* 181). The Tehuelches mendaciously agreed "to slaughter every Indian who passes to the South of the river" (*BD* 181), but there was an important caveat: "if they fail in doing this, they themselves shall be exterminated" (*BD* 181). Thinking his "friends" might some day turn on him, de Rosas always put Indian allies in the front ranks as shock troops, "so that their numbers may be thinned" (*BD* 181).

At this point in the *Diary*, Darwin denounced de Rosas' strategy explicitly. He reprised his contradictory statement of 16 August 1833. If all the Indians "are butchered," he reiterates, a grand extent of fertile land will be gained, especially for the production of corn. But he acerbically remarks that Argentina "will be in the hands of white Gaucho *savages* instead of copper-coloured Indians" (*BD* 181; italics added). And though the white gauchos were a little superior in civilization to the native, they were unquestionably "inferior in every moral virtue" (*BD* 181). Despite the immense territory over which the native populations could roam, Darwin lamented the high probability that, because of the incessant warfare, in another half century, "there will not be a wild Indian in the Pampas North of the Río Negro" (*BD* 181). With muted irony, in a letter of 8 May 1834 to Edward Lumb, Darwin would write that de Rosas had returned from a "glorious campaign," had succeeded in wiping out 3,500 native people, and he had acquired an immense quantity of land, accomplishing his grand design (*CDC* I 386–87).

By the autumn of 1834, Darwin had taken and had held a moral position, with respect to the extirpation of native tribes. This did not mean, however, that he always respected the integrity of their cultures. While in Argentina, Darwin tried his hand at archeology. One particular experience demonstrates his acute power of observation. In the record of 4–7 September, while at Bahía Blanca in Northern Patagonia, he recalled seeing a soldier start a camp fire with a piece of flint. Darwin instantly recognized the small object as being part of an arrowhead. The soldier explained that these arrows could easily be picked up near the Island of Churichoél, located along the Río Negro. Darwin estimated that it was two- or three-inches long, twice the length of arrowheads used in Tierra del Fuego. The flint was opaque and cream-colored, but its points and barbs had been purposefully broken off. Knowing that no Pampas nation currently used bows and arrows, he reasoned that there might be a tribe on that island related to forest-dwelling tribes that traveled on foot. Darwin was excited, moreover, about the possibility that the arrowheads were "antiquarian relics" of Indians who had lived on the island prior to the advent of horse culture in South America, and who were likely to have been hunters and gatherers. The presence of these arrowheads on the island also suggested to him that the horse was not indigenous to the region.

The entry is remarkable because, on the basis of a fragmentary, two-inch piece of flint and a trace of geographical information, Darwin was able to conjecture about the ethnicity, technology, and lifestyle of its presumed owner, as well as about the bio-geographical history of the horse. He speculated that the early inhabitants of Churichoél Island used bows and arrows, did not ride horses, and were ethnically related to tribes in the East. They could not have been contemporaries of the Araucanians, the largest tribe to the East who inhabited southern Chile because the latter used spears, did not have bows and arrows, and did not ride horses. In the 5 August 1833 record, written at Patagonia, Darwin alluded to how, several years before, a disciplined force of Araucanians had destroyed *estancias*, situated along the rode to Patagonia, near the northern bank of the Río Negro valley. Although the event took place in the vicinity of Churichoél Island, these Indians were armed with bamboo spears, not bows and arrows, and were on horseback. In Chile, in January 1835, Darwin would meet the downtrodden remnants of an Araucanian tribe: they, too, rode horses (*BD* 285–86). At a mission in Valdivia, Chile, in February 1835, he would re-encounter Araucanians who were spear-throwers and "good horsemen" (*BD* 290); and thirty miles north of Valdivia, while nearing Concepción, he reports, on 22 February 1835, that "several groups of Indians *on horseback* appeared to watch with interest our movements" (*BD* 293; italics added).

Who, then, were the early inhabitants of Churichoél Island? If they were, indeed, pre-equine ancestors of modern Araucanians, then the arrowheads were likely to have predated the mid-sixteenth century introduction of the modern horse to Chile and Argentina. European horses were originally transported from Spain to Peru and Chile in 1541, by Pedro de Valdivi, and Hurtado de Mendoza transported horses to Argentina (1553) and then to Chile (1557) ("Old Lima Haciendas of Peru").

The natural history of the horse in South America would prove to be of continuing interest to Darwin as he developed his evolutionary thought. In *Origin*, for example, while discussing extinction he was astonished to have found the tooth of a prehistoric horse decades earlier in La Plata, Argentina. It was embedded with the remains of extinct animals, all of these fauna having co-existed with contemporary shells "at a very late geological period" (*OS* 259). He was interested to find out what caused the indigenous horse's extinction, in light of the fact that modern horses, transported from Spain to South America, proliferated on the Pampas. Darwin, however, was operating on the incorrect assumption that the ancient horse was a lineal precursor of the European species, so these two species of horse were unrelated.

As for the arrowheads on Churichoel Island, they were indisputably of "antiquarian interest," dating back some three centuries or more from Darwin's times. But, given the evidence at hand, the mystery of the ancient residents of Churchoél Island was unsolvable. Whether the islanders were of Araucanian or of Andean ancestry (the Calchaqui, for example), could not be determined from the fragmentary evidence. What is most fascinating about Darwin's foray into archaeology is the inductive process it reflects. In this instance, Darwin's intellectual excursus is quite remarkable: he moves from a fragmentary artifact, noticed in passing but assessed in detail, to plausible, though inconclusive, ethnological conjectures on the manufacturer's material and social culture, and history.

The arrowhead-analysis described above indicates, not only that Darwin had an intuitive talent for archaeological research, but that he was also quite interested in native culture. But there was an insensitive side to Darwin's archaeology, one that cannot be accounted for by the vagaries of language. At Guanaco Island in Port Desire, on 1–2 January 1833, Darwin's "antiquarianism" devolved into tomb raiding. On an excursion, his party found a Native American grave on the top of a hill. From the remains of several fires and horses' bones nearby, it was obvious that natives occasionally visited the burial ground. On 2 January 1834, however, Darwin and a party of officers admitted "to ransack[ing] the Indian grave in hopes of finding some antiquarian remains" (*BD* 211–12). This spontaneous decision was made, despite the fact that signs of occasional visitors were present, and that the grave had a cairn, a heap of memorial or landmark stones, "placed with some care" to a height of six feet. The natives had obviously landscaped the grave with earth, hewn stone, and peat (Darwin even sketched the arrangement of the stones in the margin [*BD* 212 n.1]). It was undoubtedly a private place of remembrance. Darwin relates what follows: "We undermined the grave on both sides under the last block; but there were no bones," a finding that suggests the remains had completely deteriorated. Three other stone heaps were found, displaced by sealers or other voyagers.

After this act of forensic archaeology or of desecration (depending on one's point of view), Darwin reflected on native burial customs and on two assumptions: where an Indian dies is where he or she is buried; and bodies were exhumed and re-interred in hilltop cairns like the one they destroyed. He then reflected on the anthropological meaning of the exhumation custom. Before the importation of horses, Uruguayan Indians must have lived like Fuegians, that is, they scavenged the coastline. The ability to transport the dead inland using horses must, therefore, have permitted them to create burial grounds (*BD* 212).

In no other Darwinian context, to my knowledge, did intellect so override ethics than in the cairn incident. Darwin and company treated the cemetery as if it were an archaeological dig and tried to disinter human remains as if they were searching for extinct Megatheria. Their decision to proceed is all the more unethical in that the gravesite was not prehistoric, even though human remains had disintegrated; it had immediate significance, having been constructed with care and sensibility and had been recently visited. It would be unfair to compare Darwin's conduct to that of someone like Giovanni Belzoni (1778–1823) who, during a three-year journey on the Nile, penetrated the burial chamber of the Second Pyramid of Giza, to recover the alabaster sarcophagus of Seti I, from the pharaoh's tomb in the Valley of the Kings (Fagan 75). Darwin's activities, though not nearly as infamous, were nonetheless unethical.

In November 1834, Darwin landed at Chiloé, on the coast of Chile, and began to record observations. Once again, his observations, in the entry of 25 November, demonstrate his perceptiveness as an ethnologist. He saw a family "of pure Indian extraction," whose father looked very much like the Fuegian, York Minster. Yet some of the younger boys, "with their ruddy complexions," could have been mistaken for natives of the Pampas (*BD* 266). Although Darwin found it difficult to distinguish in their bearings important aspects of tribal heritage, he intuited that everything he had seen suggested "the close connection of the different tribes." The anthropologist Ashley Montagu states that human beings, predominantly of Mongoloid origin, had entered America in migratory waves from Siberia across the Bering Strait, made their way as far south as Tierra del Fuego, and their artifacts and remains, estimated from radiocarbon dating, show that they arrived between 15,000 and 11,000 years ago (88–91). Darwin's assumption of the common ancestry of the various tribes, despite their speaking an assortment of dialects, was plausible.

Acute observation, intuition, and fact-finding from various sources, notably census figures, recurrently characterized this phase of Darwin's ethnology. The Chiloan group he met on 15 November was friendly and "advanced to the same degree of civilization" as had the white colonists (*BD* 266). To the South, he saw many "pure Indians," notably on the coastal islands, who retained tribal surnames. Charles D. Douglas, a resident of Chiloé, employed on the *Beagle* as surveyor and pilot, furnished Darwin with population statistics. Darwin also learned about the local residents of mixed blood — the majority of the population, in fact — who, upon his arrival, had made him nervous. According to the census of 1832, 42,000 people, the majority of whom were small "copper-coloured" men of mixed races, lived in Chiloé and its dependencies (*BD* 266). Of the 42,000, 11,000 retained their native surnames, were predominantly Christian, but were not likely of pure blood. Their subsistence was limited: they grew potatoes and, like the Fuegians gathered shellfish from the low water.

Apparently, this segment of the population also retained superstitious beliefs and was said to participate in diabolic rituals, for which participants were punished by Church authorities. More that 30,000 people of mixed blood (called *mestizos*) were products of intermarriages between the Spanish and the indigenous people. According to Douglas, the Indians were Chahues and Ragunos (all of Araucanian heritage), who spoke the same Belichen dialect. Neither of these tribes, however, was considered to be the original inhabitants of Chiloé; rather, according to the historical record, the Bybenies tribe was thought to be the first to settle in the region, but they migrated with the influx of new tribes.

Darwin also understood that technology was a tribal signature. He cited William Low's experience while sealing in the channels of Cape Tres Montes, 225 miles south of Chiloé. The large party of Native Americans there had oared canoes, built of planks like those the Periaguas made, each with a cross on the bow. Darwin wondered if these men were descendants of Chiloé's ancient inhabitants. The Chahues and the Ragunos, believed to be direct descendants of a large northern tribe, had been sent south to the Chilean missions to be taught Christianity and put to work — "in short," Darwin acerbically remarks, to be "slaves to their Christian teachers" (*BD* 267). Of the original Bybenies, however, there were only remnants, chiefly in Caylen, and these people had lost their dialect. The Indians retained their own leaders but had no real power. Chilean authorities were trying to make retribution to the Indians by allocating undeveloped land to each chief, to his widow, to militiamen, and to the aged (267). Generally, as the 1 December 1834 entry points out, the Native Americans whom Darwin met in Chiloé were very poor (*BD* 234).

Although Darwin's moral indignation towards colonial policy-makers, and over the extermination of Native South Americans, was often muted and expressed in personal discourse, it was nonetheless genuine and consistent with his abolitionist views. A measure of ambivalence over race persisted, however, in the manner in which he perceived nonwhites of mixed ancestry.

# 7. "The Mysterious Agency": Darwin in the South Seas

## 15–26 November 1835: Tahiti

As the first European explorer to visit the island of Otaheite or Tahiti, Samuel Wallis, in 1767, established close relations with the inhabitants there (Heawood 216–217). His expeditions into the interior of the island brought back wonderful accounts of its natural beauty and fecundity, and those who had been sick aboard H.M.S. *Dolphin* regained their health in this congenial environment (217). Eight months after Wallis had arrived in Tahiti, the French circumnavigator Louis Antoine de Bougainville's (1729–1811) expedition anchored off the coast. Accompanied by naturalists and astronomers, he had voyaged round the world to visit Tahiti, the Society Islands, the Samoan Group, New Hebrides, and to rediscover the Solomon Islands. The French were deeply impressed not only by the luxuriance of the island but also by the good nature of the inhabitants (222–23). And, on 13 April 1769, Captain James Cook arrived at Tahiti and entered Port Royal Harbor. Although the Tahitians stole objects from H.M.S. *Endeavour*, Cook maintained cordial relations with them, and he fulfilled his navigational mission, which included charting the transit of Venus and gathering important information about the island's geography. Because of his success, navigators had valuable information about unknown regions of the South Pacific (Heawood 228–29).

On a return visit to the island on 6 August 1773, Cook noticed that many material changes had taken place since 1769, and the people remained as amicable as ever (Heawood 240). On the third voyage, commenced on 25 June 1776, Cook chose Tahiti as a vital weigh station in largely uncharted waters (246). Other major European expeditions followed suit, such as Vancouver's, in late 1791 (288). British ships, like H.M.S. *Supply* in 1788, counted on Tahiti as a haven, thanks to Captain Cook's diplomacy; the *Supply*, seriously stricken with scurvy, received a warm welcome from Cook's personal friends, the Tahitians Otoo and Oedidee, and the sick were able to recuperate, there being an abundance of anti-scorbutic fruit on Tahiti (304). The infamous Captain Bligh, commander of the H.M.S. *Bounty*, procured breadfruit trees for that purpose as well, before setting sail for Java, and before the mutiny (311).

On Sunday, 15 September 1835, the *Beagle* reached Tahiti. Once at anchor in Matavai Bay, the ship was met by canoes which guided the shore party. Darwin's party received a joyous welcome and had a fine dinner. Both Darwin's and FitzRoy's initial impressions of these people were recorded. Both agreed that the Tahitians differed markedly from the Fuegians. But whereas Darwin saw in the Tahitians incarnations of savage nobility, FitzRoy emphasized their physiological characteristics and aspects of their material culture. But the latter's descriptions, especially in regard to cranial anatomy, were unreliable since he tried to understand Tahitian behavior in the context of phrenology, which assumed that cranial formation mirrored personality and intelligence.

Darwin's descriptions were also skewed but in a different way. He tended to idealize the Tahitian. Those whom he observed bore a mildness in their facial expressions, which immediately "banishes the idea of a savage." Although their clothing was rag-tag, they nonetheless appeared intelligent, and, on the basis of this intuition, he assumed that they were "advancing in civilization." Captain FitzRoy, on the other hand, came to a different conclusion on first meeting the natives: "I shall not forget the very unpleasant impression made upon my mind, at first landing, by seeing a number of females, and children, with a few men, half dressed in the scanty, dirty, and tattered scraps of clothing, which they unfortunately prefer to their native dress" (Narr. 2 548). Physically well developed, and resembling Patagonian Indians, the Tahitian men, according to Darwin, were generally "very tall, broad-shouldered, athletic," and well proportioned. When they guided him, on 19 November, through valleys and mountains, he was greatly impressed by their agility and strength (*BD* 369–371). In imagery reminiscent of Rousseau's writings, he sketches the scene, as his Tahitian guides wend through a lower valley, "with their naked tattooed bodies, their heads ornamented with flowers ... in the dark shade of the woods [.] [They] would have formed a fine picture of Man inhabiting some primeval forest" (*BD* 375). Darwin might have had in mind Rousseau's memorable image of savage man, in the *Discourse on the Origin and Foundations of Inequality Among Men* (1755). Though the savage is devoid of supernatural gifts and education, one finds in him, "an animal less strong than some, less agile than others, but, on the whole, the most advantageously constituted of all; I see him eating his fill under an oak tree, quenching his thirst at the first stream, making his bed at the foot of the same tree which furnished his meal, with all his needs satisfied" (*Inequality* 10–11). Rousseau's natural man did not cower on a stormy beach in a makeshift hut but strode in a natural world that had been created for his support and shelter.

Rousseau's perspective on man, though idealized, was nonetheless dynamic. In fact, he had a rudimentary understanding of how man could adapt to environmental conditions, and of how nature, here compositely portrayed as a body of constant, unforgiving laws, pressured the human species to adapt or to die. If successful, man can become strong or be more in conformity with the world and more likely to survive adverse conditions: "accustomed from infancy to bad weather and the harshness of the seasons, inured to fatigue, and forced, naked and unarmed, to defend their lives and their prey from other wild beasts, or to escape from them by running, men acquire a robust and almost unalterable constitution" (11). Rousseau infers that the physical effects of adaptation are inheritable and inculcated culturally through learned behavior: "the children, bringing into the world with them the excellent constitution of their parent fortifying it by the same exercises that produced it, thus acquire all the vigor of which the human species is capable" (11). Rousseau's Nature, Spartan in its severity, renders "strong and robust those with good constitutions, and lets all the others perish" (11). The implication is that the most well adapted (not necessarily the most robust) would live to reproduce, to transmit adaptive traits to their young. The most important insight of all was that human beings who were maladapted to natural conditions perished along with their deficiencies.

Unlike Darwin, FitzRoy did not superimpose the image of savage nobility on those whom he met. The Tahitian males of the "higher classes" (their social ranking being ambiguous) were large in stature "but rather unwieldy." Different body types (stout, tall, middle-sized, and short) were seen among the lower classes. On one feature, FitzRoy concurs with Darwin: they are "well-proportioned and muscular" (Narr. 2 547). Unlike the white laborer whose musculature is "hard and knotty," that of the Tahitian is "rounded, and smooth" (Narr. 2 547–58). FitzRoy did not conjecture as to whether differences in muscle-mass were the obvious results of life in the tropics versus life in industrial or farm labor. Though the Captain makes the figurative remark that the Tahitians stride like "the giants of history" (Narr. 2 548), he is more inclined to compare the Tahitians to their closest South American counterparts, the Patagonians. The Patagonians' nobility and physical pre-eminence were most readily seen if contrasted to their diminutive, southern neighbors, the impoverished Onas.

FitzRoy attenuated the comparison, however, when he used phrenology to rate the intelligence of human groups. A typical statement follows: thus, the Patagonian male had "a large, coarse looking head, with high cheek bones, and a 'mane-like' head of hair," while the Tahitian head was "singularly well formed." "If phrenology is not altogether a delusion" — i.e., judging intellect and demeanor from cranial anatomy — the Tahitians are, therefore, likely to be fast learners, "capable of receiving instruction, or doing credit to their teachers" (Narr. 2, 548).

Captain Cook, Darwin, and Captain FitzRoy identified Tahitian tattooing to be an index to culture. The Tahitian practice of tattooing (their word is *tattau*) impressed Darwin, as much as it had Captain Cook in 1769. In a journal entry of July 1769, Cook viewed the practice critically rather than affectively. In one passage, he was oblivious to the possibility that *tattauing* either was an art-form, or a mode of cultural expression, or both, so he was content simply to describe what he saw. The inlaying of indelible black ink into the skin made the *tattau*, but the results he inspected were, at times, crude and disfiguring. Some Tahitians, for instance, had poorly designed figures of men, birds or dogs on their skin, whereas women generally had the figure Z inscribed on every joint of their fingers and toes; the men also marked up their hands and feet and had circles and crescents on their limbs. Cook discerns no meaning in the hodge-podge of shapes: "both the quantity and situation of [the images] seem to depend entirely upon the humor of each individual" (37). He mentions disapprovingly how extreme the practice is among the Islanders, many of whom covered their buttocks with deep black designs, and "over this most have arches drawn one over another as high as their short ribs which are near a quarter of an Inch broad; these arches seem to be their great pride as both men and women show them with great pleasure" (37).

On the other hand, Darwin delights in the ornate designs, especially those that gracefully follow the curvatures of the body, and that have "very elegant and pleasing effect"; one figure, in particular, was striking: the image of ramifying branches, recalling palm leaves and the surface of a Corinthian column, extended from the lumbar spine, up and around the rib cage, and looked like a "delicate creeper" reminiscent perhaps of acanthuses winding around a tree trunk (*BD* 366). Older people also displayed the tattoos of their youth, often on their feet, and were dated by these ineradicable images (*BD* 367). Although older Tahitians usually did not look their age, none could disguise it; for an old man has "his age for ever stamped on his body & he cannot assume the air of a young dandy." Darwin also noted how women tattooed their fingers.

Darwin was very grateful for the hospitality he received, as the natives attempted to communicate, albeit in broken English. They performed a bonfire serenade on the beach, in which a chorus of little girls sang melodious songs. The entire scene reinforces his idyllic expectations, making them "unequivocally aware that [they] were seated on the shores of an Island in the South Sea" (*BD* 367).

On the morning of Tuesday, 17 November, the crew of the *Beagle* was awakened by a flotilla of canoes, and a group of two-hundred Tahitians were permitted on deck. Their behavior was extraordinary. Cook had noted in his journal six decades earlier that the Tahitians whom he allowed on board, though certainly not aggressive, had the impulsive habit of taking whatever they saw with them and even picked sailors' pockets, as if they had no concept of private property and no inhibitions against theft: how hard it was "to keep them from stealing but everything that came within their reach, in this they are prod[igious] expert[s]" (April 1769 26). On 2 May 1769, natives went so far as to rob an astronomical quadrant from under a sentry's nose. Cook was so desperate to regain this valuable instrument that he contemplated detaining a chief as hostage, but before he took this drastic step the instrument was returned (30).

Darwin's experience with the Tahitian canoeists was quite the opposite of Cook's. Those who boarded the *Beagle* were merchants: they brought things to sell, mostly shells, had a sophisticated understanding of the value of money, and preferred it to practical items, like clothes. They even preferred paper tender over coins. Some of them had compiled considerable sums. One chief, for example, even purchased horses and whaleboats, paying from 50 to 100 dollars.

In the evening of 18 November, the expedition camped on the bank of a stream, near a chain of waterfalls. Like so many explorers before him, Darwin marveled at the fertility and abundance of plant life and of fruit on each side of the ravine, there for the taking. In contrast to the flimsy dwellings of the Fuegian tribes, he found several Tahitians industriously erecting an excellent house on the spot, using nothing more than strips of bark for twine, bamboo stems, and the large leaves of the banana for bedding. The explorers then built a fire to cook the evening meal. Darwin astutely noted how different was the fire-making technology of the gauchos of the Pampas who rotated a stick in a hole to create friction from that of Tahitians who rubbed the blunt point of a stick in a groove, to ignite the wood dust; the wood of the *Hibiscus tiliaceus* was ideally suited for the purpose of fire, and its light wood was also used as poles for carrying burdens or as ballast for outrigger canoes (*BD* 371, 373). Darwin appreciated the Tahitian's ability to ignite the fire. What took a Tahitian two seconds to kindle required far greater exertion from one untrained in the technique. It took about ten minutes to make a large enough fire in which leaf-enveloped beef, fish, crustaceans, fruit, and vegetables were layered between hot stones, and the open hearth was then covered by earth to trap smoke and steam. This method provided a wonderful meal in about a quarter of an hour (*BD* 372). Darwin realized that he had entered a world in which man could utilize an abundance of natural resources and not be subjugated by inclement weather.

Distinguishing between the daily plight of certain Fuegian tribes and the Tahitians, Darwin states, rather ambiguously, that "savage man, with his reasoning powers only partly developed, is the child of the Tropics"; the implication of this private statement is that, in a mild, tropical ecology, nature offered the reasoning savage material sufficient for his needs. Did this mean that, if destitute Alacaluf were relocated to a Polynesian environment, life for them would inevitably improve? Conversely, did it mean that if the robust Polynesian were transplanted to the stormy shoreline of Navarino Island, in Tierra del Fuego, would they degenerate, despite their intelligence and strength?

Darwin did not elaborate on these intriguing possibilities, but he had an opinion. If we recall, his reaction to Fuegians encountered in 1832 had been culturally conditioned: they were, at first sight, inherently savage and alien to his idea of humanity. By 1835, and after having met the Tahitians, he modified his opinion somewhat. In a deleted sentence, he reflects that, through the exercise of reason, man's propensity is to use natural resources to sustain himself: "if an animal exerts its instinct to procure food, the law of nature clearly points out that man should exert his reason & cultivate the ground" (*BD* 373n.). The implication is that, irrespective of environmental conditions, man could not be reduced mentally to an animalistic level, because his intelligence could not be entirely eradicated; furthermore, the gatherer (he implies) had the inherent capacity to become an agriculturalist. If the Fuegian could be thought of as an ignoble savage, the Tahitian, in Darwin's revised opinion, was not a noble savage, as the concept was popularly understood; rather, his lifestyle exemplified the highest level of achievement for which uncivilized mankind could hope, one in which ecology, human intelligence, and the natural laws governing organic life were in relative equilibrium.

The Tahitians took temperance to an extreme, as Darwin discovered on an inland excursion. On 19 November, he records that they sipped from his flask of spirits, guiltily putting their fingers before them mouths and uttering the word "missionary" (*BD* 373). He recounted that, in 1833, alcohol abuse was a health problem on the islands. To ameliorate the problem, the missionaries convinced a few men to join a Temperance Society, and eventually the chiefs and the Tahitian Queen Pomare cooperated. They established a law barring the importation of spirits and fined anyone who sold or bought alcohol. A period of grace was permitted for merchants to sell what remained of their stock, but after the law came into effect, a general search was conducted, even of the missionaries' quarters, and all liquor (generically referred to as *Ava*) was poured out. Darwin praised prohibition on Tahiti and the missionaries' work in this regard, particularly in light of the damage alcohol abuse caused to indigenous people in the Americas (*BD* 373).

FitzRoy was also greatly impressed by the island-wide prohibition against alcohol. He is astounded "that the people of a whole country had solemnly refrained from drinking spirits," a choice that entitled them to respect and to "high consideration." The Captain related that, having discovered a small vessel aiming to sell rum on the Island, the people went out to the vessel, "and destroyed the obnoxious liquor." Houses were searched with puritanical scrupulosity. Even the preacher, George Prichard (1796–1883), had to decide whether to destroy a bottle of brandy which he retained for medicinal purposes. Although the residents granted him amnesty, Prichard poured out its contents (Narr. 2 550).

On Sunday, 22 November 1835, the *Beagle* entered the harbor of Papeete, considered the capital of Tahiti. As the seat of government and chief resort of shipping, Papeete was the residence of the Queen (*BD* 376). In the morning, Captain FitzRoy took a party to divine services, conducted in the Tahitian language, and the missionary, Mr. Prichard, led the service. Darwin thought Prichard a sensible and good man, as he did the latter's colleagues, Mr. Wilson and Mr. Nott. Prichard had recently completed the monumental task of translating the Bible into the Tahitian language. Darwin mentioned them in passing because the character of the missionaries had so frequently and so unjustly been attacked.

As to the moral state of Tahiti, Darwin hoped to form a balanced judgment on the basis of all he had read and seen. His research on the islands came from three sources. The first was William Ellis' two-volume, *Polynesian researches, during a residency of nearly six years on the South Sea Islands* (1829). Ellis (1794–1872), himself a missionary in the South Seas, looked at everything "under a favourable point of view" (376). The second source was F. W. Beechey's 1831, *Narrative of a voyage to the Pacific and [Bering] Strait, to co-operate with the Polar expeditions: performed in His Majesty's Ship Bloss[o]m ... in the years 1825, 26, 27, 28.* Frederick William Beechey (1796–1856), who was a naval officer and geographer (President of the Royal Geographical Society, 1855–56), wrote from a neutral standpoint, according to Darwin. And the third source was the Russian explorer and navigator Otto von Kotzebue, whose three-volume, *A voyage of Discovery, into the South Sea and [Bering] Strait* (1831), Darwin found to be "strongly adverse."

A balanced understanding of Tahiti's moral state, Darwin hoped, could be gathered from a collation of the three texts. To find a via media, he rejected the idea, promulgated by both Beechey and Kotzebue, "that the Tahitians had become a gloomy race & lived in fear of the Missionaries." He saw no truth to the claim of their being fearful; in fact, the islanders respected the missionaries. Despite several excessive prohibitions, the missionaries on Tahiti had established a creditable state of morality and religion, contrary to the opinions of those who imputed failure to them. Their critics, Darwin attests, judged them unfairly and by too high a standard: "They forget or will not remember that human sacrifices & the power of an idolatrous priesthood — a system of profligacy unparalleled in the world, & consequent infanticide as part of that system, — bloody wars where the conquerors spared neither women or children have been abolished; [and] that dishonesty, intemperance & licentiousness have been greatly reduced by the introduction of Christianity" (*BD* 377).

As far as sexual immorality was concerned, the virtues of the women (harkening back to Cook) had been criticized the most. Adopting a liberal and ethnologically objective position, Darwin thought this criticism unjust because what appeared promiscuous to Europeans was, for the Tahitians, conduct for young women that was both culturally acceptable and traditional. Those who judge the Tahitian way of life, he maintains, are hypocrites who "do not give credit to a morality which they do not wish to practice" (*BD* 377). Moreover, prejudices against "a religion which they undervalue, if not despise" motivate the critics of the Pacific missions (*BD* 377). It is not clear, from this entry, what, if any, was the underlying motive for such harsh criticism. FitzRoy and Darwin, on the strength of excerpts from their respective narratives, weighed in jointly on the moral conduct and on the character of the Tahitians in the 28 June 1836 "A Letter, Containing Remarks on the Moral State of Tahiti, New Zealand, &c.," as well as in the 1839 *Journal*. They praised them for their progress under the tutelage of the missionaries from savagery to civilization.

Kotzebue's criticism of Tahitian culture recapitulated Cook's findings. In July 1769, Cook strongly denounced the moral license of the Tahitians. Young girls, as a diversion for adults, were customarily gathered together to perform a "most indecent dance which they call *Timorodee*." Along with *Timorodee*, Kotzebue decried an "inhuman" custom that he found "contrary to the first principals of human nature": the Tahitians' resolution to enjoy "free liberty in love without being troubled or disturbed by its consequences." The horror lay in the fact that children conceived through these unions were smothered. Even cohabiting couples over the years were said to practice this atrocity. Cook writes that they are overt in their actions, considering it "as a branch of freedom upon which they value themselves" (38).

Relying on the narratives of Cook's three voyages, Malthus had also found trouble in this fabled paradise, and he left these descriptions unchanged in the 1826 edition. Among the Tahitian higher classes, promiscuity and infanticide were "fundamental laws" (*1803* 48), and the size of the higher classes was checked by the practice of murdering children. As Malthus observed, infanticide was permitted on every level of society, to the degree that it might even have become a fashion rather than a last resort, necessitated by poverty. Debauchery, promiscuity, and libertinism prevailed (*1803* 49). More than disease and human sacrifice, the combination of infanticide and island warfare (and the resulting destruction of villages and livestock) effectively checked population growth; concomitantly, famine was recurrent, and the loss of life was high. Since the time of Cook's voyages, a rapid succession of depopulating wars, the affect of European diseases, and the scarcity of women had determined the levels of prosperity and of population in Tahiti (*1803* 52).

John Lubbock's survey of Tahitian civilization, which recapitulated several Darwinian opinions, treats a wide variety of topics, from technology (tools and implements, dress, weapons, furniture, housing, fire technology, cookery), to social customs and politics (meals, modes of burial, surgery, religion, government, and mores), and to language (469–488). Darwin's liberal view of Tahitian social mores adumbrated Lubbock's which was expressed in 1864. Before condemning their promiscuity, Lubbock reasons, we must consider that they did not share the same system of morality (486). He was, nevertheless, a staunch critic of the privileged *Arreoy* association, a cult in which "all the members of [the association] were regarded as being married to one another" (487). Children of these unions were usually murdered; but if a child was permitted to live, the father and mother were considered engaged to one another and were ejected from the association. The woman who chose not to kill her own child was derisively called a "bearer of children." Using an argument derived from Malthus, via Kotzebue, Lubbock suspects that the most powerful reason behind the association's propensity for infanticide is that "their numbers were already large, the means of subsistence limited, and that, as but few were carried off either by disease or in war, the population would soon have outgrown their supplies, if some means were not taken to check the natural increase of numbers" (487).

Darwin admired the fair-mindedness of the civilized Tahitians, especially as it was manifested in a local, maritime dispute. In 1833, a small Peruvian ship under British registry was apparently plundered by Tahitians living in the Low Islands. The assumption was that "some indiscreet law" of the Tahitian Queen Pomare inspired this act of piracy. The British Government, therefore, demanded compensation from the Tahitian Government — which illustrated how far the islanders had progressed, politically and legally. The Tahitians had agreed to pay 3,000 dollars to settle the issue but, after two years had elapsed, they had not yet paid the settlement. The Commodore of Lima ordered FitzRoy to pursue the issue. He was granted a parliamentary session with the Queen on 24 November 1835, and the matter was finally settled, as the chiefs and people "resolved to subscribe & complete the sum which was wanting" (*BD* 379). According to Darwin, FitzRoy sympathized with the financial burden of the Tahitians on the main island, especially since these people sacrificed their private property "for the crimes of distant Islanders." Darwin appreciated their cooperation and loyalty to the Crown, expressing his surprise "at the extreme good sense; reasoning powers, moderation, candor & prompt resolution which were displayed on all sides" (*BD* 379). After the proceedings had ended, several of the chiefs even asked Captain FitzRoy a number of "intelligent questions concerning international customs & laws," especially those related "to the treatment of Ships & foreigners." Once the Tahitians made their decision, and with the knowledge they had acquired about maritime law, they formulated laws pertaining to such matters. After some festivities, Captain FitzRoy and Darwin went on shore to acquire a deed signed by Queen Pomare and two chiefs stipulating how much of the required sum was to be remitted then, and when they intended to pay the balance (*BD* 379). Deed in hand, FitzRoy, Darwin, and the crew of the *Beagle* set sail for New Zealand (*BD* 379–80).

In Captain FitzRoy's *Journal* can be found a much different account of what had happened to the pirated vessel. According to him, the bark *Newton*, out of Valparaíso, had been sailing under Chilean (not British) colors but was owned by British subjects (Narr. 2 554). That was a significant difference, if these facts are reliable. The natives, it seems, had unknowingly seized a British vessel, for the colors were not aloft. But more important was Fitzroy's contention that Queen Pomare might not have been responsible for the seizure of the vessel in the first place. FitzRoy cited the testimony of Mr. Middleton, the ship's pilot. The Captain of the *Newton*, Mr. Clarke, had been employing Low Island natives to dive for pearl oysters and had agreed to pay them in cloth and provisions each month. Because Clarke was alleged to have repeatedly mistreated them, and because he gave them meager provisions (e.g., one cocoanut per day and nothing else), the natives thought about deserting him, but they needed the goods that had been promised.

As the story goes, Middleton requested more food for the divers, to which Clarke agreed, but, once the food was dispensed, the Captain "affected to deny his orders," gathered the biscuits, and threw them overboard. This made the divers angry, of course, but they did not react to the affront immediately. Middleton claimed to have warned Clarke of the immediate danger and to change his ways before it was too late, but the Captain arrogantly resisted the advice. Yet the divers did not react. But later that day, while Middleton was away getting shells, Clarke beat a chief. This set off a revolt: the divers took over the *Newton*, "bound all the white people," and transported them to shore. When Middleton returned, he found his crew gone. The natives, assuring him that they were friends, hailed him on board and promised not to hurt anyone. FitzRoy interjects at this point in the text: "What extraordinary mildness among savages!" None of Middleton's belongings were disturbed, though the rest of the ship had been ransacked and the furniture of the hull "torn to pieces" (Narr. 2 555). Middleton was allowed to bring the damaged bark to Tahiti where it was auctioned off to settle insurance claims.

FitzRoy points out that the practice of pearl diving was "a difficult and dangerous employment." Unlike Darwin who, on 18 November 1835, writes that the Tahitians have "the dexterity of Amphibious animals in the water" (*BD* 370), FitzRoy conveys the actual physical cost of their labor in the oyster beds: though the divers at the Paamuto Islands, for example, never descended more than four of five fathoms (i.e., 24–30 feet) and for brief dives only, the Tahitians spent one to three minutes below the surface at equal or greater depths to harvest as many as ten shells per dive. But doing this over a four or five hour stint, being "extreme labour," had alarming effects: after a long dive, natives hemorrhaged from the ears and nose and, for as long as ten to twenty minutes, they were temporarily blinded. Divers, he observes, endured these exertions, "for a small monthly pay of ten or twelve yards of calico, or coarse linen" (Narr. 2 555). If Darwin was referring to the 1833 *Newton* incident (which seems likely), and if Middleton's account was true, then the British Government owed the Tahitians an apology and significant damages, not vice versa.

# 19–29 December 1835: New Zealand

Upon arriving at the Bay of Islands, New Zealand, Darwin was surprised at how the region differed from Tahiti. Differences in the standard of living between British settlers and natives could not have been greater. The hovels of the natives, described as "diminutive and paltry," contrasted with the white-washed, neat English cottages, with their flower gardens (December 21–22, 1835; *BD* 381–82). Unlike Tahiti with its peaceful villages, the landscape of the Bay of Islands featured European-style fortifications, of which Darwin gave detailed descriptions. Surprisingly, native tribes manned these forts, used them in combat, and the natives also possessed firearms. The sophistication of the stockades, the defensive tactics natives employed, and the fact that conflicts were incessant, led Darwin to conclude that, "in no part of the world a more war-like race of inhabitants could be found than the New Zealanders" (*BD* 382). Appearances to the contrary notwithstanding, presently there was much less warfare than in the past, an improvement Darwin ascribes to "pro-gressive civilization" (*BD* 383); and muskets, once lucratively sold by Euro-pean traders, were no longer in high demand.

The inhospitality of the natives was infamous. Captain Cook is reported as have said that they customarily greeted approaching ships with "volleys of stone" and boldly defied the visitors to come ashore to be killed and eaten (*BD* 382–83). "This warlike spirit," he reflects, "is evident in many of their customs & smallest actions." Hence, if a New Zealander is struck, even in jest, "the Blow must be returned" (*BD* 383). Of the main tribes in the region, the southern-most one was reputedly the most bellicose. The visit of a chief to England illus-trates this obsession with fighting. Chief Shongi, who became a sort of celebrity in England, loved war so much that he believed it to be "the one & lasting spring of every action" (*BD* 383). Apparently (according to a missionary's account), Shongi's chief motive for going to England was to procure arms and, more important, to learn how to manufacture them. A protracted struggle between his and a neighboring tribe, it seems, had caused an armaments race, and the conflict was envisioned to be a blood-feud extending over generations. Shongi eventually had a decisive battle with the so-called Thames tribe, defeated them, and slew his counterpart. Even though Chief Shongi harbored "deep feelings of hatred & revenge," the presence of these negative emotions did not warp his personality; in Darwin's opinion, the chief remained "a good natured sort of person" (*BD* 383), or so the local missionary had claimed.

Captain FitzRoy, in a journal entry of 21 December 1835, was particu-larly impressed by the New Zealanders' energy and ferocity: "There is noth-ing in the outward character of the country corresponding to the ferocious sanguinary disposition of its aboriginal inhabitants" (Narr. 2 567–68). These visceral traits did not mean they were slow-witted. Actually they seemed quite intelligent, demonstrating "quickness of apprehension, without much reflection" (Narr. 2 567–68).

FitzRoy agreed with Darwin that the Maoris intensified their aggressive demeanor with facial scarification: "Ferocity is a striking trait in the countenances of the older men," and this expression was enhanced by "the savage style" of facial tattoos. Whereas Darwin, like Cook, did not see much anthropological significance in the practice, FitzRoy realized that it was much more than self-mutilation; in fact, it was actually a form of ornamentation. Cutting lines in the skin with "a blunt-edged iron tool" and of then staining them black certainly intimidated, creating the expression of "a demon-warrior." However crude these designs were, they were not the arbitrary marks of an incompetent operator. On the contrary, the tattooing also had heraldic significance, each design representing the rank and prominence of its bearer. The shapes on the face, FitzRoy soon discovered, were actually personal signatures. He found this out when he witnessed a legal resolution between disputing tribes. When eight chiefs signed a legal document over land rights, each made marks on the document "resembling a small part of the tattooed lines upon their faces. One man imitated the mark upon the side of his nose; another [did so] near his eye" (Narr. 2 584–86).

At times, as we have already seen, Darwin's emotional reaction to aboriginal people precluded thoughtful interpretation. His reaction to facial tattooing was an example of how hasty judgment precluded curiosity and inquiry. Unlike FitzRoy who recognized the heraldic import of the crude facial tattoos, Darwin dismisses facial scarring as an external index of savagery that lent "a disagreeable expression to their countenances." The complicated, symmetrical designs covering the New Zealanders' faces, instead of stimulating Darwin to discover their cultural meanings, led him to dismiss them as puzzling to "an unaccustomed eye." In physiological terms, he might have correctly concluded that deep scarification had damaged facial muscles and nerves to the degree that the expression seemed unnaturally rigid. Of Queequeg's demeanor and character in *Moby Dick*, Ishmael thought differently — and not as a Darwinian: "Savage though he was, and hideously marred about the face — at least to my taste — his countenance yet had a something in it which was by no means disagreeable. You cannot hide the soul. Through all his unearthly tattooings, I thought I saw the traces of a simple honest heart" (51–52). Both FitzRoy and Darwin conjectured on behavioral traits empirically. But whereas FitzRoy saw a mixture of possibilities ("energy, quickness of apprehension ... and a high degree of daring" [Narr. 2 567–69]), Darwin overreacts and generalizes, as "a twinkling" in their eyes was unmistakable evidence of "cunning & ferocity" (*BD* 384).

From his readings of Lubbock and of Tylor, Darwin realized, in 1871/74, that human expressions, tastes, dispositions, and habits were often very similar to one another. The pleasures derived from dancing, music, acting, painting, and tattooing and ornamenting the body seemed universal (*DM* 185–86). Tattooing was popular in many uncivilized societies as well, from the Eskimos to the New Zealanders (*DM* 595). The missionaries whom Darwin interviewed in New Zealand informed him that Maori women would not give up facial tattooing as they considered it beautifying. Men desire facial tattoos to attract women and to make themselves formidable warriors (*DM* 597–98). In 1864, citing John MacGillivray's Australian narrative, of the H.M.S. *Rattlesnake*'s 1848 third cruise, Lubbock observes that Maoris "tattoo themselves on the back and breast in rows, rings, and semi-circles" (446). Both tattooing and body painting, continues Lubbock, were considered kinds of clothing. Among the "Feegeeans" the practice was confined to the women, was a religious duty, and involved considerable discomfort; and, if the duty was neglected, such an infraction was punishable by death (456). To native Australians, however, tattooing was a social, not a religious, responsibility (475).

Of the English minority in the area, Darwin had little to say that was complimentary. Many of the inhabitants were escaped convicts from New South Wales. Most, he thought, were worthless in character. The missionaries in the area, faced with challenges from white and native peoples alike, had not had much success (*BD* 384). Although aboriginal tribes had been converted to Christianity elsewhere, in this area, most remained resistant to proselytizing. FitzRoy appreciated the missionaries' difficult task, too, especially in the village of Kororareka, a particularly difficult location that he called "a stronghold of iniquity." The Church here persisted in its service to the people, even though it was surrounded by "spirit-selling" Englishmen, by pandering native chiefs, and by the dregs of criminal society (*BD* 321).

After touring the Bay of Islands' villages, and after speaking to people, Darwin recorded several acute ethnological observations, comparing Polynesian New Zealanders or Maoris to Tahitians. From his standpoint, the New Zealanders resembled the Tahitians, but there were clear differences between the two ethnic groups. For example, although the New Zealander appeared "superior in energy" to the Tahitian, the "character of the former is of a much lower order" (*BD* 384). Even a cursory glance, Darwin maintains, supports the conviction "that one is a savage, the other a civilized man" (*BD* 384). In a passage of 21 December 1835, FitzRoy compared the New Zealanders both to the Fuegians and to the Tahitians. After seeing several New Zealanders in their native dress and not at their hygienic best, he pronounced them "a race intermediate between the [Tahitians] and Fuegians." Despite this superficial judgment, FitzRoy acutely observes that Fuegian, Tahitian, and New Zealander are of "one and the same race of men, altered by climate, habits and food;

but descended from the same original stock" (Narr. 2 567–68). Thus, according to his ethnic interpretation, each tribe was a variant of the human species. Although their respective lifestyles and natures differed from one another, they were closely related racially; the differences were, in part, attributable to environmental pressures and to the adaptive responses of each group to these pressures. The Maori warrior was exceptional in outward expression and bearing, and Fitzroy was impressed by to their "quickness of apprehension" and "high degree of daring" (Narr. 2, 567–68).

The lack of sanitation and of personal hygiene among the New Zealanders and of basic amenities in Maori habitations repelled both Darwin and FitzRoy, the former comparing the huts to what he had seen in Tierra del Fuego. One chief, in particular, wore a shirt, "black & matted with filth" (BD 384). The native hovels that Darwin saw had been built the same way, and all were extremely filthy. Resembling a cow shed with an open end, each hut was partitioned into two rooms. When the weather was bad, the inhabitants slept in the inner room and stored their property there (BD 388). Surveying aboriginal architecture more carefully, FitzRoy seemed to be describing a completely different, more sophisticated abode. The buildings that he saw were not Fuegian-like huts; rather, they had two wide planks, placed edgeways in front and joined at the top by nails or pegs, forming a wide angle with an interior space, and a two-foot square doorway. The walls and roof, being wickerwork, were thatched over with broad flag leaves or rushes. Each typically had a porch where the family sat, ate, and slept. The roof eaves projected several feet beyond the front, as did the side walls, to create a simple portico. Despite the details of construction, FitzRoy echoes Darwin's opinion that the sleeping area is a "sty"; surprisingly, he states that even a Fuegian wigwam was far preferable (Narr. 2 577–78).

Polity existed in the Bay of Islands but not of a government in the European sense of the term. The land was divided up between the various, independent tribes, each of which comprised free men and slaves captured in war. For the freeborn, land was there for the taking and, if vacant, could be occupied and tilled. Although proper laws did not exist, rules of conduct were recognized, to define what was right or wrong. Where an infringement occurred, retribution, rather than arbitration, was called for, whether immediately or in future. As expected, in terms of governance Darwin ranked the New Zealanders a notch above the Fuegians but below the Tahitians who had a queen and a council of elders: "If the state in which the Fuegians live should be fixed on as zero in the scale of governments ... the New Zealand would rank but a few degrees higher, while Tahiti, even as when first discovered, would occupy a respectable position" (BD 385).

Even though a codified body of law did not exist in New Zealand in 1835, and even though the natives appeared to Darwin as unreasonable and as highly volatile, an interesting event caused him to modify his negative opinion somewhat. When the first official British resident, James Busby (1801–71), was attacked and wounded at his home by irate tribesman, the cause of the dispute being unclear, the native community condemned the act, especially since it was done at night and while Mrs. Busby was indisposed. It seems that this stealthy attack was dishonorable, the native code of behavior proscribing aggression at night, and especially if the wife had retired (*BD* 386). The chiefs who convened a meeting to punish the aggressor decided to confiscate his land for the King of England. The very idea of indigenous New Zealand chiefs convening to punish one of their fellows was likely without precedent. The loss of territory, most definitely, was a serious matter. Because the aggressor lost his property, he also "lost caste in the estimation of his equals" (*BD* 386). This incident, even though it turned out well for Mr. Busby (or, as Darwin calls him, "Mr. Bushby"), was typical of the social climate early settlers had to endure. Fitzroy sympathized with Mr. Busby's predicament: "An isolated individual, not having even the authority of a magistrate, encircled by savages, and by a most troublesome class of his own countrymen" (Narr. 2 575–77). An English rabble, convicts and "democratic" revolutionaries, victimized honest settlers and missionaries alike in the struggle for power and for land (Narr. 2 580).

Although New Zealand was fertile, agricultural technology was still needed to grind out a mode of subsistence. The missionaries taught the natives how to build agricultural and farming devices — water mills, blacksmith forges, stables, threshing barns, and winnowing machines; and the natives were also taught how to use ploughshares. In the village of Waimate, for example, the missionaries and English settlers had built their own homes, but here, unlike in the Bay of Islands' district, they had not forsaken the natives. There were large gardens, good crops, and everywhere evidence of native workmanship and of an improved way of life for all residents. Darwin admired the profound effect this instruction was having on the indigenous people. The moral effect of instruction on the natives, more than the success of the British in establishing civilization, impressed him (*BD* 380). By necessity, the missionary system in New Zealand had to employ tactics that differed from those used in Tahiti. Whereas, in Tahiti, the missionaries paid attention, primarily, to religious instruction, in New Zealand, where the land had potential but needed work, the emphasis was on the "arts of civilization." The Tahitians had an advantage over the New Zealanders in terms of the progress towards civilization since the basic needs of the former were more readily satisfied.

For this reason, Darwin thought, in comparison to the aborigines of New Zealand, the mind of a Tahitian was certainly "one of a higher order." Darwin speculated that the intellectual disparity between two ethnically related groups was due to the fact that Tahiti was more hospitable than New Zealand. The Maoris, therefore, needed to establish an agrarian economy before considering cultural refinements (*BD* 390).

On Christmas day, 1835, Darwin visited the house of Mr. Williams, where he found a large group of native children, and a nicer and merrier group he had never seen, nor had expected, in a land once-notorious for cannibalism, murder, and "all atrocious crimes" (*BD* 391). But Darwin's sentiments in the 30 December entry cancelled the benevolent gesture out. As the *Beagle* sailed out of the Bay of Islands, bound for Sidney, he reflected that they were all probably glad to be leaving New Zealand. For Darwin, it was not a "pleasant place." The natives lack "the charming simplicity" of Tahiti. Of the English settlers, most are "the very refuse of Society" (*BD* 395).

## 12 January–14 March 1836: Australia and Tasmania

On 16 January 1836, Darwin met a group of native Australians for the first time. The group was pleased to demonstrate spear-throwing skills for a shilling. Partly clothed and speaking some English, the natives were good humored, pleasant, and "appeared far from such utterly degraded beings as usually represented" (*BD* 398). Though intelligent and sociable, they had, however, no desire to settle anywhere, to cultivate the ground, to raise sheep given them by the English, "or build houses & remain stationary" (*BD* 398). Despite their itinerancy, Darwin positioned them on his scale of civilization "some few degrees higher" than the Fuegians." But, on the scale of barbarism, they stood a few degrees lower than the inhabitants of Tierra del Fuego (*BD* 398). Precisely what these poorly defined categories meant is uncertain; for example, was Darwin basing his distinction primarily on material and social culture? But Darwin explored other issues in greater depth.

Because aboriginal society seemed marginal to the growing British colony on the Continent, Darwin was curious about how the natives survived — about how, "in the midst of a civilized people, a set of harmless savages wander[ed] about without knowing where they will sleep, & gain[ed] their livelihood by hunting in the woods" (*BD* 399). More ominous was Darwin's observation that their numbers seemed to be dwindling; as he continued on his journey; he saw "only one other hunting party." It was obvious that the natives lived in a state of independence from the whites, but he also discovered that they engaged in inter-tribal warfare, which had a pernicious effect on population (*BD* 399). In the 1839 *Journal*, he offers a partial explanation for the apparent decrease in the aboriginal population: "As the white man has traveled onwards, he has spread over the country belonging to several tribes. These, although enclosed by one common people, keep up their ancient distinctions, and sometimes go to war with each other" (*JR* [1839] 375). In the *Diary*, and before reading Malthus' *Essay* in 1838, Darwin had ascribed the decrease in numbers explicitly to alcohol consumption, to European diseases, such as measles, and to the gradual extinction of game (*BD* 399). Because the natives had lost their lands to colonists and have had to endure epidemics, famine, and warfare, their population had diminished considerably. Furthermore, because of their wandering life, more children died in infancy than would have under less itinerant circumstances (*BD* 399).

In the 30 January 1836 entry of the *Journal*, Darwin wrote about the treatment of aboriginal people in Hobart Town, Van Diemen's Land (Tasmania). His rhetoric suggests that the moral conflict at the center of his ethnology was reaching some degree of resolution. Bass's Strait, which was the size of Ireland, had become the new home for aboriginal people. Consequently, the white population of Van Diemen's Land "[could enjoy] the great advantage of being free from a native population" (*JR* [1839] 387). He acknowledges that the transportation of indigenous people was a "cruel step" to take, but, in his view, it was unavoidable because of a succession of "robberies, burnings, and murders, committed by blacks" (*JR* [1839] 387). However, the criminal activity, he recognized, was the effect of colonial policy against blacks.

The transported natives continued to resist the colonists until, in 1830, the island was placed under martial law and the white population was enjoined "to secure the entire race" of indigenous people. The method of doing so was copied from the hunting matches in India. A line of pursuers drove the natives (approximately 200) into a cul-de-sac on the Tasmanian peninsula. The natives evaded the trap, but they surrendered eventually and were deported to Flinder's Island in 1835. By 1842, there were only fifty-four survivors (*JR* [1839] 388).

In the 1839 edition of the *Journal*, Darwin elaborated the 16 January 1836 *Diary* entry, with two large paragraphs on the subject of aboriginal demography. He writes that, along with the obvious causes of destruction stated above, "there appears to be some more mysterious agency generally at work" (*JR* [1839] 376). With a scope encompassing the southern hemispheres where European expansionism was active, he concluded that, wherever Europeans have gone, indigenous people died off. This has been particularly true for the Americas, for Polynesia, for the Cape of Good Hope, and for Australia. But the white colonist was not the only human competitor to be blamed, for "the Polynesian of Malay extraction has in parts of the East Indian archipelago" driven out "the dark-coloured native" (*JR*.[1839] 376). This hegemonic phenomenon was biologically motivated, as the "varieties of man seem to act on each other in the same way as different species of animals — the stronger always extirpating the weaker" (*JR* [1839] 376). This sentence contains a very interesting ambiguity of terms. Here, Darwin was trying to compare the struggle between varieties of human beings, all of whom were members of a single species with the struggles between "different *species* of animals." Contrary to the opinion of contemporary racists, the conflict between colonists and aborigines in Australia was between two human *varieties* or racial communities.

Darwin was definitely thinking here in naturally selective terms, as we shall see in chapter 10 and 11; that is, the human groups uprooted by colonists were widely believed to be weak and inferior — people who were historically maladapted to the ecological niche in which they lived, and therefore unable to resist, or to accommodate themselves to, the arrival of a stronger human group. The moral question was rhetorical: because of their weakness, should they have been or did they deserve to be displaced?

The plight of the Tasmanians left Darwin ambivalent. On the one hand, in the light of historical events and consistent with his inchoate apprehension of natural selectivity, he perceived that the native Tasmanians were dying out. On the other hand, his acknowledgment of natural laws did not prevent him from recognizing the enormity of the situation and from expressing sympathy for the native Tasmanians. He was genuinely moved to learn that the Tasmanians were cognizant of the facts that their land was irretrievably lost and that they were dying off.

Although Darwin was affected by the pathos of the Tasmanians, their passivity disturbed him, almost to the point that it seemed to justify their displacement. On 19 January 1836, while in New South Wales, he was surprised to find that the indigenous people seemed to accept their situation and were pacified by the settlers' meager "peace offerings," such as the borrowing of dogs and the reception of cows' milk (*BD* 401). He concluded from this apparent behavior that the "thoughtless Aboriginal" was "blinded by these trifling advantages," and that they were delighted when the "White Man" approached them, oblivious to the likelihood that the British seemed "predestined to inherit the country of [their] children" (*BD* 402).

Darwin visited King George's Sound, an important seaport that had been only recently colonized. On 6 March 1836, he was impressed by the "good disposition of the aboriginal blacks" who desired to work. In their habits, manners, general appearance and tools, they resembled the natives of New South

Wales, but, unlike their counterparts in the other Australian colonies, Darwin found them to be quite industrious. In this realization, he had come a long way from the tendency to denigrate natives, solely on the basis of physical appearance. And even though he found the New South Wales inhabitants to be physically repulsive (their bodies being unusually hairy and filthy), and even though he called them "true Savages," he could not help but feel "an inclination to like such quiet good-natured men" (*BD* 411).

A large tribe called the White Cockatoo men visited the town where Darwin was staying and was supposedly asked to hold a dancing party. That night, Darwin witnessed the fascinating event: the tribe lit fires, painted themselves with white spots and lines, joined the King George's tribe in a dance, each party answering to the other in their movements and gestures. Each line of tribesmen scampered sideways in choreographed unison or in "Indian file into an open space," stamped the ground with great force, grunted, beat their weapons and clubs, extended their arms, and wriggled their bodies (*BD* 412). Darwin's first reaction was to consider the display as a meaningless, rude, and "barbarous scene." Seeing the obvious pleasure of native women and children as they watched the proceedings, however, he sensed that there was more here than met the eye. "Perhaps," he writes, "these dances originally represented some scenes such as wars & victories [?]" (*BD* 412). Actually, his guess was close to the truth: it was a peace-making dance between two warring tribes. Darwin witnessed two dances. In one, the dancers imitated the movements of the Emu. In the second, a kangaroo hunt was pantomimed.

Another indication of Darwin's maturing ethnology was that, in the case of the performing tribes, he did not resort to demonic epithets to describe what he did not fully understand, although the animal costumes, the loud sounds, the wild movements, and the naked figures, silhouetted against blazing fires, seemed to move "in hideous harmony" (*BD* 412). A sense of dramatic interaction was evident, as the dancers and the audience were all "in high spirits." Though the ground trembled with the stomping, and though the air resounded with native cries, Darwin was able to suppress a spontaneous reaction to what appeared to be a primordial scene and to modulate his tone. Thus, he described the dance objectively as "a perfect representation of a festival amongst the lowest barbarians" (*BD* 412). He would later write approvingly of the aborigines' energetic and natural manner: "In Tierra del Fuego, we have beheld many curious scenes in savage life, but never ... one where the natives were in such high spirits, and so perfectly at their ease" (*JR* [1845] 450–51).

FitzRoy was a perceptive ethnographer, for he understood that the dance was a ritualized means of conciliating two warring tribes. Unfortunately, the spectacle overloaded his senses. Even a clear thinker like FitzRoy had difficulty analyzing the performance. Although the animal choreography, cacophony, and regalia were extraordinary, he likened the scene to pandemonium; and the aborigines, to degraded caricatures of humanity. Ironically, Darwin and FitzRoy seemed, in this instance, to have exchanged ethnographic vocabularies and outlooks. While Darwin degraded the savages he met in the early 1830s and moderated his language by 1835, FitzRoy's moderation in the 1830s seems to have given way to less tolerant language by 1835, at least in this particular instance. For the Captain, the evocative scene was degrading:

> When all was ready, the fires burning brightly ... the spectators collected together, a heavy tramp shook the ground. A hundred prancing demon-like figures emerged from the darkness, brandishing their weapons, stamping together in exact accordance, and making hoarse guttural sounds at each exertion. It was a fiendish sight, almost too disagreeable to be interesting. What pains savage man takes, in all parts of the world where he is found, to degrade his nature; that beautiful combination which is capable of so much intelligence and noble exertion when civilized and educated. While watching the vagaries of these performers, I could not but think of our imprudence in putting ourselves so completely into their power: about thirty unarmed men being intermixed with a hundred armed natives ... their imitation of snakes, and kangaroos, in a kind of hunting dance, was exceedingly good and interesting [Narr. 2 625–27].

Darwin reconsidered regional demography in 1839. He could not understand why aboriginal populations throughout the South Pacific declined so precipitously, even in temperate islands like Tahiti, where infanticide was proscribed, where profligacy was diminishing, and where homicide was declining (*JR* [1839] 376). The Reverend J. Williams speculated that communicable diseases, to which colonists were immune but which they carried, was likely the chief cause of these alarming trends (*JR* 1839] 376–77). Epidemiological instances of this abound in the historical literature. In 1768–1769, for example, an outbreak of venereal disease was recorded in Tahiti. Before Captain Samuel Wallis in H.M.S. *Dolphin* arrived there in 1767, the islands were apparently free of these diseases. But it is more likely that de Bougainville's expedition to Tahiti, which followed Wallis' nine months later, was responsible for communicating the disease. The French expedition, it seems, had been traveling to other South Pacific Islands prior to arriving in Tahiti and might have acquired venereal diseases on the voyage, transmitting them to the Tahitians later. Bougainville denied responsibility and blamed Wallis. Cook found rampant V.D. at his arrival in 1769, but both gonorrhea and syphilis had declined by 1773 on his second voyage. Unfortunately, by July 1769, more than forty members of the *Endeavour* had V.D. After a three-month stay in

Tahiti, Cook sailed to New Zealand, arrived in October 1769, and brought gonorrhea there (G. C. Kohn 337). Epidemics such as dysentery, influenza-like illnesses and unspecified lethal infections erupted in New Zealand between 1790 and 1800. When European ships arrived in the Thames area of New Zealand in 1820, most of the Maori population had already been wiped out by an unspecified contagious disease. Not long after the arrival of H.M.S. *Coromandel*, from Sydney, Australia, in 1826, a major epidemic of some kind struck the Bay of Islands. Whooping cough ravaged Maori and European children alike in the Bay of Islands, from September–October 1828 to early 1829 (G. C. Kohn 240).

Expressing interest in colonial society, especially among the higher and the convict classes, Darwin acknowledged how difficult it was to form reasonable opinions and conclusions, considering the brevity of his stay. But he was disappointed with what he saw. The rancor of the community, its political factiousness, the "open profligacy," and the jealousy that pitted descendants of rich emancipationists against free settlers, whom the former considered "interlopers," were factors that weakened white society (*BD* 405–06). Social stress and what Darwin thought to be a "preponderant interest" in money-making enterprises and in the wool industry particularly, affected the intellectual culture directly: "The very low ebb of literature" was reflected by the "emptiness of the book-sellers shops" (*BD* 406).

The life of the convicts, though an object of dread in England, was actually not very severe, as their corporeal needs were being met, and for some there was the possibility of probation for good behavior. But these years of exile were, for the most part, "passed with discontent & unhappiness." The government's offer of free pardons and the fear of being remanded to secluded prisons deterred crime, but it did nothing to ameliorate the moral state of the convicts. Those who wished to change their lives were inhibited by their peers, especially among the servant class, where "intolerable misery & persecution" would be their reward (*BD* 407). The Australian penal system, in his view, was an abject failure (*BD* 407).

Though settling Australia was an opportunity to gain riches, and though the luxuries of life were abundant, these charms were lost because the country was "uninviting." The habits of the people and the decline of intellectual pursuits, in Darwin's opinion, will cause the national character to "deteriorate" (*BD* 406). The Australian economy puzzled him as well. On the one hand, their chief exports, wool and whale oil, were limited in quantity. The transportation of wool to coastal ports was hampered since there were no canals, and since the cost of transporting wool overland barely exceeded the cost of tending to and of shearing the sheep. To make matters worse, the pastures were so thin that settlers were forced to move deeper and deeper into the interior where the country appeared to be extremely poor. Given the apparent limits of agriculture and husbandry, Darwin conjectures that Australia must ultimately depend for its economic survival on becoming a maritime nation, "the center of commerce for the Southern Hemisphere" (*BD* 406–07).

# 8. The Making of Humboldt's Ethnology

Darwin's immediate experience with aboriginal societies evoked a conservative reaction from him, one that differed greatly from the kind of openness and relativism that characterized Humboldt's writings. Darwin, of course, thought highly of Humboldt's work, but the latter's reactions to natives encountered in the Amazon Basin did not impress him as much as had the natural descriptions, such as that of Tenerife. But the sentiment Darwin expresses in a letter of 6 August 1881 to J. D. Hooker, I think, was heartfelt: that it is right to call Humboldt "the greatest scientific traveler who ever lived" (*L&L* [1887] Vol. 3 247).

This chapter has a practical, twofold purpose: first, to abstract the development of Darwin's Humboldtian ethnology — his study of the origin, distribution, characteristics, and relations of races, from a perspective that was neither judgmental nor demeaning; and second, to facilitate a contrast between Darwin's emergent ethnology and the post-voyage theory on man as an evolutionary creature.

Whereas Humboldt did not approach natives with preconceived notions and even discounted assumptions about savagery and primitivism, Darwin was so shocked by the appearance of certain Fuegians that popular assumptions and conventional theories were momentarily validated in his mind. The Alacaluf who lined the ridges or who stood in canoes were not human beings at all, and he clumsily tried to account for their characteristics analogically, contrasting savage and civilized man to one another, and correlating the former to wild animals; the latter, to domesticated ones. Analogies and superficial comparisons validated, in his mind, the popular assumption that Fuegians such as these were, at best, only remotely akin to Western man. In one context, he conjectured that natives were either unable, or disinclined, to exercise their evolutionary advantages to render their conditions more hospitable. The paucity of material culture strengthened the suspicion that some were either mentally inferior to civilized man or not human, in the Western sense of the term. In particular contexts, Darwin even went so far as to dislodge the people of the Archipelago, zoologically, from the human genus.

Darwin hastily and wrongly concluded that coastal tribes were wretched gatherers, even though some manufactured and utilized bows, arrows, and spears. Unlike Humboldt who found convincing evidence of cannibalism among the Amazon tribes, Darwin accepted unsubstantiated allegations of cannibalism among the Fuegians, which corroborated pseudo-ethnological opinions about them; and he propagated these rumors in his correspondence (30 March 1833). Rightly outraged at the enslavement and degradation of women in Alacalufan society, he directs his disgust of "miserable savages" to all tribes and genders (March–April 1833). One year later, Darwin's emotions and assumptions again precluded a deeper understanding of Fuegian tribes. Canoeists off Wollaston Island were "hideous" to behold. Fuegian nakedness, painted bodies, tangled hair, and discordant voices continued to overwhelm his sensibilities and, in his mind, confirmed their sub-humanness; thus, he referred to them in animalistic terms as "unbroken savages" and as "gifted animals" — as creatures somewhere between man and beast. Their poor diet and squalid living conditions propped up this assumption (25 February 1834), and he recapitulated this view in a later notebook entry (March–July 1838), drawing a closer affinity between savages and higher primates than between the former and Western man.

By the late 1830s, Darwin's opinion of Fuegian cultures, which corresponded to Malthus' depiction of them as desultory, uncultured cannibals, had reached its nadir. Gradually, as Darwin began to understand that dismissive stereotypes of native humanity revealed nothing about their struggles to survive or about their place in the natural history of mankind, his opinions changed. Although it is difficult, precisely, to date when Darwin grew disaffected over contrived models — i.e., with taxonomic scales, hierarchies, axes, or polar dialectics — the kinds commonly found in the writings of eighteenth- and of early nineteenth century naturalists, and although he would never completely repudiate dehumanizing assumptions or clichés about native mankind in the post-voyage years, humanistic insights began to appear in his writings, even as early as 1834. He began to inquire about Fuegian intelligence, in order to account for their technological inertia. His aim was certainly meritorious, but the analogical method, once again, proved to be not up to the task. A simplistic analogy between Fuegian intelligence and the visionary genius of Sir Isaac Newton, for example, stated the obvious, while explaining nothing about Fuegian mentality, inventiveness, and potential. A hackneyed analogy, he eventually realized, could not comprehensively answer questions regarding tool industries, hut making, hunting, social structure, politics, diet, or spirituality; for detailed analyses in these areas were important, as they would allow one to draw inferences and to make cross-cultural comparisons between tribes. To understand who the Fuegians were as a people, then, one had to understand the intricacies of their respective lifestyles. Only on this basis, thought Darwin, could one define their humanness, know why natives differed from Europeans and from one another, and speculate on the chances of a Newton arising from their ranks.

Intermingled with retrogressive or intemperate comments in the *Diary*, in the *Journal*, and in the correspondence, were penetrating observations about human behavior. As early as 6 February 1833, for example, Darwin wondered why some Fuegians preferred theft over the exchange of goods, and he speculated that the equality of the inhabitants and the absence of central authority precluded their becoming more civilized in this regard. After finding the Rev. Matthews' mission ransacked, he questioned the assumption that Fuegians educated in England would, in the long run, benefit from what they had learned or be able to resist backsliding to uncivilized habits. By February 1834, Darwin had begun to record details of Fuegian material culture, a practice reflecting the understanding that observations not only of their daily activities but of their geographical environment were needed if their history was to be understood.

Since there was much more to be learned about these human beings, he articulated a number of insightful questions about them, adumbrating the 1839 Questionnaire of the British Association for the Advancement of Science. Understanding native origins, migratory history, social development, and ethnic heritage, it was widely believed, would dispel misconceptions. Like Humboldt along the Amazon, Darwin questioned widely held assumptions, one of which was that, in view of their harsh living conditions and scavenging lifestyle, the Fuegians were in steady decline. He states, instead, that they were in equilibrium with their environment, and, despite their primitive way of life, did not face imminent extinction.

The need to revaluate primitive societies was felt by his contemporaries. The 1839 proceedings of the British Association reflected an acute awareness of this issue, and its endeavors were dedicated to the preservation of primitive cultures and traditions. To this end, I have noted, Darwin collaborated with James Cowles Prichard and with five other prominent religious and scientific figures to compile an 89-point Questionnaire for the use of missionaries, naval personnel, and others during their visits to native lands.

Even with the 6 November 1859 *Allen Gardner* Massacre, which Jemmy

Button and others planned and carried out, Darwin did not give up on the Fuegians. His dialogue with the missionary Thomas Bridges on the expressions and gestures of the Keppel Island Yahgans contributed to the success of *The Expression of the Emotions in Man and Animals* (1872). In the late 1830s, Darwin noted in *N*64 and *N*65 that human groups were naturally inclined to struggle against each other for primacy, an idea recapitulated in the 31 January 1862 Kingsley correspondence and again in *Descent*.

Darwin's ethnological sensitivity and the moral rectitude of his thought were voluble in the writings on the inhumanity of slavery and on the genocide of South American tribes who inhabited the plains of Argentina and the mountains of Chile. The *Diary* contains nearly two-dozen anecdotes about the plight of the blacks under Brazilian slavery, and about how their degradation was ideologically rationalized. Morality and the psychology of oppression were aspects of Darwin's maturing humanism. *Diary* entries of March 1832, for instance, contrast the dignity and decorum of the impoverished blacks with the moral hypocrisy and depravity of the Brazilian planters. Though slave plantations varied logistically from one to another, they were all fundamentally aberrant establishments. Even though plantations, such as that of Socêgo, in Rio de Janeiro (13 April 1832), displayed a subtle and paternalistic kind of slavery whereas that of Patrick Lennon's on the Río Macae (15 April) was openly cruel and depraved, Darwin saw the inhumanity common to both variants, despite the limited economic freedom slaves were accorded in the former. The bounty hunters or Maticans who tracked runaway slaves through the remote Corcovado Mountains (30 May 1832) deserved Darwin's ire. Their economic motivation was obvious, as was that of the plantation owners who paid them to recapture or to murder runaways.

Underlying enslavement was a moral disorder that Darwin identified as having desensitized slavers to the sufferings of captive human beings. In Note *C*154, he articulated the moral paradox of slavery: that the enslaver considers the slave an animal and, in so doing, debased his own nature. However appalled Darwin was, he continued to observe steadily and to record interesting aspects of slave personality and behavior. He wrote about mannerism, expressions, courage, uplifted spirits, obstinacy, and good nature (3 July 1832). His experience in Brazil convinced him that humanness was not contingent on either race or skin color. He recorded the deprivations of primitive living and no longer accepted misconceptions about tribal people at face value.

Darwin's antiquarian interests of 1832 to 1833, a Humboldtian aspect of his narrative, are noteworthy. In Patagonia (August 1833), for example, he correctly identified an arboreal landmark as a cultic altar and, from arrowhead fragments, commented perceptively on native technology and on equestrian culture (February 1835). Despite lapses of judgment, exemplified by the tomb desecration of 2 January 1834, he studied human beings carefully and treated them amicably. One instance of his ethnological perceptiveness was his ability to differentiate one ethnic group from another. In the faces of Patagonian tribal members, he correctly noted similarities to Fuegians. The Pehuenche of Patagonia were, indeed, related to the Onas of the Archipelago, but, as he further noted, crucial differences existed between the two peoples. Whereas the Pehuenche were noble and civilized, for environmental reasons the Onas were not as well off. In this observation, Darwin may have been reminded of the risk of making categorical judgments based on superficial characteristics. Pehuenchen nobility evaporated from his mind when he learned that in their patriarchal society women were treated poorly. November 1834 observations recorded at Chiloé, off the Chilean coast, compare and contrast Chiloan natives, Fuegians, and natives of the Pampas. Linkages such as these convinced him that these tribes had a common origin in the distant past. His intuition of common ancestry was to be confirmed archaeologically. Using available demographic data, he pursued his ethnological work, reviewing census records, tribal nomenclatures, religions, and lifestyles.

Darwin condemned the war of extermination undertaken by General de Rosas against the tribes of the Pampas, yet he recognized and admired its laissez-faire rationale as a means of expanding the cattle industry (August 1833). Any admiration he might have entertained for de Rosas' grand scheme, however, dissipated when he learned that a military operation north of the Río Colorado wound up massacring men, women, and children. For Darwin, human dignity was unassailable, and loyalty was a high virtue. He respected the noble patriotism of captured Indian ambassadors who chose to die rather than to reveal the location of their camp; and he loathed an Indian chief who betrayed the Andean location where 1200 Indians were to gather for a counterattack. An Indian informant told Darwin of other massacres, one that did not spare women of child-bearing age and that sold children into slavery. Darwin denounced these crimes as unbefitting a Christian nation (September 1833). The butchery of native South Americans, some 3500 in all, for the purpose of acquiring fertile land, led Darwin to allude to the "white Gauchos" (with Humboldtian irony) as the real savages, and de Rosas' war derisively as a "glorious campaign."

The *Beagle*'s voyage to the South Pacific furnished Darwin with an extraordinary opportunity to develop his understanding of native populations. In Tahiti, he recorded the natives' material culture and food preparation, how they expeditiously constructed sturdy huts and efficient hearths, and how their fire-making technique differed from that used by the gauchos.

The Tahitians' mastery over their environment was impressive and their temperance laudable (November 1833). He adopted a relativistic opinion of traditionally sanctioned promiscuity and appreciated the civilizing strides the people had taken: with the guidance of the missionaries, they proscribed idolatry, human sacrifice, profligacy, infanticide, and internecine war. Darwin made acute ethnological observations while in New Zealand, and he compared Maoris to Tahitians, and with some accuracy; the latter, he thought, were more civilized than the former (December 1835). He deplored how Tasmanian aborigines were cruelly transported from the mainland and understood that conflict between white settlers and indigenous people had set into motion a terrible cycle of violence and of reprisal: colonial misconduct precipitated black violence which, in turn, was answered with transportation. Aboriginal demography in Australia and Tasmania he found especially interesting. In January 1836 and in the 1839 *Journal*, he corroborated Lyell's 1832 comment that European expansionism destroyed native populations, but he also observed that colonial invasion, irrespective of ethnicities or race, had the same effect on indigenous people. In lamenting the decline and extinction of the "aboriginal blacks," Darwin in 1836 had come a long way from the impressionistic young man who demonized native Fuegians. Although the aborigines of New South Wales were "true Savages," he still saw their humanity and was inclined to like "such quiet good-natured men" (March 1836).

    In the post-voyage years, a new and more important challenge arose for Darwin: could the Humboldtian ethnology be reconciled to the idea of man as a competitive and evolutionary creature? His response to this ethical challenge is the focus of Part III.

# Part III.
# The Post-Voyage Ethnology

## 9. Allied Kingdoms, 1836 to 1870

Darwin recognized the Fuegians' humanity, unequivocally, in the document, "A Letter, Containing Remarks on the Moral State of Tahiti, New Zealand, etc.," coauthored by Captain FitzRoy. The Letter was written on 28 June 1836, on board the *Beagle* as it was about to cross the Tropic of Capricorn for the sixth and last time. In terms of its portrayal of aboriginal man, however, it is a regressive document because it adheres to obsolete ideas with respect to behavior, customs, and way of life. Despite their hope for social progress in native communities, its authors describe aborigines, such as the natives of New Holland and of Tierra del Fuego, as degraded tribes ("Moral State" 221). FitzRoy and Darwin note that the Fuegians are amenable to European influence and are of "good disposition," even though they exhibit "failings inseparable from a thorough-bred savage"; the adjective "thorough-bred," a *double-entendre*, either means being well educated or having the traits of a wild animal.

Though Darwin and FitzRoy categorized natives as savages, they were genuinely amazed at how far the Fuegians had progressed socially. The Christian education and practical training of Fuegia Basket, of Jemmy Button, and of York Minster, had reputedly transformed these "degraded ... human beings" into productive citizens. FitzRoy and Darwin are gratified at how far the natives under their tutelage had come: the Fuegians "once went naked, destitute of any covering, except a small piece of seal skin, worn only upon their shoulders; that they had devoured enemies slain in battle; or that they had smothered, and afterwards eaten, the oldest women of their own tribe, when hard pressed by hunger during a severe winter!" ("Moral State" 222).

After spending three years in England, the three surviving Fuegians were clothed in European attire and believed to be cured of cannibalistic tendencies. If "cannibal wretches" such as these native can be transformed into "well behaved, civilized people, who were very much liked by their English friends," then it is possible "that a savage is not irreclaimable, until advanced in life; however repugnant to our ideas have been his early habits" ("Moral State" 222). In all likelihood, the Fuegian "companions" never practiced cannibalism, but FitzRoy and Darwin could never have foreseen their unexpected backsliding to savage ways, York Minster's theft of his companions' belongings, or the shocking events of 6 November 1859, to which we will turn in this chapter.

In contrast to the paternal optimism of Darwin, of FitzRoy, and of others about the redemption of modern savages was the idea that, irrespective of circumstances, the indigenous people of the region were irreclaimable to civilization. The belief that natives were less than fully human remained entrenched in popular and in scientific thought. An index to this pervasive opinion was the use of generic term *Fuegian*, which tended not to differentiate one ethnic group from another, and which was notoriously conducive to caricature. This opinion infiltrated the most authoritative and influential writings of the times. Malthus, who relied on a few well-known sources, propagated it:

> The wretched inhabitants of Tierra del Fuego have been placed, by the general consent of voyagers, at the bottom of the scale of human beings. Of their domestic habits and manners, however, we have few accounts. Their barren country, and the miserable state in which they live, have prevented any intercourse with them that might give such information; but we cannot be at a loss to conceive the checks to population among a race of savages, whose very appearance indicates them to be half starved, and, who, shivering with filth and vermin, live in one of the most inhospitable climates in the world, without having the sagacity enough to provide themselves with such conveniences as might mitigate its severities, and render life in some measure more comfortable [*1803* 20].

By the late eighteenth century, a substantial amount of information had been accumulated in regard to the Fuegians, ever since Cook's 1769 first impression of the Onas. Indeed, for decades, the distinction between indigenes of the region was being gradually clarified; and appropriate attention was being paid to their linguistic and cultural characteristics. Malthus, having gotten his information secondhand from Cook and others, portrayed native Fuegians in the worst possible terms. Not consulting firsthand texts seriously limited his viewpoint on the Fuegians. Notable among the valuable primary texts was Edward Cavendish Drake's, *A new universal collection of authentic and entertaining voyages and travels* (1768). Drake's anthology contains extracts from two narratives: that of 1577 by Sir Francis Drake (1540?–96), while at Cape of Good Hope; and that of 1592, by Thomas Cavendish (1560–92), while in the Strait of Magellan.

Darwin unfortunately subscribed to the Malthusian image of these natives, that is, as an undifferentiated population of cannibals. The armchair literature appeared to corroborate the rumors he had heard on the voyage. Influenced by the opinions of travelers, by popular stereotypes, and by muddled translations, he accepted rumors about cannibalism, even as late as the 1870s.

Although the presumption of savagery skewed Darwin's earliest comments on the Fuegians, his post-voyage ethnography features reflective passages. Notebook entries *C*77, 78, and 79, written between March and July 1838, for example, incisively convey the philosophical problem at the center of his ethnology (*CDN* 263–64). On the one hand, he portrays man, conventionally, as a creature sharing general instincts and moral feelings with higher mammals. On the other hand, man is intellectually exceptional. Although animals are capable of some reasoning, man has excessive reasoning powers that replace unalterable tendencies in the human "mental machinery." Darwin also meditates on the circumstances necessary to have made man, intuiting that generations of animal species were man's evolutionary precursors; and, rejecting the theory of special creation, he speculates on a time when rude and uncivilized man did not exist, and when the earth was populated by animals, now extinct (*C*79, *CDN*, 264).

Along with these ruminations, Darwin again endorsed the undignified image of the Fuegians as rude, cannibalistic savages. His comments in early post-voyage texts exemplify an ethnological and taxonomic problem with which he had to grapple, namely the misconception that nonwhite natives and apes were more zoologically akin to each other than the former were to Europeans. One basis for this line of reasoning, for many naturalists, was that being human was contingent on gaining mastery over one's environment. The cryptic statement concluding the entry — i.e., "not understanding language of Fuegian, puts [natives] on par with Monkeys" — suggests that Darwin erroneously interpreted the guttural exclamations of the Fuegians as inhuman jabbering (*C*79, *CDN*, 264).

The proclivity for ethnic generalization, for conflating physical anthropology and ethnology, and for the use of spurious models to measure cultural and technological sophistication, in the late 1830s, interfered with the development of Darwin's thinking on man's place in nature. Specifically, these factors hindered a sympathetic understanding of primitive people and the development of a critical ethnology in the private discourse of 1834. Old assumptions lingered in the writings of the late 1830s: the association of cannibalism with tribal communities; the presumed affinity of apes and aborigines; and the blurring of cultural distinctions between native tribes. On the latter point, it appears that Darwin had indeed recognized the distinctiveness of the tribes that he met, and a comment appearing as notebook entry *B*33 supports this contention. While he tended in some contexts to subsume Yahgan, Alacaluf, Ona, Aush, and Southern Patagonians, along with others, under the *Fuegian* nomenclature, he nonetheless recognized that the "*distinctness of the tribes* in T[ierra] del Fuego" was ascribable to the fact that extant primitives from different tribes did not cross readily (*CDN* 179; emphasis added). The assumed affinity between higher apes and aboriginal man, along with the cultural generalizations of *B*33, clearly were inconsistent with an ethnology based on relativism, on respect for the integrity of natives, and on careful observation.

Primitive man was often thought of as a living link to human prehistory and, through deep time, to our ape-like ancestors. Naturalists like Thomas Henry Huxley and others, accepting the premise that Europeans, nonwhite natives, and the great apes were closely related to each other, created taxonomic models in which living savages, on the grounds of ethnicity and culture, were made to fill the fossil gap between modern man and apes. Because man and the higher apes, on the basis of anatomical similarities, were presumed to be collateral descendants of a common ancestor, and because the human fossil record had not definitively revealed an intermediate link between man and ape, the modern savage was conveniently identified as a living artifact of prehistoric humanity; consequently, natives were degraded into a human sub-species (Eiseley 43; Stocking [1987] 147).

One approach to human origins, diversity, and behavior, popular at the time, was to observe primates. Darwin's primate notations adumbrate his extraordinary study of animal and of human expressions in the 1870s. In the late 1830s, however, his primate observations, especially with respect to orangutan behavior, tended towards anthropomorphism and, as such, lent credence to the prevailing theory that apes were more closely related to nonwhites than the latter were to whites.

In comparing mankind to the great apes, Darwin was working within the taxonomic category or family now called the *Hominoidea*, a group encompassing lesser apes (the *Hylobatidae*), the great apes, and humans (Andrews 248). He was particularly captivated by the orangutans that he observed at the Zoological Gardens of London. His aim was not to observe and record behaviors randomly, but rather to test several propositions: that apes and men had co-descended from a common ancestor, and that aborigines were evolutionary intermediates between man and ape.

Studying primates, comparatively, was not in itself a flawed approach; rather, it was Darwin's use of Linnaean taxonomy that led him astray. On two counts, his approach to the superfamily *Hominoidea* was actually *counter-evolutionary*: (1) it artificially ranked human races on a graduated scale; and, on the basis of this scheme, (2) taxonomically related nonwhite human beings to animals — specifically to nonhuman *hominoids*. To Darwin, in form and expression the orangutan *looked* like man's closest relative. But looks were deceiving. The fundamental choice of the orangutan as man's closest relative would prove to be wrong; ironically, unlike the gorilla and the chimpanzee, the orangutan has been determined to be a distant relative of man and has been segregated to its own subfamily, the *Ponginae* (Andrews 40).

Even today, primate taxonomy is an extremely complex subject. This is obvious if we look at where human beings rank in the Primate Order. Man occupies the apex of an inverted triangle having ten levels, his membership at each level becoming progressively more exclusive, until, as a species and in all of his racial diversity, he stands alone. The ten levels follow: Order (*Primates*), Suborder (*Anthropoidea*), Infraorder (*Catarrhini*), Hyperorder (*Eucatarrhini*), Superfamily (*Hominoidea*), Family (*Hominidae*), Subfamily (*Homininae*), Tribe (*Hominini*), Genus (*Homo*), Species (*Homo sapiens*) (Tattersall, "Classification," 137). To complicate matters, the Latinate categories are not entirely free of ambiguity; for example, the sub-familial category *Homininae* sometimes groups humans, chimpanzees, and gorillas together, but is more commonly used to signify extant and ancestral human beings only (Andrews, "Homininae," 247). Darwin's view of man as an evolutionary creature, at least in the transitional period from 1836 to 1840, continued to be influenced, and confounded, by the prevailing theories of his milieu.

Darwin's theoretical interest in and employment of racist anthropology in the private discourse, from the 1830s to the 1860s, seems to have operated on an intellectual rather than on an ethical plane. On the one hand, he was inclined to downgrade the African anthropologically, but then, having been an eyewitness to their long-suffering and fortitude, expressed sympathy for slaves, interest in their ethnological character, and contempt for enslavers. By the 1870s, and in great measure, Darwin's conscience would override theory, as a more modern approach to human diversity prevailed, directed not by pre-conceived models but by reason, morality, and hypothetical deduction.

Darwin's tendency to anthropomorphize the orangutan was a common practice of the times, and the contemporary lexicon reflects the mistaken tendency to search for our past selves in them. It is interesting to note that the adjective *anthropomorphous* (coined in 1753), which literally means "Of human form, having the form of a man" (*OED* [1933] I 361), was widely used to describe the great apes. Huxley's essay "On the Natural History of the Man-Like Apes" (1863), illustrates how homology (the finding of structural similarities in animals by studying corresponding parts) was used to compare apes to each other and to man. One of the earliest proponents of this methodology was the Swedish naturalist and physician Carolus Linnaeus (1707–1778), whose long-standing classification of organisms, in the tenth and definitive edition of his *Systema Naturae* of 1758, *correctly* groups man, apes, monkeys, and lemurs together under the category "Order I. Primates" (Tattersall 136–37). The difficulty arises when Linnaeaus subdivided Homo sapiens into five, ranked categories (Farb 254): thus, four primary races are arbitrarily classified and ranked according to physical, psychological, and cultural characteristics; and a fifth grouping is reserved for wild-men that were reputedly quadrupeds.

The opposite inclination — to differentiate man from the great apes — became popular in 1861, as is suggested by the archaic term *Hominal* (from the Latin *Homo*, for Man), "Of or relating to man (in natural history)" (*OED* VII 355), from which derived the zoological term for man, *hominid*, first appearing in print in 1889 (*OED* VII 355). The word *anthropoid/al* (*anthropos*, man; + *-oid*, like or resembling), which had entered the lexicon in 1832, now referred exclusively to a creature that was "human *in form only*" (*OED* I 361; italics added). The adjective *anthropoidal*, supplanting *anthropomorphous* in everyday usage, emphasized the reality that great apes physically resembled humanoid but were not human. Another pair of terms, *Quadramana* (four-handed, for nonhuman primates grasping with hands and feet) and *Bimana* (two-handed, exclusively for man), also distinguished between man and ape and did so morphologically, but these terms were also abandoned (*DM* 155).

In the 1830s, Darwin's preference for the older adjective *anthropomorphous* over the more precise *anthropoid/al* (1832) in the primate descriptions indicates that he was as-yet relying on obsolete paradigms. He believed, as well, that man and ape were descendants of a common ancestor and, as such, were closely related to one another zoologically. Darwin's immediate concern, especially in the notebooks, was to define this affinity. If he were successful in this regard, he would have broken away from Linnaean taxonomy, to see humanity in a new light.

Notebook *M*, which Darwin wrote from July to early September 1838, contains one-dozen entries on the behavior of the orangutan and on the erroneous assumption of its zoological affinity to uncivilized, modern man. These comments exemplify Darwin's inclination to anthropomorphize the great apes while *implicitly* dehumanizing uncivilized man.

Despite Darwin's misdirected aim, the anecdotal notes on orangutan behavior in the Zoological Gardens are interesting in and of themselves. One animal that was teased with a nut became frustrated and behaved like a child.

From this display, Darwin wondered if monkeys cried (and, by implication, if they had emotions similar to humans); in addition, the monkeys screeched like children (*M*107, *CDN,* 545). Apparently expressing displeasure and other emotions, a young orangutan in the Zoological Gardens pouted while protruding its lips, a facial expression Darwin thought comparable to the human expressions of contempt, of disgust, and of defiance. In Notebook *N,* opened October 1838 to December 1839, he recorded that both orangutans and chimpanzees appeared sullen and that the former whined like a child. He wondered why both children and apes pouted, while adult humans did not (*N*88, *CDN,* 587). Citing an 1834 report in which a male gibbon, while on board a ship, is said to have undergone a tantrum on deck, Darwin describes the animal behaving like a spoiled child, rolling on the deck and swinging its arms and legs wildly (*N*94, *CDN,* 590). In a related entry, although Darwin states that, like human beings, some animals think before they communicate orally, he does not appear to mean that primates developed in the same way as children did, and he expressed some reservations about the analogy (*N*13, *CDN,* 567). Describing Jenny's removal of ears of corn from straw with her teeth, in *M*13, he reiterates that she behaves like a child when, bewilderedly, she handed the cobs to Darwin. At that moment, the indisposed orangutan Tommy is said to have borne an expression of lassitude and pain (*M*13, *CDN,* 567).

Darwin recognized that the incipient tool-usage of an orangutan as it pounded the earth with a stone suggested its affinity to man (*M*129, *CDN,* 551), and the zoologist William Yarrell (1784–1856) came to a similar conclusion. In the Keeper's absence, Jenny the orangutan, when unable to open a door manually, picked up a chair and banged it against the door with sufficient force to open it (*M*138, *CDN,* 553–54). When Jenny untied a difficult knot using teeth and hands, she displayed manual dexterity. Darwin was so impressed by this behavior that, at a later date, he connected Jenny's display directly to his work on human descent (as evidenced by the abbreviated interpolation, *Descent 1838*) (*M*139, *CDN,* 554).

Observations such as these made it clear to Darwin that Jenny was quite intelligent, but at times he went too far. On one occasion, with a mere facial expression the ape is thought to have requested the Keeper's permission to eat a piece of bread, a gesture Darwin interprets as evidence that the ape connected thoughts causally (*M*139, *CDN,* 554). Jenny was also mischievous and disobedient; yet, afterwards, supposedly understanding her transgression, she shamefacedly or fearfully hid. When she expected to be whipped, she covered herself with straw or a blanket, which, if anything, illustrates the brutality to which these animals were subjected. Instead of calling this a case of animal cruelty, however, Darwin was more interested in it as evidence of the evolutionary kinship of man and higher primates, in that apes regularly used objects, such as chairs, stones, and blankets, with conscious intent (*M*140, *CDN*, 554). Alexander Miller (1829–1852), superintendent of the Zoological Gardens, from independent observations, also found that primate facial expressions reflected consciousness and emotion, and that noises and gestures were characteristic of certain primate species; however, as in the case of the pig-tailed baboon, for instance, an expression that one might take as sulkiness need not necessarily correspond to the human feeling of gloom or moroseness (*M*137, *CDN*, 553).

To state that a young orangutan exhibited behavior comparable to that of a child implied some degree of zoological kinship between them; however, in entry *N*64, equating the tastes of man to those of the apes and suggesting that both man and orangutan find the texture of silk handkerchiefs pleasing to the touch drifts precariously towards anthropomorphism (*CDN* 581).

Though of some use, the anecdotes surveyed above reflect Darwin's misdirected effort to bring the orangutan into emotional and cognitive kinship with uncivilized man, as opposed to trying to understand the ape as belonging to a genus, zoologically distinct from man. Further along in *N*64, Darwin's strategy to dehumanize aborigines while humanizing apes is more explicit: whereas the members of "Allied Kingdoms" (a euphemism for the great apes) share basic tastes with civilized man (such as the tactile appreciation of fine silk), "in savages other tastes [are] few." To attribute human sensitivity to an ape, while diminishing the sensitivity of natives, suggests that in the late 1830s the old anthropology, with its stratified image of human evolution, still appealed to Darwin (*CDN* 581).

The juxtaposition of the 1836 Darwin-Fitzroy "Letter" to notebook reflections of 1838 exhibits the conflict of ideas at the center of Darwin's early ethnology. Even though he knew that native people living under the worst conditions in the wilderness were irreducibly human, he still had great difficulty coming to terms with this fact and with his kinship to them. Although he acknowledged the specific kinship of civilized and of savage man, at the same time, he persisted in exiling some nonwhites to a low rank in the homo-sapient lineage, a tactic consistent with eighteenth-century ethnology.

One adherent to this old viewpoint was Charles Kingsley. In a 31 January 1862 letter to Darwin, he explicitly describes in mythological terms the idea of the aborigines as lesser human beings. Conjecturing that early modern man's racial memory of an atavistic, missing link has survived in legends and in tales of monstrous beings, Kingsley asserts that extant natives, "especially conquered inferior races," were direct descendants of aggressive, pre-human beings, of creatures intrinsically different from an original white race. The correlation of mythological beings of this kind to uncivilized people, who are disparagingly referred to as *"conquered inferior races,"* indicates that Kingsley was a proponent of the old anthropology and of the Linnaean system. From this perspective, he speculated not only that Fauns and Satyrs might be the products of racial memory and the legendary composites of early Homo sapiens' experience with prehistoric beast-men, but that contemporary native populations directly descended from this monstrous breed; and he based this conjecture on the absurd assumption that legendary beings and uncivilized man were lascivious (*DCP* Letter 3426; italics added).

Kingsley's positioning of modern primitives in the void between ape and man, his description of a missing link that was part man and part beast, and the conflation of mythological monsters, of proto-human creatures, and of "inferior" extant races, perpetuated the zoological paradigms of the milieu, to which Darwin and FitzRoy subscribed in the late 1830s. This way of looking at the human species and at its racial variants, moreover, reinforced in the minds of Europeans the belief that nonwhites were inferior to them: whites were at the apex of the racial hierarchy, while nonwhites were positioned on lower, qualitative levels.

To exemplify the kind of taxonomic model popular in Darwin's milieu, we can consider one that Johann Friedrich Blumenbach (1752–1840) had devised. A German historian, anthropologist, and comparative anatomist, from 1776 to his death Blumenbach was professor of medicine at Göttingen University (*Chambers* 141). Darwin commented on a translation of Blumenbach's 1792 *An essay on generation* (*C*204, *C*269, *CDN*, 303, 323). In conjunction with Blumenbach's essay, he read William Lawrence's 1822 *Lectures on physiology, zoology, and the natural history of man,* and the third edition of James Cowles Prichard's *Researches into the physical history of mankind,* published from 1836 to 1847. Darwin's specific focus in *C*204 was on the physical characteristics of different racial groups. Differences between human groups, he recognized, lay chiefly in size, skin color, head form and features, form of limbs, type and quantity of hair, and kind of intellect. He abstracts information on the subject "from Lawrence, Blumenbach, and Prichard" (the three-page abstract is in the Darwin Archive, Cambridge University Library).

In the belief that aborigines were descendants of prehistoric humanity and that human diversity was a biological fact, Blumenbach had devised a dialectical model to differentiate the primary racial groups from each other and to position them on a graduated scale to convey the presumed inferiority of one to another and of all nonwhites to whites. In short, he broke up the human family. As early as 1770, he had constructed an axial model, with

Caucasians at the evolutionary focus as the original race and other races as degenerate offshoots. In *Über die naturlichen Verschiedenheiten im Menschengeschlechte* (1770, 1st edition), he subdivided the human race into four racial subcategories, and in the 1781 edition, into five. There, he writes that "The Caucasian must, on every physiological principle, be considered as the primary or intermediate of these five principal Races. The two extremes into which it has deviated are, on the one hand, the Mongolian, on the other the Ethiopian. The other two races [form] transitions between them: the American [Indian] between the Caucasian and Mongolian; and the Malayan between the Caucasian and Ethiopian" (190).

Allusions to the racial conventions of the times in Darwin's discourse, from the late 1830s to the early 1860s, suggest that he accepted as valid the claim that nonwhite races were direct descendants of primordial Homo sapiens or of more primitive forms. During this period, although expressly sympathetic towards, and respectful of, uncivilized or enslaved human beings, he envisaged the genus Homo as a racially defined infrastructure of human beings, with reputed levels of intelligence and of physical characteristics determining the evolutionary status of each group. As late as 1859, he writes that, "We have a very fine gradation in the intellectual powers of the vertebrata, with one rather wide gap ... between say a Hottentot and an Orang ... even if civilized as much mentally as the dog has been from the wolf" (*L&L* [1913] Vol. 2 211).

Even though the Hottentot (more appropriately the Khoikhoi of Southwest Africa) and other ethnic groups were made to occupy the lowest rungs of the human hierarchy, Darwin had no doubt that modern primitives were a world apart from the apes — but the crucial distinction was that they were closer to the ape than was the European. The analogy he constructs — that the Hottentot is to the orangutan as the dog is to the wolf— literally means that Africans and orangutans, like dogs and wolves, belong to the same zoological *family*. According to the *International Code of Zoological Nomenclature*, this is an *accurate* statement: Hottentots or Khoikoi and the great apes *are* members of the zoological *family* called *Hominidae*. But whites and members of all other racial groups are *also* members of this family. The problem lay with Darwin's ambiguous use of the word *family* in the 1859 analogy above. In it, he appears to have extracted whites from the *Hominidae* family, while leaving dark-skinned human beings with the great apes. There is reason to believe that, from the late 1830s to the 1860s, Darwin straddled two philosophical traditions: one that envisaged human variation in terms of a graduated hierarchy, with whites at the evolutionary apogee and blacks at its nadir; and one that recognized, and defended, the inherent dignity of all human beings. This contradiction mirrored an interior debate, with Darwin's moral character hanging in the balance

In the post-voyage years, perhaps because no other method was at hand, Darwin employed racially based paradigms to make sense of human origins, of man's natural history, of man's place in nature, and of human diversity. But progress came, gradually and thankfully, through a renewed interest in his *Beagle* experiences with the nonwhites who were enduring great hardships, both natural and man-made. He realized, indisputably, that human behavior, expressiveness, and suffering were natural but unique.

One aspect of his ethnological inquiry was to work on the facial expressions of man and animal. In a letter to Thomas Bridges, 6 January 1860, he studied human expressions, correlated them to behavior, and observed his children's reactions in this regard, explaining them generally by natural selection (*DCP* Letter 2640 note 2). In comparing the expressiveness of children and of higher primates, Darwin explored the common heritage of man and ape; but, at this time, he did so neither to vindicate conservative anthropology, with its racial ranks and selective dehumanization, nor to segregate nonwhite human beings in a twilight world between man and beast. Instead, he hoped to find affinities *between races*. Thus, in comparing white to nonwhite facial expressions, he sought to demonstrate the commonality of their expressions and that these were defining, human characteristics.

The recurrent tendency in Darwin's writings on man was for old and new ideas to be intermingled and to be alternately emphasized. This alternating emphasis suggests that his contradictory view of man was difficult to resolve. From the 1830s to the early 1870s, in order to vindicate his humanism, he needed either to modify or to reject the long-standing idea that the modern genus Homo comprised subclasses of human beings whose alleged inferiority to the Caucasian was measurable in terms of physiological variations, such as nonwhite skin color, skull shape, brain size, skeletal features, level of civilization, and depth of culture. In this effort, he achieved a measure of success. The old metrics, though never dislodged, would be gradually superseded by a sympathetic and objective ethnology, inspired largely by his experiences four decades earlier with native societies.

A significant public expression of this humane ethnology came in 1840 when Darwin participated in professional forums on ethnology and contributed to the drafting of a Questionnaire to assist field workers in the collection of information in native countries. In 1839, while attending the meeting of the British Association for the Advancement of Science, held in Birmingham, he heard James Cowles Prichard read the paper, "On the Extinction of some varieties of the Human Race," which was subsequently published in the December issue of the *Edinburgh New Philosophical Journal*. Prichard examined human groups that had become extinct and predicted that the same fate awaited other isolated societies. The irretrievable loss to psychology, physiology, and philology, resulting from the disappearance of so large a portion of the human race would be disastrous. Thus, every effort had to be expended to rescue them and to preserve important information related to their cultures. To this end, the National History Section of the Society, to which the paper was delivered, funded the printing of a Questionnaire, designed for the use of travelers or residents in contact with "the threatened races." A Committee was, then, appointed by the same Section to prepare a list of questions modeled in format and content on a questionnaire that the Ethnographical Society of Paris had already completed.

The Committee consisted of eight prominent naturalists, physicians, and clergy: Charles Darwin; James Cowles Prichard (1786–1848), physician and ethnologist; Thomas Hodgkin (1798–1866), physician; James Yates (1769–1871), Unitarian clergyman and naturalist; John Edward Gray (1800–1875), botanist and zoologist; Richard Taylor (1781–1858), naturalist and publisher; Nicholas Wiseman (1802–1865), Roman Catholic clergyman; and William Yarrell (1784–1856), London stationer and naturalist. Of the seven committee members, two directly influenced Darwin's thought: he had recently read and briefly commented on the zoological research of Gray (on shellfish and ruminants) and of Yarrell (on birds and the Irish Hare) (*Bibliography, CDN,* 670, 692).

"Queries respecting the Human Race, addressed to travelers and others" was intended to gather data on aboriginal people, to preserve their cultures, and to establish their humanity, beyond question. The Questionnaire took an ideological stand on the monogenetic side of the human-origin debate, its drafters subscribing to the idea of "the unity of the human species" (Gruber 222). Approaching race from the direction of culture and language, Prichard believed that ethnology, more a historical than physiological discipline, had as its aim to trace all human migrations back to a common origin (Stocking [1973] xcix–c).

The Questionnaire did include some comparative physiology. Of its 89 questions, numbers 1 to 12 ("Physical Characters" being the first of ten categories) are concerned with the structure of the head, extremities, facial features, dentition, skin color, hair color and texture, skeletal bones. Observers are reminded to think comparatively: in the case of two or more varieties of the human race, the typical characters of each in the most distinct form should be noted.

Although only five numbers are designated for language (that is, 12–16), pertinent questions are to be asked on inflection and pronunciation: to identify languages carefully, one must differentiate one dialect from another, and to approximate regional limits; for hitherto unknown languages, vocabularies should be compiled, along with parts of speech, and orthographic data; specimens of native writing (conversational prose and metrical composition) should be gathered, even if not yet translated; efforts should be made to find out how extensively a language is spoken and understood, whether a language is prominent in a specific racial group or geographical location; and, accompanied by political, and social details, whether more than one language exists among a single group of people.

The third section of the Questionnaire, "Individual and Family Life," the largest but most disorganized of the ten divisions, consists of 32 questions (numbers 17–49): 17–23 deal with infants and children (birth ceremonies, gender-related differences in treatment, infanticide and its causes, culturally authorized deformation of children's bodies, modes of education, especially with respect to behavior, and sports and amusements); number 24 asks at what age puberty begins, the leap being from infant-toddler to adolescent; numbers 25–26 inquire about family size and gender of offspring; and number 27 focuses on the rearing of children. Textual reorganization is needed at this point, as topics are bunched together and in need of logical segues from one to another: number 28 has to do with evidence of unusual sensuous acuity; number 29, with the median age for childbirth and nursing; number 30, with menstruation and gestation; number 31, with ceremonies and life-stages; numbers 32–33, with chastity and accompanying customs; numbers 34–37, with marriage ceremonies, polygamy, divorce, and treatment of widows. The focus shifts abruptly, in number 38, to diet, nutrition, and culinary practices; in number 39, to clothing and bodily ornamentation; numbers 40–41 asks about adult amusements and games of chance. Then, in number 42, longevity is the subject; in number 43, treatment of the sick; number 44, veterinary medicine; number 45, entozoan (i.e., intestinal parasites); mortuary practices are broached in numbers 46–48; and finally, in number 49, religious beliefs of the after-life.

The fourth category of inquiry, "Buildings and Monuments," though brief, consists of three questions with multiple follow-ups. This very important topic, which encompasses not only habitations, but also the wider concern of technology, requires suitable development. No other category, except perhaps language, can reveal more about a level of civilization than architectural invention. Question 50 involves the types of habitations, their interior structures, and how they are deployed, but nothing is mentioned as to materials or variations in construction. Question 51 amounts to a digression on monuments and sarcophagi and belongs with numbers 46–49. Question 52 absurdly reminds the inquirer to preserve the skeletal remains of human or animal, a topic connected more with comparative anatomy than with architecture. Titled "Works of Art," category five is technologically orientated: number 53 asks for the preservation of art, metal, bone implements; number 54 reminds the investigator to describe "works of art," their material composition, the modes by which the materials are obtained, how the materials are prepared, and the instruments used to shape them. This industrial information is intended to illuminate "the character and origin of the people" and to suggest commercial opportunities or colonial incentives. The Committee points out that, with reference to question 54, the information contained therein can point out advantages, obtainable "by preserving, instead of annihilating, the aboriginal population." Darwin may have annexed to number 54 the snippet on "Domestic Animals," which poses the fourfold question about types of domestic animals, about their species, about their origins and variations, about their modification or degeneration, and about how these animals are used in the community.

The seventh category, "Government and Laws," comprises individual and multiple questions. Travelers are instructed to ask about the form of government, whether monarchic, democratic, or theocratic (number 55); whether chiefs exercise authority, either absolutely, electively, or hereditarily (number 56); if a clan or caste system determines the government, one should ascertain whether certain rights are accrued or lost according to one's social position, whether groups are segregated from one another, and whether physical and moral effects are incurred from segregation (numbers 57–59). Numbers 60 to 63 pertain to the law and to the rights of citizenship: observers should try to identify the laws, if a legislator creates them (number 61), how these laws are observed, whether they are preserved, rescinded, augmented, or modified, and how they relate to property ownership. Justice and the penal code are to be treated in numbers 64–67.

The eighth category, "Geography and Statistics," is of value to the ethnologist attempting to understand migratory history and demographic patterns (numbers 68–69) (census figures with respect to village and location). The limits and character of an inhabited region should be described (number 68), as well as what is known in regard to migrations within the area (number 70). Malthusian thought seems to have influenced number 71: where the population has decreased, one should state the causes, such as diseases, starvation, war, and emigration. Conversely, an increasing population should be explained (e.g., "an excess of births over deaths").

Prichard and Darwin more than likely framed numbers 73–74: in a colonial state, how are uncivilized natives affected? And how do the aborigines relate to the settlers (number 73)? In addition, "any tendency to the union of races" should be considered fully: (number 74). The ninth category, "Social Relations," is important, although its questions (numbers 75–76) treat international or inter-tribal relationships primarily and overlap with the previous category. The issue is how, for example, Tahitians relate to other island communities, how Australian tribes relate to those of Tasmania, and, as we have seen, how Fuegian tribes, such as Onas and Alacaluf, Yamana, or Yaghan, interact with each other. Question 76 presents with disorganization and imbalanced emphases; it treats warfare to excess, while, in a detached sentence, a far more essential question is treated as an after-thought: the inquirer is to state "whatever particulars respecting their origin and history are derived, either from traditions among themselves or from other sources."

Category ten, "Religion, Superstitions, &c," consisting of thirteen questions, addresses religious fervor (number 77), the nature of the deity or deities worshiped and of secondary spiritual entities (numbers 78, 84), liturgical practices, notions of witchcraft, magic, prophecy (numbers 79, 85), sacred calendars (number 80), orders of prelates and mode of election (number 81), comparative religion and attitudes, neighboring or remote (numbers 82–83), and astrology (numbers 86–88). Appended to this category, as question 89, is the reminder that one who achieves fluency in the native tongue should assess the "psychological character" of the host nation, including their level of intelligence, sociability, independence, morality, and degree of docility. The purpose is to determine if it is worth the effort to help them develop and improve their characters.

Because neither traveler nor British seaman "elicited much systematic information" from the Questionnaire, ethnologists, such as E. B. Tylor and James Frazer, had little choice but to rely on secondhand information from a variety of well-known sources (Stocking [1987] 79). Even though the Questionnaire had little impact on cultural anthropology, in the late 1830s and early 1840s Darwin's humane ethnology, despite inconsistencies, gradually progressed. And even though contrived schemes persisted into the 1860s, it was clear to him that, to understand primitive society in its own right, one had to observe native societies without prejudgment and, essentially, to evaluate the human group in its own material, social, and cultural terms.

From the late 1830s to the early 1860s, as I have pointed out, Darwin's ethnology had two conflicting elements, one static and the other progressive. The static element, exemplified by Malthus' writings, promulgated the idea of uncivilized man in the pejorative sense. Its most extreme form, derived from Linnaean taxonomy, assumed that Africans and other nonwhites had more in common with apes than with Europeans, considered natives of various races to be the descendants of degenerate nations in antiquity, and viewed some natives as unclassifiable intermediates between man and ape.

The progressive component of Darwin's ethnology, aligned with Humboldt in its relativism, in its critical objectivity, and in its sympathy for indigenes, recognized the ineradicable humanity of natives of every race and challenged historical assumptions about their mentality and social life. The obligation of civilized nations, thought Darwin, was to reclaim from the uncivilized world the scattered remnants of the human race. This redemptive impulse motivated missionaries and naturalists alike to preserve fragile societies, to expose their oppressors, and to preserve their cultures from extinction. In this respect, Darwinian naturalists and Christian missionaries, though their motives and methods differed, shared a common goal. Unanticipated events in a mission country, however, would subvert this noble endeavor and compromise Darwin's progressivism.

A critical event in the development of Darwin's ethnology occurred in 1859 and its effects resonated into the 1860s. On Sunday 6 November 1859, Jemmy Button, his brother, and other native parishioners massacred missionaries and the entire crew of the vessel, the *Allen Gardiner*. When a rescue party arrived, they found the ship completely dismantled. On shore, they came across the only survivor, ship's cook Alfred Cole, who had been driven mad, was naked, starving, and in ill health. Cole testified that on Sunday, 6 November 1859, the crew and the missionaries had constructed enough of a new building to conduct their first church service in Tierra del Fuego. Everyone, with the exception of Cole who remained on board, was to attend the service. Three-hundred natives crowded into the building with the white men. In the midst of the opening hymn, mayhem broke out. The natives murdered the defenseless missionaries with spears, clubs, and stones. Tommy Button, Jemmy's brother, hurled a stone, killing the catechist Garland Philips who had made it to the beach and was trying to escape into a longboat. Cole abandoned ship and took a dinghy to the opposite harbor, pursued by the murderers, but he managed to come ashore and flee into the jungle. Eventually Cole was captured, was tortured, but, for reasons unknown, was spared. He lived with the savages three months until his rescue.

Cole identified Jemmy Button as the ring-leader, although the latter denied responsibility and tried, unsuccessfully, to blame the incident on the Onan tribe on Navarino Island. E. L. Bridges writes that Button was indeed proven to be the chief instigator. The attack might have been caused by resentment and jealousy (so Bridges speculates), because he had not received all that he demanded from the missionaries, while other natives had received much more (E. L. Bridges 41–8). Whatever Jemmy's motivation, it is clear that his friendship with the crew of the *Beagle* and all that was learned while in England had been forgotten.

It is difficult to ascertain Darwin's precise reaction to this catastrophic event. He certainly knew about it, but he made no timely public comments on the subject in a major work. But remarks made in an 30 June 1870 letter to Lieutenant Bartholomew James Sulivan (1810–1890), shipmate aboard the *Beagle* who would become a Rear-Admiral in 1877 (*Biographical Register, BD*, 455), gives us some idea as to his reaction to the subject. Referring to Sulivan's surveying of the Falkland Islands, 1838–1846, and to his association with the South American Missionary Society, Darwin writes that he had not heard anything with respect to the success of the mission on Tierra del Fuego. Its growing success in the summer of 1870, however, was changing his earlier opinion. His faith increasingly renewed in the mission, Darwin expressed his gratitude that Sulivan's Committee saw fit to elect him an honorary member of the Society. In a footnote to the correspondence, Francis Darwin alludes to an article that Sulivan wrote for the 24 April 1885 edition of the *Daily News*. It provides a clear account of Charles Darwin's connection with the Society. Sulivan explains that, from the time of the 1859 *Allen Gardiner* massacre and into the 1880s, Darwin remained intimately involved in the Society's activities. Sulivan paraphrases Darwin as having often expressed the conviction that "it was utterly useless to send Missionaries to such a set of savages as the Fuegians, probably the very lowest of the human race." But, apparently, accounts of native behavior under the guidance of the missions, *from 1867 on*, began to change Darwin's mind. In 1867, he admitted to having been wrong in judging the Fuegians so harshly, and he donated a modest sum to the support of the missions. Darwin is also said to have expressed interest in the linguistic work of Thomas Bridges, in correspondences to Sulivan of 6 June 1874, of 10 June 1879, of 20 March, and of 1 December 1881. One can reasonably infer from this information that Darwin's pessimism about native amelioration, beginning with the Rev. Matthews' departure on 6 February 1835, had been vindicated by the *Allen Gardiner* massacre. As it turned out, he was not entirely convinced that missionary work in the region was utterly futile (*L&L* [1887] Vol. 3 126–128)

In 1860, as I mentioned, Darwin renewed his research on Fuegian emotional states and on how they were manifested in facial expressions and in gestures. In light of the massacre, he could just as easily have given up on serious research in this area and have simply regarded the Fuegians as morally incorrigible and as socially irremediable. He was leaning in that direction, for sure. Well before the massacre, in 19 March 1845, there is evidence, in a letter addressed to J. D. Hooker, that his interest in "savage mankind" had already waned (*DCP* Letter 842).

Despite remarks of this kind, Darwin pursued the project earnestly, and he contacted the missionary Thomas Bridges. Bridges who had begun his work at the Keppel Island mission in the Falklands, in 1858, then moved to Ushuaia. The missionary work in Tierra del Fuego, by 1859, had been an exercise in futility. Bridges' predecessors had met with great difficulties: Richard Matthews was driven out, Allen Gardiner died of starvation, Garland Philips and his colleagues were murdered, and George Pakenham Despard simply gave up (E. L. Bridges 47–8). Undaunted, Thomas Bridges learned the language of the Yahgans, and, with the indispensable help of a native family who lived on Keppel Island, began to compile a phonetic dictionary (presently in the possession of the British Museum), and to write twenty, generically diverse works in the field (articles, memoirs, dictionaries, biblical translations), published intermittently from 1862 to 1884 (Cooper 72–4).

A ship left Keppel Island bound for the Fuegian channels, in 1863, with Bridges on board. The last contact the British had had with the natives of Ushuaia was on 6 November 1859, so there was apprehension for everyone and, no doubt, the temptation to abandon plans to convert them. But Bridges was equipped with an inestimable resource: he could speak the Yaghan dialect. Disembarking from the ship, he courageously visited the native settlements alone in a dinghy. The correspondence between Darwin and Bridges actually began only *eight weeks* after Garland Philips, his coworkers, and all but one of the crewmen on the *Allen Gardiner* had been murdered (E. L. Bridges 46).

By 1860, Darwin had, indeed, renewed his interest in Fuegian ethnology, and the focus of his attention, appropriately, was on communication and gesture-language. As early as 1838, he had begun to observe and record observations on the expressions of his own children and of animals (see *M*96, *CDN.*, 542; and *DCP* Letter 2640 n.2). His 6 January 1860 letter to Bridges, transcribed from a memorandum and copied by an amanuensis, consists of fifteen specific questions on Fuegian facial expression (*DCP* Letter 2640). Bridges responded, point for point, in a letter dated October 1860 or later (*DCP* Letter 2643). The expressions of the Keppel-Island Yahgans exhibited nothing unusual: they nodded for, yes, shook their heads for, no; blushed when embarrassed; expressed astonishment with wide eyes, uplifted brows, and open mouth; conveyed anger like Europeans, and even stamped their feet, paced and inflicted physical injury on themselves; they showed dejection in the same way as Europeans, turning down the corners of their mouths; when angry, turning noses up, puffing out breath, and spitting (Bridges adds that they hissed through their lips, but ignored Darwin's question about sneering); they frowned when deep in thought (Bridges ignored Darwin's question of shoulder shrugging to communicate lack of specific knowledge); on feminine beauty, Bridges confirmed Darwin's suspicion that Caucasian women were in their estimation very beautiful.

Darwin incorporated some of these responses into his 1871 *The Expression of the Emotions in Man and Animals*, specifically comments having to do with assent, dissent, blushing, and anger (*DCP* Letter 2643 and notes 2–6). Bridges informs him that Fuegians "nod their heads vertically in affirmation, and shake them laterally in denial," and the discussion included North American Indians (*Expressions* 276). Expressions of astonishment or surprise, with eyes and mouth wide open, were remarkably uniform in undeveloped countries, notably among the Abyssinians, the Ceylonese, the Chinese, the Fuegians, the North American Indians, and the Australians (*Expressions* 279). Bridges also discovered that the Fuegians, when angry, had the habit of stamping the ground, of walking distractedly around, and of crying and growing pale (*Expressions* 248). To express contempt, Fuegians, whom Bridges observed, protruded their lips, hissed, and turned up their noses; but spitting at someone was the highest form of contempt (*Expressions* 260–1).

Darwin's work on Fuegian behavior and gesture language in the 1870s was in keeping with the renewed, popular interest in the people of the region. The literature on Fuegian cultures, from missionaries and explorers, gradually invalidated, but did entirely eliminate, preconceived models, generalizations, and racial assumptions. Valuable ethnography, especially on Tierra del Fuego, continued to appear. Captain William Parker Snow published, in 1857, an important travelogue of his two years' cruise off Tierra del Fuego, contributing cultural observations of the Yahgans, whom he visited in the region of Beagle Channel and Lennox Island (*Cooper* 128). Another resource on Tierra del Fuego was the South American Missionary magazine that, during Darwin's lifetime, appeared in more than forty volumes, and that contained an abundance of material on the cultural life of indigenous people (129). Works surveying the opinions of explorers and of naturalists were always needed. Franz Theodor Waitz's *Anthropologie der Naturvolker* is an example of such a survey. The third of the six volumes, which appeared in 1862, treats Fuegians and Chonos extensively, although factual data and other material are entirely derivative, having been culled, ironically, from the writings of King, of Fitzroy, of Darwin, and of others (133). Sarah Ann Myers, in her book, *Self-sacrifice, or the pioneers of Fuegia* (1861) recounts the early efforts of British missionaries in the area (114). One of the most important writers of the period on Yahgan culture and language was the Reverend George Pakenham Despard. Despard lived in the region from 1857 to 1862, compiled an unpublished 1000-word lexicon, and wrote extensively on cultural matters (82–3). From 1863 to 1869, Bishop Waite Hockin Stirling and J. W. Marsh who served at the Falkland Mission and on native islands wrote about the moral culture of the Yahgans (131). Mrs. Phebe Anne Hanaford, in her book, *The captive boy of Tierra del Fuego* (1867), tells the story of a shipwrecked father and son who fall into the hands of Alacaluf: the natives murdered the father but spared the boy who remained in captivity from February to May 1855. Mrs. Hanaford gathered firsthand cultural information from the boy which she included in her narrative (95).

Although the corpus of Magellanic literature, in the period of the 1850s to 1870s, showed signs of modern ethnological thinking, especially with respect to Fuegian cultures, distortions persisted. I would like to conclude this chapter by focusing on several representative works of the decades leading up to Darwin's *Descent*.

One of the most popular ethnological books of the period was Sir John Lubbock's, *Pre-Historic Times as illustrated by Ancient Remains, and the Manners and Customs of Modern Savages* (first edition 1865; third edition 1872). Born in London in 1834, Sir John Lubbock, 1st Baron Avebury (1834–1913) was a banker who served on educational and currency commissions, and who, from 1886 to 1900, was a Liberal-Unionist. His purpose in *Pre-Historic Times*, through twelve of its sixteen chapters, was to elucidate "the principles of prehistoric archaeology," using material unearthed, from 1861 to 1864, at human habitations in Denmark, Switzerland, North America and elsewhere. Chapters XIII to XVI, dealing with the manners and customs of "modern savages," discuss the lifestyles of extant tribes that had not progressed to the use of metal. Assuming that extant savages were incarnations of prehistoric mankind, Lubbock hoped to use this data to gain some understanding of "the remains of savage life in ages long gone by" (Preface v–x). Cooper observes that, between 1865 and 1913 [7th edition], little had been done to update the portrayal of the Fuegians in Lubbock's book, which relied on outdated sources, from John Hawkesworth's collection of narratives (1773–74) to James Weddell's 1825 description of the Yahgans, met in 1823–24 at St. Martin's Cove, Hermit Island (68, 96, 134).

Lubbock cites a number of well-known texts, namely the writings of Falker (1774), Byron (1741), Hawkesworth (1773), Weddell (1825), and (to his credit) FitzRoy (1839) and Darwin (1839). Like Malthus, however, he reiterates the general opinion that, "The inhabitants of Tierra del Fuego are ... more degraded than those of the main-land: in fact, they have been regarded by many travelers as being the lowest of mankind." Along with his reliance on arcane sources was his tendency to generalize; consequently, important differences between tribes and their unique qualities were blurred. This was true, even though Lubbock distinguished the Fuegians from both the North American Indians and the Chonos of South America. Since his sources were limited to the period from 1741 to 1839, (the first edition of *Pre-Historic Times* was published in 1865), the writings of Snow, of Despard, of the Missionary Society, and of many others, revealing the rich cultural traditions and diversity of Fuegian tribes, could not figure into his survey. Lubbock's use of earlier sources, of Adolph Decker (1624) who saw the Fuegians as beastly cannibals and of a text divesting them of government and religion, was counter-productive. His description of the women is startling but typical of the age: "About four feet and some inches is the stature of these *she-Fuegians—* by courtesy called women" (538; italics added). The natives of Tierra del Fuego, in Lubbock's view, "certainly appear to be among the most miserable specimens of the human race" (543).

In the copy of *Pre-Historic Times* that he annotated, Darwin remarks that the chapters on modern savages are "very interesting." Lubbock's influence extends to *Descent* (*DCP* Letter 4858 note 3). Using Lubbock as a resource, however, had both negative and positive consequences. In one passage, for example, Darwin employed one of Lubbock's generalizations to support his strategy of distancing savages ethnologically from modern man but *without* denying their humanness. Darwin distanced human from animal intelligence at the primate border: cognitively, the highest ape could not be compared to the lowest savage (*DM* 66). Nevertheless, some maintained that savages were inherently deficient in abstract cognition. The notion that natives could not formulate abstract ideas was based exclusively on the writings of Johan Baptist von Spix (1781–1826) and Karl Johan von Martius (1794–1818) who had studied Brazilian tribes. Although certain tribes had lexicons, they were, in Lubbock's words, "entirely deficient in words for abstract ideas." What Spix and Martius related about "the *Brazilian tribes*," he avers, "appears also to be true of *many*, if not *most*, savage races" (573; italics added).

On the subject of computation, Lubbock was more convincing. Rather than to generalize from scant evidence, in this instance he read sources thoroughly and based his conclusions on a larger cross-section of cultures. For example, he referred to a paper by the Scottish philologist, surgeon, colonial administrator, and polygenist, John Crawfurd (1783–1868), "On the physical and mental characteristics of the Negro," recently published in the *Ethnological Society's Transactions* ([1866]: 4:212–39]). Crawfurd concluded, after examining thirty Australian languages, that none of the tribes there had the ability to count beyond four (*Pre-Historic Times* 575). The surgeon and artist, Isaac Scott Nind (1797–1868), who discovered that the natives of King

George's Sound could count to five (although the fifth integer is translated as *many*), was also referenced (575); additionally, the Australian Cape Yorkers, whose numerical vocabulary Lubbock annexes for review, could go beyond the number two (575). For Darwin's purposes, the citation on counting was legitimate support, whereas the one for abstract thought was not.

Lubbock's research on superstition was used in *Descent* but to negative effect. Darwin suspected that poor reasoning led to superstition and to strange customs, both of which plagued savage man (*DM* 99). To support this generalization, he cites Lubbock's hyperbole that "the horrible dread of unknown evil hangs like a thick cloud over savage life, and embitters every pleasure" (*Pre-Historic Times* 583). The context of the reference, specifically, was to sorcery, practiced in the New Hebrides, as described in the missionary George Turner's (1818–1891) *Nineteen Years in Polynesia: Missionary Life, Travels and Researches in the Islands of the Pacific* (1861). Lubbock writes of how illness could be induced through sorcery and spells reversed through bribes. Darwin appropriated the notion that the fear of supernatural power in the hands of wizards, a kind of witchcraft, constitutes an "unknown evil" that depresses savage mentalities in all quarters of the world (*DM* 99).

Lubbock's claim that savage life was universally embittered by superstition was unfounded. Among Fuegian cultures, for example, the wizard or medicine-man was a member of every clan or family among Onas and Yaghans. Although a form of sympathetic magic was practiced (a lock of hair to force tribute), and although they were believed to have power to take a life, they also were invested with life-giving and curative powers and were believed to have the gifts of divination and prophecy, exercised for the communal welfare (Cooper 159–160). The superstitious practices of savage life, as the Fuegian example illustrates, had many purposes, not all of which were malevolent and depressing. Throughout the late nineteenth century, however, the two-dimensional image of the Fuegian persisted in popular and in professional literature alike.

Darwin had an advantage over men like Prichard and Lubbock. He had visited native lands, had gathered firsthand experiences, and could use this information to explain man's place in nature as an evolving species. Though Darwin subscribed to the belief in the indivisible unity of the human species, as well as to the need of preserving human culture, he struggled for years with the refractory idea of the cognitive, socio-cultural, and technological equality of all human beings. But his ethnology had emerged.

# 10. Natural Selection: The Bio-Ethical Dilemma

Men such as Prichard and Darwin, as we have seen, were genuinely concerned with the preservation of tribal cultures and hoped to prevent the destruction of isolated societies. As Darwin's ethnology developed, he faced contradictory propositions emerging from his evolutionary work, one of which was moral and the other biological. In the Humboldtian spirit, he gradually came to value indigenous cultures and viewed their way of life dispassionately. This humanistic attitude was an outgrowth of his moral and egalitarian convictions. In the opposing, Malthusian spirit, he understood, as well, that man as a biological creature was subject to the laws of nature and therefore had to compete with other living beings in order to survive. But in the case of humanity, unusual circumstances obtained, notably when civilized and uncivilized societies confronted one another. The competition arising in this instance, whether overt or subtle, was not between separate species, but rather between ethnic and racial varieties of the *same* species. This was the incongruity with which Darwin had to contend.

Darwin gave this bio-ethical problem considerable attention in the late 1830s. In a salient notebook entry, he reiterates the idea that a decreasing population sometimes foreshadowed extinction, but the reference in *B*147–48 is explicitly to extant *human groups* (*CDN* 206). Reflecting on Prichard's 1839 paper on human extinction, he considers, in another entry, that migration, whether forcible or voluntary, could lead to human extermination and that those who were responsible have varied racially (*T*81, *CDN*, 465). In another notebook entry, Darwin finds racial competition and conflict to be consistent with natural selection. The most intelligent human beings, he states, will invariably seek dominion:

> When two races of men meet, they act precisely like two species of animals.—
> they fight, eat each other, bring diseases to each other &c, but then comes the

more deadly struggle, namely which have the best fitted organization, or instincts (i.e. intellect in man) to gain the day.— In man chiefly intellect, in animals chiefly organization: though Cont. of Africa & West Indies shows organization in Black Race there gives them preponderance. intellect in Australia to the white.— The peculiar skulls of the men on the plains of Bolivia — strictly fossil in Van Diemen's land — they have been exterminated on *principles*, strictly applicable to the universe.—... Man acts on & is acted on by the organic and inorganic agents of this earth[,] like every other animal.— [*E*63–65, *CDN*, 414–15].

In the 1839 *Journal*, Darwin found Australian aborigines to be nothing like "the utterly degraded beings as they are usually represented"; in fact, their arts were admirable (*JR* [1839] 376). The victims of colonization, they have suffered from diseases to which they are not immune: "Wherever the European has trod, death seems to pursue the aboriginal," and this has been true in the Americas, in Polynesia, in the Cape of Good Hope, and in Australia (*JR* [1839] 376). Contrary to popular thinking, the white man has not been the sole destroyer of native civilizations. For example, in the East Indian archipelago, the Polynesian of Malayan extraction has uprooted indigenous people (*JR* [1839] 376). Darwin's most insightful deductions in this period were that colonialism was a selective process, comparable in its effects to the struggle for existence among animals and plants, and that in this struggle neither race nor ethnicity was necessarily the determining cause.

The survival of the fittest human beings had a moral dimension, which was not the case for animals and plants. For Darwin the naturalist, it is likely that, "The varieties of man seem to act on each other in the same way as [do] different species of animals — the stronger always extirpating the weaker"; but, at the same time, Darwin the moralist is saddened to hear "the fine energetic natives [of New Zealand] saying, that they knew the land was doomed to pass from their children" (*JR* [1839] 376). It is clear, then, that from 1837 to 1839, Darwin was thinking of the human species in naturalistic terms involving competition and the domination of one group over another. In the early 1840s, however, his earliest reflections on what he would later call the theory of natural selection focused primarily on lower animals and plants.

Darwin deduced from his observations of animals and plants that all living things competed with one another for existence. This deduction and what he had presumably learned from Malthus and others indicated that, under natural circumstances, population levels tended to exceed subsistence, that creatures in a common environment struggled with each other for resources, and that favorable variations tended to be preserved and unfavorable ones destroyed; moreover, these processes sometimes caused the elimination of some species and the creation of others.

Exploring these crucial ideas in essays of 1842 and 1844, which were early drafts of *Origin*, Darwin was primarily concerned with understanding the mysterious mechanism by which organisms descending from the same stock tended "to diverge in character as they become modified" (*Autobiography* 120). At Down, he recalls having realized that "modified offspring of all dominant and increasing forms tend to become adapted to many and highly diversified places in the economy of nature" (*Autobiography* 121). By the 1860s, as we shall see, this concept would be applied to man explicitly: the offspring of European colonialists will become adapted to diversified places in the economy of nature which was conducive to their aim of global dominion.

In 1856, acting on the advice of Charles Lyell, Darwin expanded his writings in what was aptly titled the *Big Species Book*, an ambitious project that wound up being an unfinished abstract of the collected materials. He recollected other ideas, enumerated below, that had contributed to his understanding of the theory of modified descent. While exploring the Malay Archipelago in the summer of 1858, Wallace sent Darwin the groundbreaking essay, "On the Tendency of Varieties to depart indefinitely from the Original Type," known also as the "Ternate Paper" (February 1858). This essay proved that Wallace had independently arrived at conclusions, four in all, that were similar to Darwin's: (1) varieties progressively diverged from the original form; 2) living conditions affected progressive divergence; (3) living things underwent modified descent; and (4) new species appeared, and old ones became extinct (*IT* 61–2).

Darwin forwarded the Ternate essay to Lyell who, in collaboration with J. D. Hooker, arranged for the joint publication of the relevant documents in the 1858 *Proceedings of the Linnaean Society*. The issue included an extract from Darwin's manuscript, Wallace's Ternate paper, and a 5 September 1857 Abstract of a pertinent letter from Darwin to Asa Gray (1810–1888), the American botanist and taxonomist. The documents were read on 1 July 1858 in London. Although the publication of the theory as an aggregate of documents elicited little immediate interest, Lyell and Hooker nevertheless encouraged Darwin, in September 1858, "to prepare a volume on the transmutation of species, using the manuscript material of 1856." This material eventually was published as *Origin*, in November 1859 (*Autobiography* 122). In this text, Darwin defines natural selection or the survival of the fittest (the appositive phrase being Herbert Spencer's), as "the preservation of favorable individual differences and variations, and the destruction of those which are injurious" (*OS* 59).

Returning to the ethnological strand of his thinking, Darwin applied the theory of natural selection to humanity so as to demonstrate how beneficial variations arise, to assist human beings under their "conditions of life" (*OS* 59). In correspondence of 11 October 1859 (to Charles Lyell), of 31 January 1862 (Kingsley to Darwin), and of 6 February 1862 (Darwin to Kingsley), Darwin alluded to the extirpation of human groups as being part of the natural course of things and theorized that natural selection affected the intelligence of races, with the logical implication that the most intelligent variants will flourish, while the least intelligent would be annihilated.

In the 11 October 1859 letter to Lyell, Darwin finds no difficulty accepting the notion of the "most intellectual individuals of a species being continually selected; & the intellect of the new species [being] thus improved, aided probably by effects of inherited mental exercise. I look at this process as now going on with the races of man[,] the less intellectual races being exterminated" (*DCP* Letter 2503). Expounding on this subject, in a 25 September 1860 letter to Darwin, Lyell conjectured that modern man had emerged ca. 50,000 years ago from an original and intellectually inferior race. The descendants of this original race were likely to have been isolated, globally, and more diversified racially than their modern descendants. But the most interesting observation he makes is that the most powerful and "cosmopolite" or globally diffusive would "exterminate inferior ones" (*DCP* Letter 2927a).

Another important correspondent of the period was Charles Kingsley (1819–1875), then professor of Modern History at Cambridge University and an enthusiastic supporter of Darwin's evolutionary theory (Stocking [1987] 63, 147). Darwin's 6 February 1862 letter to Kingsley is largely concerned with human expression and with the wider discussion of how man relates to the lower animals. In regard to the moral paradox of his anthropology, Darwin acknowledges its weightiness, as being "a grand & almost awful question on the genealogy of man" (*DCP* Letter 3439 note 2). He recalls how unnerving the idea was that he had descended directly from prehistoric antecedents — from forebears very similar to the "barbarians" whom he had encountered while on the voyage. When Darwin first saw a Fuegian, naked, body-painted, and pitiful, he was revolted by the thought that his ancestors were like these natives and that a more primitive forebear was a forerunner of modern man (*DCP* Letter 3439 note 2).

While Darwin accepted racial equality as an unassailable truth, in select instances he still found it difficult to accept, and this was as true of his thinking in the 1860s as it was in the 1870s. On one level, and perhaps evasively, he and Kingsley agreed with an idea, expressed by Lyell in 1832, that "the higher races of men" will eventually clear away "the lower races" (*Principles* Vol. II [1832] 175). Darwin dourly predicted that in five-hundred years the Anglo-Saxon race will have expanded and wiped out entire nations (*DCP*

Letter 3439). Undoubtedly, Anglo-Saxon hegemony and the concomitant assimilation or effacement of indigenous people was consistent with an ethnology based on racial gradation. But, in this context, it is possible that Darwin was speaking from an evolutionary rather than from an imperial perspective about the struggle for existence between human groups.

If the comments in the 6 February 1862 correspondence represent Darwin's racial opinions at that moment, then it seems that he subscribed to three propositions which were, to varying degrees, incongruent with Humboldtian ethnology. The first was that British maritime expansion was legitimate and necessary, on nationalistic, economic and scientific grounds; the second, that the "extermination" of native communities was an inevitable, but unfortunate, by-product of this policy; and the third that the elimination of natives will be an evolutionary advantage for the dominant Anglo-Saxon race. The letter to Kingsley, as I suggested above, shows that Darwin was aware of what natural selection meant for aboriginal man, and the views he expresses in the letter are consistent with thoughts recorded in *B*169. In the 1860s, Darwin understood precisely that the struggle between human variants meant that native man was endangered. This conclusion, from the perspective of Lyell, of Kingsley, and of others, was consonant with evolutionary biology.

Before proceeding to Darwin's ethnological thought of the 1870s, we need to review Alfred Russel Wallace's (1823–1913) important contribution to the discussion on human origins and his idea of how natural selection affects man. Wallace's 1864 essay appeared at a critical point in the discussion.

A British naturalist, Wallace developed a unique understanding of evolutionary theory. Both he and Darwin considered the idea that human competition was the catalyst of natural selection. His 1864 essay, "The Origin of Human Races and the Antiquity of Man Deduced from the Theory of 'Natural Selection,'" published in the *Journal of the Anthropological Society of London*, treats issues that Darwin had been working on since the 1830s, but in 1864 Wallace focused exclusively on man.

One of Wallace's aims was to see if natural selection could be applied to the origin of races (*IT* 181). Like Darwin, he believed that it accounted for the modification of all organic life but that, as far as man was concerned, there was a significant difference in the way its effects were manifested. Wallace theorized that, at some time in human prehistory and once human intelligence had reached a sufficient level of complexity, natural selection no longer affected human physiology: the mental faculties, in other words, had become modified to the degree that physical modification was obviated (*IT* 192). He reiterates this theory in a 29 May 1864 letter to Darwin: the intention of the 1864 paper, Wallace explains, was to distinguish between lower animals that had been physiologically modified through natural selection and man who will no longer undergo major, physical modification (*DCP* Letter 4514). The superiority of the human mind renders man impervious to selective pressures that in lower animals induce constitutional changes, as in the axial skeleton, in cranial architecture, and in physiology. Modern man, regardless of race, has undergone minor variations only — e.g., in pigment, in physical proportion, and in hair texture — which are expressions of localized adaptation.

Wallace addressed ethical problems, too. One was the widespread assumption that the material deficiency of uncivilized society was traceable to a mental deficit in its inhabitants, a supposition that brought their human identity into question. In 1864 he established three criteria relating the intelligence of civilized to uncivilized man: (1) advanced intelligence, a defining human trait, led to technological adaptation on all levels, increasing the chances of survival and the propagation of inherited propensities related to intelligence; (2) all human beings, irrespective of race or of geography, have inherited an unparalleled intellectual endowment, far superior to all other animals, and have achieved this prominence through selective pressures; (3) because the human species displays a multiplicity of intra-specific variations, such as skin color, hair texture, or height, all of which are naturally selected modifications largely corresponding to habitat, aboriginal cognition should be assessed relatively, that is, in terms of *how* "the mental requirements of savages" *are fitted* to life in their respective regions; otherwise, the erroneous conclusion for the European beholding indigenes at first sight would be that they are barely human (*IT* 206).

Wallace believed that by observing modern primitives one could learn about human prehistory. To witness the varied behavior and lifestyles of natives, however meager and primitive their achievements might seem, was to behold the effects of natural selection on prehistoric man and, specifically, how diminutive man learned to survive through reason and artifice. Thus, native communities offered a glimpse into the prehistoric past and exhibited man's perennial resilience. The ability to use natural resources and to resist both climate and predator were essential to long-term survival. Wallace took this line of argument further. Anatomically, the most primitive Fuegian was essentially no different from the European. Although Darwin struggled with initial presuppositions about particular natives, especially about those who appeared intimidating and alien, he, too, realized that the mind of a savage *potentially* was no different from his own. For Wallace and Darwin, that was a startling admission to make, but predictably qualifications ensued.

Wallace had no difficulty admitting that all human beings, whether civilized or not, were potentially the same, but there were undeniable differences between the two that he attributed to adaptation and to bio-geographical factors. There was no denying that the uncivilized mentality *in its current state* was radically different from that of civilized man and that both mentalities were the products of different migratory patterns and adaptive processes. Over time and through decision-making, natives had learned to survive, becoming fitted to, and in equilibrium with, their ecology. This notion brings to mind Lyell's distinction, in 1832, between having inherent intelligence and being able to apply this capacity in problem-solving and in the transformation of material resources to sustain and defend oneself. Reflecting on the contest between races, Lyell observes that each is "gifted with equal capacities of improvement," yet, despite their intelligence, natives will be quickly exterminated by Europeans because their aptitude or ability to learn was in some respect deficient, rendering them less able to resist or adapt to changing conditions brought on by the appearance of colonists (*Principles* Vol. I 175).

Wallace knew that aborigines were resourceful, and he respected them. To judge a Fuegian by Western standards, in his view, was to ignore the natural principle actively at work in human history that had brought mankind into equilibrium with the world. Tribal life, whether on a remote island, on the plains or savannahs, or in the distant Arctic, he reminds his reader, had no practical need either for morality and refined emotion or for abstract reasoning and idealism — such higher sensibilities and intellectual pursuits having been supplanted by a preoccupation with survival. This implies that native aptitude was sufficient and appropriate to their *immediate* needs and that the absence of abstract reasoning or of a stringent moral code should not be used as a criterion by which to define humanness (*IT* 206).

On the basis of two premises, Wallace defined what it meant to be human. The first was that the intellectual capacities of civilized and of native man were equal to one another; and the second was that the anatomy of the human brain had remained stationary for tens of thousands of years. These were logical inferences. Had selective pressure not brought on the evolution of human intelligence, primitive man living in limited and hostile environments would have wound up having ape-like intelligence, and likely would have become extinct, as a result; instead, by virtue of their humanity, savage man, whether he was cognizant of it or not, possessed a mind comparable to that of a philosopher (*IT* 206). How the intellect was applied to the exigencies of a specific habitat accounted for the differences between civilized and savage man: for hunters and gatherers, higher levels of thought and creativity simply had no practical benefit effect for the community (*IT* 207). Of course, Wallace was making these claims seventy-six years before the discovery of the Caves of Lascaux, but his relativistic view on intelligence is, nevertheless, a modern one.

Wallace conveyed these ideas to Darwin personally. In a 10 May 1864 correspondence, he maintains that the savage's perceived inadequacies, in abstract reasoning and morality, were not deficiencies at all; rather, they were simply less relevant to their daily struggle to survive (*L&R* 1 152). In his 28 May response, Darwin acknowledges the novelty of Wallace's principal idea that the mind had been modified more than the body. He then applies Wallace's theory to the struggle between various human groups: the ultimate triumph of one over another depends, not on physiological advantages, but rather on intelligence and on morality (*L&R* vol.1 153; Darwin's emphasis), the implication being that the savage's conforming of intelligence to situation proves that he is human and has learned how to survive in his world. But conformity to the wilderness has rendered the native adaptively inferior to civilized man in terms of the reasoning faculties and material culture.

Darwin, unlike Wallace, believed that native aptitude was inheritable, an idea he exemplified with reference to the Eskimo's expertise as fishermen and as canoeists (*L&R* vol.1 53). The idea was that, without instruction or the ability to emulate practitioners, an Eskimo child bore innate knowledge of fishing and of canoe-making; apparently, Darwin was not thinking of the oral transmission of traditions. Wallace, however, did not agree with the idea of the inheritability of specific knowledge. He thought that, unlike technical aptitude, human intelligence was an irreducible constant. The transmission of knowledge through a division of labor and through learned skills might benefit its users; but, hypothetically, under social duress technical methods could be lost, unless preserved through instruction. Wallace's divergent point is that the *intelligence* needed to reconstruct an industry, such as fire- or arrow-making, was an evolved human trait, and mankind, regardless of geographical history, retains the capacity to reinvent (*L&R* vol. 1 240). Lost or forgotten technology, therefore, could be reconstituted, in Wallace's view, as an adaptive response to environmental contingencies, and not necessarily retrieved, in the Darwinian sense, as a genetically encoded artifact.

The 1864 essay, in sum, proposes that, if contemporary savages were fit enough to survive in the wilderness, this measure of intelligence confirms their humanness. It also attests to their resilience and to their ability to learn from, and to communicate with, one another. It logically implies, moreover, that their prehistoric forebears survived through their social skills and lived well enough to have propagated the species under adverse conditions. Conversely, had prehistoric man *not* been able to exercise his high intelligence in a hostile world, even minimally, the species would have faded into extinction. In Wallace's judgment, a sense of social welfare and of cooperation had, from the beginning, to have been inherent in modern man's consciousness.

Human sympathy and sociability were the keys to survival and to dominion over nature. Even in the rudest extant tribes, according to Wallace, the infirm are fed and cared for, and neither weakness nor lack of vigor was a death sentence. Whether that might be true for gatherers whose survival depended upon small-group cooperation and on rapid and frequent migrations, Darwin might have doubted. Wallace was probably thinking more of a settled community in which a division of labor between hunters, fishermen, and farmers was customary, and in which food was regularly exchanged or apportioned.

The refinement of social attitudes in primitive communities was another factor obviating the need for physiological adaptation. Survival was easier for communal man: weak or maladapted animals disappeared into the food chain, but in human communities the disadvantaged were not abandoned (*IT* 181). While physical characteristics no longer bore evolutionary importance, mental capability and the moral sense had become increasingly more important to the well-being of the human race (*IT* 181–82). Mutual defense, food acquisition, and shelter construction, a sense of right, restraint of destructive inclinations, the ability to anticipate, all were qualities that Wallace believed essential to early communities.

Wherever dissention and self-destructive behavior prevailed, a community could be put at risk, so cooperation was essential to survival. Conversely, wherever external enemies were repelled, internal dissensions quelled, inclement weather, disease, and famine resisted, communities survived and flourished. Efficient use of natural resources was essential; in addition, a successful population was unlikely to rise above the level of subsistence. Furthermore, if highly developed moral qualities were the norm, a community would have an advantage in the struggle for existence. It would prosper while competitors would decrease in number and eventually disappear (*IT* 182).

Wallace's imaginative retrospective of human prehistory surveys two consecutive periods. The first dates back forty millennia, to a nebulous point in time when natural selection, presumably, had ceased to affect human evolution in any significant anatomical degree, and when the human mind had reached its evolutionary zenith. At that point of humanization, if you will, man had become a physiologically "stationary" animal: the intellectual, social, and moral qualities, however, continued to evolve. Wallace seems to have anticipated the discovery of the Cro-Magnon man, an early *Homo sapiens* living 40,000 years before the present, in the upper–Paleolithic period. Cro-

Magnon's skeletal remains and artifacts were first discovered, in 1868, in Les Eyzies, Dordogne, France. In a rock shelter, the remains of five individuals were found, having modern features: a high-domed cranium and a small jaw, features characteristic of modern humans (Leakey and Lewin 30). This was a major find, although it was not acknowledged as being such until the early twentieth century.

Wallace was envisaging the Aurignacian culture. An early upper–Paleolithic industrial complex, ca 34,000 to 29,000 years before the present, it was known for its cave-wall paintings, bone and ivory art, and technological inventions (Brooks 63–4). If we look further back in time, the latest pre-human beings of which we have fossil evidence are believed to have disappeared 1.6 million years ago (the earliest, dubbed *Ardipithecus ramidus*, is said to have lived 4.4 million years ago in what is modern-day Ethiopia [Schmid 1]). Over the vast 1.6-million-year interim, between the disappearance of Homo erectus and the appearance of modern precursors of man, variations in mental and in moral character adapted certain stocks of emergent man to natural circumstances. Among them, a spirit of cooperation probably was evident; as a result, the best-adapted races increased in number and migrated to hospitable regions, while upper Paleolithic man became extinct (*IT* 184).

Wallace's historical retrospective moves forward to 8000 to 5000 B.C., when in five geographical regions — Western and Continental Europe, Iran-India, the Far East, and the Americas — hunting and gathering gradually gave way to farming, herding, and fishing. In continental Europe, more specifically, the gradual settlement of communities brought with it the emergence of primitive religion, the manufacture of flint tools, weapons, axes, nets, traps, bows, and arrows, and the appearance of small encampments featuring flimsy huts, along with rock engravings (Hawkes 53, 58–9).

The idea that in aptitude, productivity, and creativity Europeans were superior to native people had immediate consequences for Wallace's humanistic position even though, in other contexts, he was sympathetic towards the people whom he met in Brazil and in the East Indies. Scholars have rightly pointed out that Wallace's pro-colonial opinion raised serious ethical questions with respect to indigenous people (Stocking [1987] 100; Brantlinger 182–88). In fact, a conflict of ideas appears unexpectedly in Wallace's essay. On the one hand, he contends that extant primitives are inarguably human and perhaps, like Europeans, the direct descendants of rugged forebears. On these grounds, it would seem logical that Wallace would portray the intelligence of extant primitives as being equal in kind *and* in degree to civilized man. But, on the other hand, he differentiates between the two human populations on the basis of material achievement.

Although egalitarianism and ethnic supremacy appeared irreconcilable, this did not stop Wallace from trying to define his ethnology in regard to primitive man. The uncivilized and the civilized mentality were identical in kind, but, because of radical differences in geographical history, extant primitives are fundamentally different from the "Teutonic race" and its forebears. Whereas extant primitives are indisputably human and, as such, have high intelligence, in certain of "qualities" of mind and behavior, they are inferior to "the wonderful intellect of the Germanic races" (*IT* 184). The distinction Wallace is making here involved evolutionary biology and the idea of civilization, not racist theory. He reasons that, although Europeans and the Indians of southern Brazil are both inventive tool-makers, the European is mentally superior to the aborigines because he has interacted with, and transformed, his environment with greater efficiency and inventiveness than has his uncivilized counterpart.

If this is an accurate representation of Wallace's thinking, then it raises an interesting point. If the adaptive distinction between civilized and uncivilized man, as a measure of material achievement, is a matter of degree, then if Amazonian tribes had lived in Europe for thousands of years, they will invariably have built cities industrial and urban centers. Conversely, if ancient Europeans had been isolated in, or had migrated to, tropical and sub-tropical environments, they would currently be hunters and gatherers or rudimentary agriculturalists, at best.

Despite the contradiction between the egalitarian and imperial views, Wallace speaks of native man in the highest terms as a resilient and efficient survivor who, because of geographical circumstances, has had to endure natural hardships. The esteem in which he held native man extended to all ethnic groups, from the Uaupés to the Papuans: all were descendants of migratory bands who, for tens of thousands of years, had withstood the rigors of sub-equatorial geography. Their conquest of, or accommodation to, nature evidenced their intellectual parity with Europeans, but their circumstances had impeded progress beyond the point at which they had become adapted to their habitat.

Despite the inherent equality of all races, and according to natural law, competition was expected among human beings. The best-adapted will survive in the greatest numbers and, in multiplying widely, will propagate genetically transmissible traits. If one considers the future of human history, the dominion of the European is a biological certainty. This inescapable conclusion derived from observations of how species, or variants thereof, interacted with each other:

It is the same great law of "the preservation of favoured races in the struggle for life" which leads to the inevitable extinction of all those low and mentally undeveloped populations with which Europeans come in contact. The red Indian in North America, and in Brazil; the Tasmanian, Australian and New Zealander in the southern hemisphere, die out, not from any one special cause, but from the inevitable effects of an unequal mental and physical struggle. The intellectual and moral, as well as the physical qualities of the European are superior; the same powers and capacities which have made him rise in a few centuries from the condition of the wandering savage with a scanty and stationary population to his present state of culture and advancement, with a greater average longevity, a greater average strength, and a capacity of more rapid increase,— enable him when in contact with the savage man, to conquer in the struggle for existence, and to increase at his expense, just as the more favourable increase at the expense of the less favourable varieties in the animal and vegetable kingdoms [*IT* 184–85].

In the conclusion of the 1864 essay, Wallace applies natural selection strictly to human populations and reasserts that the annihilation of aborigines is a tragic inevitability: the morally and intellectually superior will displace "the lower and more degraded races." As a result, natural selection will have rendered man's "higher faculties" more perfectly adapted to environmental conditions and to social exigencies (*IT* 190). Wallace argues that the exploration and conquest of nature will ultimately refine man's reasoning faculties until dominion over nature is fully achieved. But if "lower" and "inferior" human beings are to be acculturated, removed, or expended in the process, then the vision of European global dominion that he entertains is certainly not *ethnological*, at least not in the sense it was understood by Darwin, Prichard, and others.

In *Descent*, Darwin also illuminated complex problems in the natural history of man, the most fundamental of which had to do with human origins. Unlike Wallace in 1864, he went back to man's zoological beginnings. Man, ape, and higher mammal exhibited so many constitutional similarities that all must have descended from an original form. Man, therefore, is likely to have descended from "an ancient marsupial animal," a creature that, through a long lineage of diversified intermediates, had descended from an "amphibian-like creature." The amphibian, in turn, hailed even further back in time to a hermaphroditic, "fish-like animal," a precursor of the extant marine Ascidian larvae, and a creature having primitive lungs but undeveloped heart and brain (*DM* 632). The line of human descent was logically traceable to an arboreal quadruped that lived in the Old World (*DM* 632). The 1983 fossil remains of a 47-million-year-old creature, called "Ida," has proven to be one of the most complete specimens ever unearthed. In the spring of 2009 (a serendipitous find in Darwin's bicentenary year), it was determined to be an early primate and possibly the ancestor of all primates. Appropriately dubbed *Darwinius masillae*, the tiny juvenile female, having the features of lemur and monkey, dates back to the Eocene Epoch, ca. 35 to 54 million years ago (Wilford A11; Szalay 180–81).

In notebook entries *N*63, 64, and 65, as we recall, Darwin suggests that the conflict between strong and weak human groups was inevitable and consistent with natural selection. In 1871, he follows with this line of argument, observing that the competition between tribes and races was a cause of extinction. Competition of this order affected weak societies adversely by lessening fertility and by causing ill-health (*DM* 191). Itinerant tribes were especially susceptible to altered conditions or life habits, such as the re-location to unfamiliar surroundings, brought on by the pressure of a more robust neighbor or invader (*DM* 196). Thus, he predicted that sterility and illness would result, if an uncivilized society were forced by a conquering tribe to leave their homes and to change their patterns of behavior radically (*DM* 199). Consistent with the principle of natural selection was the idea that the extinction of savage tribes, the dying off of the weakest members of the species, will leave the Anglo-Saxon, presumably the most strident, to pursue global dominion and at the expense of indigenes.

The contradiction in Darwin's bio-ethics, exemplified by the contrast between the humanistic discourse of the 1830s and the ideological tenor of the Darwin-Kingsley correspondence, instead of being hopelessly irresolvable, can be thought of as a dialectical opposition of ideas. On the one hand, we have the naturalistic outcome of colonialism, historically conceptualized as involving the expurgation of native culture, the destruction of newly discovered or ancient civilizations, and the acculturation of surviving remnants. On the other hand, while Darwin acknowledged these trends and outcomes as consonant with natural selection, he forthrightly condemned the high cost in human suffering that they entailed. Judging from his sympathy for slaves, for downtrodden Native Americans, and for transported Tasmanians, and considering the politically sensitive language he used to criticize the policy of General de Rosas, his use of the odious verb *exterminate* in the Kingsley correspondence might have been intended to underscore, and not necessarily to endorse, the adverse effects of colonial policy. If Kingsley and Darwin were using verbs like *exterminate* in a naturalistic sense, they were conceding that the global hegemony of the Anglo-Saxon race, along with the consequent displacement of aborigines, was inexorable. But it is entirely possible that Darwin was drawing a logical although tragic deduction, one based upon his observations of how competition between organisms favored the survival of the fittest.

Darwin differentiated the naturalistic from the ethical viewpoint extensively in *Descent*. As Lyell had in 1832, he suspected that the extinction of
ethnic groups could also be the result of tribal or of racial competition for
resources. The Malthusian parallel here is apparent. Checks to population
growth, says Darwin, are intensively at work among savage tribes. These
include periodical famines, nomadic habits, wars, accidents, sickness, infanticide, a high infant mortality, and infertility. When civilized nations contacted barbarians, in time the struggle between the two usually ended badly
for the latter. Ironically, where savage lands were cultivated, the native populations ordinarily declined, perhaps (as Humboldt had suggested) because
they could not, or refused to, adapt to the new circumstances by changing
their behavior and by abandoning their customs (*DM* 190).

By far, the most insidious causes of extinction, thought Darwin, were
infertility and ill-health, particularly as these affected children. Decreases in
this regard among the Maoris, from 1858 to 1873, for example, had been
blamed on diseases, on the profligacy of women, and on drunkenness and war;
but the chief causes, Darwin suspected to have been infertility and the high
rate of child mortality (*DM* 192–93). On the basis of gathered evidence, Darwin concludes that uncivilized societies were likely to suffer the most in terms
of health when subjected to altered conditions or habits of life; transportation alone to a new climate, however, could not cause this level of suffering
(*DM* 196). Regardless of race, natives who were forced to change their habits
of life were prone to sterility, and their children's health suffered. Whereas
these deficits were especially true for aboriginal people living on islands, civilized races had a greater ability to resist changes in lifestyle (*DM* 198).

Darwin's interest in extinction dates back to his work with fossils in
South America. Along with Kingsley, with Wallace, and with many others,
he recognized it to be consistent with natural law: that is, the weak and infirm
were dislodged, subsumed under, or destroyed by, a better adapted and more
robust competitor. The blatant moral dilemma confronting Victorian naturalists such as Darwin, however, stemmed from the fact that human beings,
and not plants or animals, were being adversely affected in this way and that
the intrusive human variety (whether European colonist, Malayan invader,
or Oens raider), was simply better adapted to the struggle.

Darwin endorsed British maritime expansionism for scientific and
nationalistic reasons but was conscientiously distressed over the effects of
imperialism on human beings, whether in slavery, in the policies of the
*estancias*, in the British or French domination of Polynesian culture, or in the
systematic displacement and eradication of natives in New Zealand, Australia,
and Tasmania. It is not surprising that he reserved his most trenchant criti-

cism for colonists who abused natives and that he spoke favorably, at every turn, of British missionaries who tried to provide native people with a better life even though the conversionary and educational measures that they employed either modified or eradicated indigenous cultures.

Darwin's evolutionary understanding of aborigines' place in nature conflicted with his sympathy for them. Conceptualizations tended to reduce them to ideas and to physiological measurements, relegating them to the surveys and racial digests of armchair ethnologists. Geographical isolation rendered native tribes more susceptible to intellectual segregation, as did caricature and hyperbole; thus, natives were regularly caged in diagrammatic niches, their skulls triangulated, and their physical forms and behavior atavistically stereotyped and made into museum exhibits.

By far, the most serious consequence of this way of thinking was the moral insensitivity it caused in many European minds — an anti-spirit of the age, if you will, against which reformers such as Clarkson, Wilberforce, and the missionaries in the Pacific islands, had waged lifelong struggles. Darwin realized that enslavement and cultural attrition persisted largely because the victims, in the context of scientific discussion and in popular literature, were depicted as being less than human, and because they were made to conform to preconceptions that Europeans had about them. The mid–1860s was an ethical juncture in the development of Darwin's ethnology. He had a choice to make: either he could forsake the Humboldtian perspective of his early writings on man, or he could abandon aborigines to imperialism and to the cycles of natural law.

# 11. Transportation and Census

Through the use of census data, Darwin emancipated himself from the ethnic assumptions and illusory paradigms of late-eighteenth and early nineteenth century cultural anthropology. By the 1870s, he could allow the incontestable facts to speak for themselves. Thus, the greatest breakthrough in his ethnological thought, heralded by the Questionnaire of the British Association three decades earlier, was his use of demographic statistics in *Descent*. This information proved, unequivocally, that the native communities in Australia, in Tasmania, in New Zealand, in the Sandwich Islands, and elsewhere were gradually being wiped out. Data of this kind grounded his speculative commentary and dramatized the fact that human competitiveness, though the driving force of natural selection, could cause ethnic genocide. Ironically, unlike Malthus, Darwin used demographic trends and statistics to support his humanistic ethic.

While Darwin understood that man was a creature subject to natural and to man-made pressures, he abhorred the tragic consequences of human competition and the destruction of ethnic communities. Conditions disadvantageous to native enclaves could be improved systematically, he theorized, through the exercise of the reasoning faculty and of the conscience. Wherever native people were being exploited, Darwin believed there was a moral obligation to intervene on their behalf.

A prime example of Darwin's use of census data to support a native community concerns the Tasmanians. He derived important information and data from James Bonwick's 1870 publications, the *Daily Life and Origin of the Tasmanians* and *The Last of the Tasmanians*. Bonwick, as he points out, documented the ongoing conflict between whites and blacks, and argued that white cruelty precipitated black reprisals — a cycle of black massacres of settlers and of white reactions that Bonwick called the Black War.

Was there a naturalistic reason behind the destructive behavior? Bonwick turned to the naturalist Franz Waitz's opinion for an explanation: the American school of anthropology, in the name of religion, taught that "the higher races are destined to displace the lower," whose eventual extinction is "predestined by Nature" (Bonwick 375). Evolutionary biology accounted for this behavior as well. Bonwick cites a familiar authority in regard to the Tasmanians' decline: their diminution "sadly demonstrates Mr. Darwin's philosophy that 'the varieties of man seem to act upon each other in the same way as different species of animals; the stronger always extirpates the weaker'" (Bonwick 377). It is intriguing to imagine how Darwin reacted to this 1870 reference to the *Journal*. Did Bonwick's citation of his view on human-competition theory, which Darwin definitely read, intensify his inner conflict over egalitarianism and the deterministic outcome of human selection?

Decades before Bonwick's research was published, Darwin, as we know, had been well aware of the Tasmanians' plight. Of the conditions existing before the transportation of aborigines, he had written incisively in the *Diary* entry of 5 February 1836: "The Aboriginal blacks are all removed & kept (in reality as prisoners) in a Promontory, the neck of which is guarded. I believe it was not possible to avoid this cruel step; although without doubt the misconduct of the Whites first led to the Necessity" (*BD* 408). In 1836 Darwin understood that white inhumanity had incited black crime. In the *Journal*, he recalls that these difficulties amounted to a "train of evil": "This most cruel step [i.e., transportation] seems to have been quite unavoidable, as the only means of stopping a fearful succession of robberies, burnings, and murders committed by the blacks; and which ... would have ended in their utter destruction. I fear there is no doubt that this train of evil and its consequences, originated in the infamous conduct of some of our countrymen" (*JR* [1839] 387). Bonwick arrived at similar conclusions. He had no illusions about British policy vis-à-vis the Tasmanians, namely the stealing of native lands, the deprivation of their rights, and inhumanity towards them (Stocking [1987] 283):

> The Aborigines ... are pronounced by the laws of civilized England to be without right or title to the land they have first occupied, and occupied as a people for some thousands of years; they are forced into the condition of subjects to the Crown, without the recognition of civil rights; and they are ... admitted to have no claim to rest their foot upon the soil which they had supposed their own. It was reserved for modern Christian civilization to advance, and act upon, a theory, which ancient heathen philosophy would have declared inhuman and unjust [Bonwick 333].

Knowing that demographic statistics were more convincing than descriptions and anecdotes, in 1871 Darwin interpolated Bonwick's data directly into *Descent*, as he made a case in defense of the aborigines. When colonized in

1803, the island had a population somewhere between seven- and twenty-thousand natives. Though the numbers here are woefully inexact, the precipitous decline of the race was indisputable (*DM*. 191–92). Sir George Murray, in a 5 November 1830 dispatch to Governor Arthur, had comprehended the moral and political implications of the occupation:

> The great decrease which has of late years taken place in the amount of the aboriginal population, renders it not unreasonable to apprehend that the whole race of these people may, at no distant period, become extinct. But with whatever feelings such an event may be looked forward to by those of the settlers who have been sufferers by the collisions which have taken place, it is impossible not to contemplate such a result of our occupation of the island, as one very difficult to be reconciled with feelings of humanity, or even with feelings of justice and sound policy; and the adoption of any line of conduct, having for its avowed or secret object the extinction of the native race, could not fail to leave an indelible stain upon the British Government [cited by Bonwick 390–91].

By 1832, only one-hundred twenty Tasmanians were known to be alive. This remnant was subsequently transported to Flinders Island, which is situated between Tasmania and Australia. Initially, this decision did not seem incommodious to its planners, for Flinders Island was hospitable and rather spacious (500 to 700 square miles). Moreover, the Tasmanians were said to have arrived at Flinders in a healthy state and were well treated. But, in their isolation, they slowly began to suffer in health, and their numbers inexplicably declined: in 1834, one-hundred and eleven were left (48 women, 47 men, and 16 children); one year later, only one-hundred remained. With this continual decline, they were re-transported, as the colonial government tried desperately to increase their numbers. Their new home was in Oyster Cove, in southern Tasmania. The census of 20 December 1847 dismally indicates that there were only fourteen men, twenty-two women, and ten children left; apparently, the re-location had done no good. Disease and death had taken their toll until, in 1864, one man and three women were left. Infertility was suspected as being a major factor in this tragic story.

From Bonwick's data, Darwin deduced that too many deaths and too few births had combined to cause the Tasmanians to dwindle in number, but it was the change in living conditions and in diet, their banishment from the mainland, and their "depression of spirits," that, more than likely, had artificially selected them to extinction. William Lanne, or King Billy, as he was called, was the last of the Tasmanian men. He died of cholera on 3 March 1869, and, despite efforts to protect him from being autopsied, he was eventually beheaded; and the body was rumored to have been stolen, although the headless skeleton mysteriously wound up in the hands of the Royal Society of Tasmania. The last Tasmania Woman was Truganina, also known as Lalla Rookh (Bonwick 398–99).

Similar demographic trends had been taking place in New Zealand and in Australia, according to the findings of Mr. Fenton, as they were recorded in a 1859 government report, "Observations on the Aboriginal Inhabitants of New Zealand," Darwin's primary source (*DM* 192–93). According to Fenton, since 1830 the Maoris had been experiencing a steady decline in population. From 1844 to 1858, tribes living in different locations and with different diets and habits declined in numbers by 19.42 percent. The 1858 census of 53,700, by 1872 declined to 36,359, a drop of 13.29 percent (recorded in the 1874 edition of *Descent*). Fenton cited, as the main cause of this decline, infertility and a high infant mortality (in 1844, 1 non-adult per 2.57 adults; in 1858, 1 non-adult per 3.27 adults). Fewer females than males were being born, and the overall adult mortality was also on the rise. The Maoris themselves attributed these trends to the introduction of new food, clothing, and habits. In December 1835, Darwin had observed that even though New Zealand had an abundance of nutritious natural resources (fern, roots, and sea food) that prevented malnutrition, and even though the British community had introduced fine crops of barley, wheat, potatoes, asparagus, cucumbers, rhubarb, apples, pears, figs, peaches, apricots, grapes, corn, olives, gooseberries, currants, and hops, the Maori population continued to decline (*BD* 387, 389).

Darwin analyzed the data and concluded that infertility was blamed on the profligacy of women, but this cause did not account for infertility either in New Zealand or in Tasmania. Infertility in all colonized regions, he surmised, could be more readily ascribed to changed conditions of life and that wherever this occurred, sooner or later, extinction would follow (*DM* 196). Darwin set these passages against the background of evolutionary theory. Since changed conditions affected reproduction significantly in lower animals, and since animals taken into captivity became sterile, it followed that aborigines risked sterility and poor health if their way of life were to change drastically (*DM* 198).

Attempting to discover exactly why indigenous societies declined under colonial rule, Darwin focused on the family. He learned that two reasons for small tribal families were hypothesized. The first and least convincing was that the women breast-fed their young longer than expected, which today is thought to confer immunity on the child. A more likely cause of their being less prolific than civilized man was their marginal existence — that is, their makeshift habitations, their daily hardships, and especially their poor diets. In contrast, because civilized men were highly domesticated, living as they did under more predictable conditions and with adequate subsistence, they tended to be more prolific than those living in the wilderness (*DM* 45–6); furthermore, he speculated that the increased fertility of man in a domesticated world could become an inherited propensity (*DM* 46).

Severe famine, which occurred periodically among savage people, severely impacted procreation, forcing tribes such as those in Australia to wander as hunters and gatherers. Under these insufferable conditions, infant mortality was high. Since famine occurred periodically, especially during seasonal extremes, tribal populations fluctuated proportionately; over time, and without an artificial increase in the food supply, their numbers dwindled progressively, and re-population in the intervals between famines could not adequately make up for the losses. Made desperate by these circumstances, wandering tribes invaded each other's territory. In this case, human competitiveness for territory and for natural resources was intensified by the life-and-death struggle — one that also pitted tribes of the *same* ethnicity against each other.

At this juncture, as I have pointed out, Darwin's ethnological philosophy had reached a point of moral crisis. Two concepts predominated. One was the constancy of natural law, dictating that the stronger life form — plant, animal, or human — inevitably extirpates the weaker in the struggle to survive. But, for mankind, this struggle had moral consequences since, in Darwin's view, human dignity was inviolable. Combined in a single statement, Darwin's evolutionary *ethnology* reads as follows: the immoral destruction of indigenous people, though *consistent* with evolutionary biology and natural selection, must be condemned by advanced civilizations.

We observed that, from the late 1830s to the early 1870s, Darwin's opinion of aboriginal man became more sympathetic and less theoretical in its emphasis. In terms of his methodology, old preconceived schemes were gradually, although not entirely, superseded by the relativism and objective fact-finding, exemplified by the writings of Humboldt. Darwin's research and the development of his evolutionary philosophy made it clear to him that all human beings, irrespective of race, of skin color, of geographical origin, and of tribal affiliation, belonged to a single species. In zoological terms, therefore, all human beings had a common origin and, despite external variations, were equal.

Like Wallace in 1864, Darwin believed that, in terms of civilization, of culture, and of intelligence and social life, profound differences existed between races and especially between Europeans and aborigines. Perhaps for want of a more systematic approach to the understanding of non–Western cultures, and since the Questionnaire project was never brought to fruition, Darwin resorted to the racial hierarchy; thus, in *Descent* he alludes to "the grade of civilization" (*DM* 198). Furthermore, he continues to observe an implicit, three-tiered model to represent human ethnology: the upper level was assigned to white civilization, the undifferentiated middle tier to non-white populations worldwide, and particular ethnicities were relegated to the lowest tier; and he even used the comparatives *low, lower,* and *lowest* in ethnographic contexts, as if these terms had some inherent meaning. The "lowest" people, once again, are the Fuegians. A racial composite, the Fuegians are unjustly portrayed as barely eking out an existence, as being communally unsettled, as possessing only rudimentary tools, and as being devoid of culture (*DM* 66).

I made the point that, in *Descent,* Darwin had taken an ethical stance on behalf of native populations, having expressed his position demographically through census data that certified the downward trajectory in numbers. He could have easily have ignored these alarming statistics, avoided controversy and public ire over colonial governance, and safely archived his criticism in private contexts. But he chose, instead, to stand with Prichard, Bonwick, and others in the public square.

But Darwin's progress in the ethical arena did not ensure the same for his methodology. Conscience and intellect, for Darwin, were as-yet unsynchronized. How, then, can one account for the ethnological contradictions that persist into the 1870s? In *Descent,* he resorts to racist paradigms even though he rejects degeneration and multiple-species or polygenetic theories of man's origin because they divest nonwhite people of their human identity. On the basis of a number of criteria, however, he rejects the theory that humanity consists of sub-species, some superior to others, and subscribes to the idea of the species comprising racial variants. First, arguing on geographical and on genetic bases, he maintains that all the races of man not only belong to a single species but are "not sufficiently distinct to inhabit the same country without fusion" (*DM* 180). Interracial reproduction evidenced the indivisibility of the species. Second, invalidating racial paradigms, he asserts that all races "graduate into each other"; and because of this blending, it was "hardly possible to discover clear distinctive characters between them" (*DM* 181). External variation, such as skin color, did not define membership in a species. To argue otherwise was to ignore the zoological lesson Darwin had learned from the Galápagos Archipelago, namely that "species within the same large genus by no means resemble each other to the same degree" (*DM* 182). Evolution, therefore, points directly to the fact "that all races of man are descended from a single primitive stock" (*DM* 183). Third, on the basis of comparative anatomy and through homology, Darwin found the multiple-species theory of man to be untenable. If contemporary races had descended from two or more distinct species, obvious differences in bones could be found in modern man. But this is not the case, although for divergent species of higher apes it is (*DM* 185). In effect, this statement contravened the close affinity that was imagined to exist between the Hottentot and the orangutan. A fourth criterion of the unified-species theory was the close disposition in taste, in habit, and in artifice of all races of man, which was evidence of their common origin; the pleasure uncivilized people worldwide found in music, dancing, acting , painting, adornment, and body-art was definitively human. The same could be said for their "mutual comprehension" of gesture-language, for similar vocalizations, emotional reactions to common stimuli, and for burial and other customs that anthropologists recorded, and which archaeologists continued to uncover (*DM* 185–86). Fifth, similarities in internal anatomy and in mental faculties attested not only to the humanness of tribal people, but, as was commonly believed, also offered insight into the state of prehistoric man before wide-ranging migrations had taken place.

It is interesting at this point to compare Captain FitzRoy's opinion, expressed in the 1830s, on human origins and migrations with Darwin's. Each was a monogenist, but FitzRoy's theory of origins was based, not on natural history, but on *Genesis* and on the genealogies descending from Noah. In Narrative 2, FitzRoy presented his views in two chapters entitled, "Remarks on the Early Migrations of the Human Race" (chapter XXVII) and "A Very Few Remarks with Reference to the Deluge" (640–57 and 658–83). Darwin, too, was a monogenist, but his version of human descent was natural rather than supernatural. Man's extraordinary penchant for adaptability and innovation, in his view, was the key to his survival over millennia (*DM* 187); above all, he reiterates that "the races of man have been similarly produced," with modifications being the direct consequence of being exposed to different conditions or the indirect consequence of natural or of sexual selection (*DM* 188–89). The external difference between the races of men, therefore, cannot be explained in Lamarckian terms as arising from the conditions of life, from the continued use of parts, or from the principle of correlation (*DM* 206). Moreover, none of the physical differences between the races of men "have an immediate benefit." The great external variability between races is insignificant. Had it been important, then long ago these variations would have been either "fixed and preserved" or "eliminated" through natural selection (*DM* 206).

Darwin was reluctant to abandon the idea of the superiority of some cultures over others, even though he believed that barbaric communities could be civilized through European intervention. In his ethnology, as in Wallace's, an impassable *cultural* and *civil* border remained between nonwhites and whites, even though his moral sensibility and compassion inspired him to champion the anti-slavery and anti-colonial causes. Darwin's ambivalence in these matters persisted over decades. An obvious symptom of his inner struggle was inconsistency. On the one hand, he disassembles multiple-species constructs, while, on the other hand, he classifies racial and ethnic groups with the descriptors *low*, *lower*, and *lowest*. In discussing the "mental powers" of man, for example, he refers to "lower races," a subdividing of nonwhite populations on the basis, not of biology, but of mentality, measured subjectively and by undefined criteria (*DM* 584). All men sing and dance, but the song and dance of "the lowest races of men" can not be equated with European performing arts. Indeed, so different from European standards of taste are those of the savage races, that aborigines are indifferent to European music, and their music is cacophony (*DM* 590).The arts of singing and dancing, which may ordinarily be thought of as defining the humanness of uncivilized man, are currently practiced "by all or nearly all the *lowest* races of men," and yet the "Hottentots and Negroes" are renowned musicians (*DM* 591; italics added).

Darwin subscribed to a modified form of degeneration theory, one that posited the primal unity of all races but also their uneven cultural and civil progress. His subscription to this idea is revealed in the discussion on ornamentation in which he compares the ancient barbarians of Europe during the upper–Paleolithic period to contemporary savages. Whereas ancestral Europeans brought to their caves aesthetically appealing objects that they happened to find, in similar fashion present-day savages adorn themselves with feathers, necklaces, amulets, and ear-rings, along with practicing body-art (tattooing, scarification, and perforation) (*DM* 595). The implied distinction, consistent with degeneration theory, was that ancestral Europeans progressed to their present status of advanced civilization, while aboriginal tribes did so unevenly relative to each other, and at differing rates.

In the case of adornment, Darwin, again, drew a bold line of cultural demarcation between societies. Seeming to have forgotten his insightful observations on body-art in the South Pacific, in facial scarification he saw nothing elegant: among Europeans, the face is admired for its beauty, but for savages it is "the chief seat of mutilation." He is referring specifically to disfiguring procedures, like facial piercing and carving or to the insertion of bones in lips and nose. Once again, for Darwin, idea and emotion are at cross-purposes. He realizes that self-mutilation had social, political, and personal significance, making warriors appear formidable, as well as communicating rank and prowess, family identity, ritual observance, or rite of passage, but the suffering it caused disturbed him (*DM* 597).

Whereas in several contexts in *Descent*, intellect and conscience seem disjoined from one another, in other places he remained dispassionate and thoughtful: if uncivilized people endured repeated procedures and intense pain, then these practices had to have deeper significance pertaining to culture and personality. He learned from what he had read, and possibly recalled from the *Beagle* voyage, that these practices, however alien and distasteful to his sensibilities, did indeed represent traditions and deeply held beliefs, attesting to the humanity of the practitioners. Intermittent comments such as these show that, occasionally, Darwin was the imperturbable ethnologist: that is, an observer who tried to understand an experience in its own terms, and who was less likely to judge the experience precipitously and by external standards.

Despite the regressive and inconsistent elements, Darwin's ethnology was informed by sympathy and good will. The extirpation of native people, dramatized by the rapid dissolution of the Tasmanians, moved Darwin in the direction of modern ethnology and set his humanitarianism on solid ground. The decline of the Tasmanians and of other Pacific natives was documented in census data for all to see. Darwin employed these data in the text, strategically, to define his ethical position on the treatment of native islanders. Instead of engaging in heated rhetoric or in pious declamations, he communicated his disapproval statistically and adduced evidence to support his humanistic stance.

Darwin the ethnographer apprehended human experience in depth and from two perspectives simultaneously — or stereoscopically, if you will. In terms of evolution by natural selection, the displacement of aborigines was the predictable result of biological competition and of European expansion. But, as Darwin's experience dramatized, the inhumane effects of colonialism were unwarrantable. Whereas in the 1860s, he seemed to have been resigned to the extinction of colonized tribes as the irreversible effect of imperial expansion, in 1871/74, he publicized the destructive consequences of overseas policy. Informing the chapters on race in *Descent*, therefore, is the resounding conviction that all human beings are equal in their dignity and that intra-species extinction of this order was commercially, militarily, scientifically, and morally indefensible.

# 12. Descent *as Synthesis*

*Descent* holds a significant position in the history of British anthropology. In order to demonstrate its historical and substantive importance, I will outline the history of events in British anthropology, from 1843 to 1871, and in this context review Alfred Russel Wallace's definition of "anthropology" and the aims of the discipline, as set forth in his 23 August 1866 Address to the British Association for the Advancement of Science ("Anthropology" Section D). *Descent*, published in 1871, improved upon this definition and incorporated these aims. Envisaging anthropology to be much more than an assemblage of loosely related fields, Darwin understood it to be a synthetic discipline, combining the physiological, cultural, and ethnic aspects of humanity.

The history of British anthropology took shape in the period between the founding of two societies: in 1843, of the Ethnological Society of London, and, in 1871, of the Anthropological Institute of Great Britain and Ireland (Stocking [1987] 238–7). From 1863, the Society and the Institute had been separate entities and its members were popularly known as *ethnologicals* and as *anthropologicals*, respectively. Their perspectives on the study of man differed from each other in significant ways. The *ethnologicals* were opponents of slavery and, like FitzRoy, initially subscribed to the Mosaic interpretation of Creation and of human origins. The *anthropologicals*, who were predominantly polygenists, thought that human diversity was evidence of there being multiple species of man. The multiple-species theory, to which some subscribed, was used nefariously to support slavery, to divest nonwhite human beings of their humanity, and to claim, in Henrika Kuklick's words, "that supposedly congenitally inferior people would learn elevated habits only if compelled to do so" (76).

Monogenism, which posited the common origin of man, eventually gained wider acceptance once the Anthropological Institute came into being in 1871, although in this circle adherence to the Bible as an authoritative text was becoming increasingly debatable. Because Darwin's theory that all human beings are members of a single species was essential to the Institute's scientific agenda, naturalists in the group recognized that the religious orientation of monogenism was inconsistent with geological and fossil evidence, as well as with evolutionary biology, and, for these reasons, had to be revised in secular and scientific terms (77). Thus, among liberal humanists, the theory of evolution as it applied to man pointed towards the separation of science and religion

From 1864 to 1871, the Institute defined its intellectual aims, ultimately reaching a compromise with dissenting members of the *anthropological* group. George W. Stocking, Jr., to whom I am indebted for this historical outline, writes about these years in some detail ([1987] 238–73). During the 1850s, the period of the Darwinian revolution, the Anthropological and Ethnological Societies seemed to be irreconcilable, as each vied for primacy over the other. The *anthropologicals*, for example, tried to obtain recognition for their viewpoint at the 1864 meeting of the British Association, where they argued, unsuccessfully, for the inclusion of ethnology and geography into Section E of the Association. A similar plan was set forth at the 1865 Birmingham meeting, but at the meeting the *ethnologicals* compromised. Thomas Huxley, John Lubbock, and their ethnological colleagues decided, prior to the 1866 meeting, that a re-ordering of loosely connected disciplines was in the best interest of all concerned — and a prudent gesture it was, since the *ethnologicals* could not out-vote the *anthropologicals*. It was agreed, finally, that a Department of Anthropology was to be formed within Section D, of the British Association. The new Department was subsequently reorganized and, in 1866, named "Biology." Ethnology and geography were assigned to Section E (Stocking [1987] 238–73).

The redefinition of anthropology as a discrete field took place gradually against an extraordinary background of scientific activity. The year 1866 was an auspicious moment in the history of natural and of engineering science. Gregor Mendel published his investigations on plant hybrids that year, but his fundamental discoveries would be ignored until 1900. Ernst Haeckel invented the word *ecology* and, in his *Generelle Morphologie der Tiere*, popularized the erroneous embryological idea that ontology recapitulates phylogeny. Sir Thomas Clifford Allbut, M.D. invented the thermometer, and William Budd, M.D. proved that limiting the contamination of the water supply stops cholera (Hellemans and Bunch 338–39). And in this year, Alfred Russel Wallace became the first President of the Department of Anthropology of the British Association for the Advancement of Science.

Wallace's Address of 23 August 1866, delivered in his capacity as the first President (Section D, "Biology," of the British Association) indicates that, at that moment, anthropology was an aggregate of disciplines. Despite Wallace's enthusiasm, the prospect of a unified field was hindered by an undefined research methodology, proposed for the common use of eleven or more sub-disciplines ("Anthropology"). I would like to deal with these two problems separately, and as a prelude to considering the importance of Darwin's contribution to the field: in single context, to answer both disciplinary and theoretical needs.

Wallace begins with a rather nebulous definition of the field: "Anthropology is the science which contemplates man under all his varied aspects (as an animal, and as a moral and intellectual being) in his relations to lower organisms, to his fellow man, and to the universe." From this general perspective, he enumerates specific disciplines, for inclusion into the field. The first is *physiology*, the study of man as "a wondrous and most complicated machine, whose parts and motions, actions and reactions he seeks thoroughly to understand." As a branch of biology dealing with the organic processes of life, physiology, nowadays, belongs to medicine. *Comparative anatomy* and *zoology*, essential to physical anthropology, relate man to other beings, physically and taxonomically. In zoology, man's uniqueness as a species can be presented, along with his relation to lower animals. Wallace recognizes the importance of comparative anatomy and zoology to the study of mankind: scientists can compare man's "structure with that of other animals, note their likenesses and differences, determine their degree of affinity, and seek after the common plan of their organization and the law of development." Thomas Henry Huxley, for one, was certainly aware of how essential these disciplines were to taxonomy. In "On the Relation of Man to the Lower Animals" (1863), he writes:

> A careful study of the resemblances and differences presented by animals has, in fact, led naturalists to arrange them into groups, or assemblages, all the members of each group presenting a certain amount of definable resemblance, and the number of points of similarity being smaller as the group is larger and vice versa. Thus, all creatures which agree only in presenting the few distinctive marks of animality[,] form the "Kingdom" ANIMALIA. The numerous animals which agree only in possessing the special characters of Vertebrates form one "Sub-kingdom" of this Kingdom. Then the Sub-kingdom VERTE-BRATA is subdivided into the five "Classes," Fishes, Amphibians, Reptiles, Birds, and Mammals, and these into smaller groups called "Orders"; these into "Families" and "Genera"; while the last are finally broken up into the smallest assemblages, which are distinguished by the possession of constant, non-sexual, characters. These ultimate groups are Species [83–84].

The investigative field of *psychology*, as the study of the human mind, of its mode of action, and of its development, for Wallace as it would be Darwin in 1871/74, extended beyond man to include all mammals. Wallace was inclined to think that a study of intelligence in animals would illuminate the origin and nature of the human mind. *History* had anthropological relevance, for the knowledge it brought of "man's progress in recent times" (from a present perspective, the inclusion of recorded history, though it bore a logical connection to prehistory and therefore to human origins, seems unwieldy and inappropriate to a natural-science category). *Geography*, which is grouped with recorded history, determines "the localities of the various races that now inhabit the earth, their manners, customs, and physical characteristics." This definition of *geography* departs from the eighteenth-century usage. In the 1843 edition of Samuel Johnson's *Dictionary of the English Language* (1775), for example, a geographer "describes the earth according to the position of different parts" (311). But Wallace's definition of geography, conceived of in the light of Darwinian thought, stressed the mutability of life and the interactivity of organic beings, with each other and with the environment. In the 1855 paper, "On the Law Which Has Regulated the Introduction of New Species," Wallace defined geography explicitly in terms of the evolutionary relationship between various animals and their respective environments. His natural-selection hypothesis, in fact, was founded on three propositions in *Organic Geography*. He pondered several probabilities arising wherever large groups of animals were diffused over the earth, and wherever others were confined to certain districts: (1) if families were widely distributed, genera tended to be limited in range; and widely distributed genera would present markedly distinct species, peculiar to each geographical range; (2) among a confined group of animals having diverse species, the most closely allied occupied the same or a nearby locality; and (3) wherever a wide sea or a lofty mountain separated countries having similar climates, close resemblances would be found between the families, genera, and species in each of the countries (*IT* 38). Wallace, in 1866, used the phrase *human geography* to describe migrations and population centers. Huxley, in similar fashion, based a four-fold classification of racial types (i.e., Australoid, Negroid, Mongoloid, and Xanthochroid), specifically, on geographical distributions ("Modifications of Mankind" 1–7). But Wallace overloaded the idea of geography with ethnological weight, namely with the "manners, customs, and physical characteristics" of natives.

The *archaeologist*, whose enterprise coincided with the ethnologist's, studied the remains of human artifice, such as relics, monuments, implements, and, in the process of studying antiquities, learned about specific cultures. Wallace recognized the close affinity and interdependence of archaeology and anthropology, as both were concerned with "the remains of man and his works, to supplement written history and to carry back our knowledge of man's physical, mental, and moral condition into prehistoric times." Unlike the modern paleoanthropologist who is concerned with prehistory and with the fossil remains of man, Wallace was thinking of historical mankind and was anticipating the kind of scheme John Lubbock would devise in 1872, namely the Four Ages of civilization (i.e., Paleolithic, Neolithic, Bronze, and Iron [*Pre-Historic Times* 2–3]).

The work of the *geologist* extended the archaeologist's retrospective vision "to a still earlier epoch by proving that man coexisted with numerous animals now extinct, and inhabited Europe at so remote a period that the very contour of its surface, the form of its hills and valleys, no less than its climate, vegetation, and geology, were materially different from what they are now, or ever have been during the epoch of authentic history." In this context, Wallace might have had Lyell's 1863 *The Geological Evidence of the Antiquity of Man* in mind.

Even *philology*, the study of human speech, of linguistics, and of cultural history, is enlisted as a means of disclosing man's migratory past and "the common origin of many of the races of mankind." Some of its proponents had used language to support religious convictions. The Philological Society of London even detached itself from the controversy over science and natural theology that had arisen in the 1830s when Cardinal Wiseman and the Rev. W. B. Winning used language as a means of support the idea of the inerrancy of Scriptures and of the veracity of revealed religion (Aarsleff 223–24). Contrary to orthodox views on language and on human origins, Robert Chambers, in the 1844 *Vestiges of the Natural History of Creation*, proposed that mankind had originated in a barbaric rather than civilized state, and that mammals were endowed with a form of gesture and sign language. Not of miraculous origin, speech was, in truth, a refinement of animal communication, having "a material source in man's constitution" (Aarsleff 224). Chambers' syllogism about the origin of language, which follows directly, is interesting for the way it anticipates ideas Darwin would enunciate and develop in *Descent* and in *The Expression of the Emotions in Man and Animals*: If language, in its most comprehensive sense as the communication of ideas by whatever means, can communicate ideas by looks, gestures, and signs of various kinds, as well as by speech; and if animals possess some of those means of communicating ideas and existed before man, then language existed upon earth "ere the history of our race commenced" (311).

Wallace accords prominence to phrenology and to craniology. Pseudoneurosciences that presumed the brain and skull to be indices to personality and behavior, they were often used in support of racist claims about the mental faculties of nonwhites. The phrenologist attempts "to connect mental peculiarities with the form and dimensions of the brain as indicated by the corresponding form of its bony covering," whereas the craniologist limits his attention to the skull as indicative of race, and in so doing "trace[s] out the affinities of modern and ancient races of men, by the forms and dimensions of their crania." An example of how phrenology could be used to support racial pre-conceptions is Dr. Wilson's report, written during the *Beagle*'s voyage of 1826–1830. The phrenologist Karl Vogt's (1817–1895), in the 1864 *Lectures on Man: His Place in Creation, and in the History of the Earth*, argued for the direct correlation of cranial structure and intelligence, and his views were typical of the racist philosophy of the *anthropologicals*:

> On looking at a characteristic Hottentot or Negro skull in profile, the face projects like a muzzle, and the incisors are obliquely inserted, so that their edges meet as at projecting angles. On viewing a German skull, on the contrary, we see that the incisors meet perpendicularly; and that on closing the mouth, the lower incisors are a little behind the superior, whilst in the Negro they are rather in advance. This formation, the oragnathous, has been accordingly distinguished from the prognathous, and it has been observed generally that this development of the jaws is in direct relation to the intellectual capacity of a people, the prognathous being confined to the lowest races of man [Lecture II, 51–52].

Two factors undermined Wallace's enthusiastic Address and his plan for a unified field. One was the obvious need to emend the disciplinary list, so as to eliminate misplacement, incorrect emphasis, redundancy, and overlap. It would take a century to iron out many of these problems and to reach clarity. In the nineteenth century, the definitions of anthropology and of ethnology were imprecise and varied from nation to nation. Nineteenth-century scholars, for example, used *ethnology* to mean the study of cultural differences and of characteristics identifying the "common humanity" of all mankind (Barnard 2). In North America, however, a more structured approach obtained, one in which anthropology would come to include four sub-disciplines: biological anthropology, archaeology, anthropological linguistics, and cultural anthropology (Barnard 2–4).

Wallace's scope and method hampered his redefinition of *anthropology*. He claims that an "anthropologist" collects and systematizes facts and laws, taken from all humanistic disciplines. Yet this would be pointless exercise, unless one had already established clear objectives and reasonable hypotheses. It seems that, here, Wallace is calling for the induction of laws from generally amassed observations about mankind, that is, from an aggregate of information taken from a mixture of disciplines or, in the case of phrenology, of pseudo-disciplines (philosophy, medicine, and theology being conspicuously omitted). Such an approach, if this were indeed Wallace's intention, is inherently flawed. Karl R. Popper, in 1963, elucidates the fallacy of inductive reasoning — the formulation of inferences based on many observations. He found this to be an erroneous and illusory method of reasoning in that a hypothesis or ordering principle, one ultimately subject to testing, to modification, and to verification, must logically precede these procedures, and direct the mind as it discriminately gathered observations (178–200). Conversely, Wallace's call for the indiscriminate amassing of human facts in the Address was inefficient and promoted the unselective gathering of data.

In Wallace's prospectus, however, anthropology was to have objectives, though they tended to be far-sighted. One was to discover the nature of man (zoological, moral, and intellectual); a second objective was to determine man's relationship to other animals; and the third was to reflect on man's destiny; the mention of "destiny," perhaps a misnomer, contradicts Wallace's assertion that all problems under consideration in new anthropological symposia should be treated as "purely questions of science, to be decided solely by facts and by legitimate deductions from facts." In this regard, Wallace and Popper are in accord; the latter, writing one century later of a "critical attitude" towards ideas, implies that the scientific investigator is to a theory as a breeder is to a breed: critical thinking in science, whether in the search of a pure breed or to establish a scientific law, consciously attempts to make theories and conjectures "suffer in our stead in the struggle for the survival of the fittest." Critical thinking, in Popper's opinion, allows the thinker "to survive the elimination of an inadequate hypothesis" (191). Wallace's inclusion of words such as "destiny" (with respect to man's future) or "universe" (with respect to man's place in the cosmos) invests the natural history of man with a predetermined and extra-natural aspect, so these words are incompatible with Wallace's call for empirical science in anthropology

But the Address also contains practical advice and aims vis-à-vis native mankind. Wallace was thinking specifically about human origins, about the relatedness of human groups, and about the amelioration of native lifestyles. In a Prichardian vein, he reminds his colleagues, especially the *ethnologicals*, of the importance of valuing the customs, the beliefs, and superstitions of uncivilized and civilized man, as these insights "may guide us towards an explanation of their origin in common tendencies of the human mind." "Each peculiarity of form, color, or constitution," furthermore, "may give us a clue to the affinities of an obscure race." And from the knowledge thus gained can be derived not only ways of governing and of improving uncivilized tribes, but also ways of obtaining "guidance in our own national and individual progress."

The Anthropological Institute, as an independent organization comprising the rival societies mentioned above, was founded in 1871, when the first edition of *Descent* was published. To suggest correlations in intent and in content between the Institute's agenda and Darwin's groundbreaking contribution, I will list the major papers delivered and published in Volume I of the Institute's *Journal*. The list of major papers shows that the *ethnologicals* dominated the floor and that the emphasis had been placed on social, demographical, archaeological, philological, and religious matters. Of the twenty-six papers delivered and published in the new journal, more than ninety percent of them are ethnological in orientation, with the remainder given to miscellaneous notes pertaining to comparative anatomy, zoology, phrenology, and Mosaic history, areas and methods traditionally of interest to the *anthropologicals*:

**Part I.** John Lubbock, "On the Development of [Social] Relationships" Inaugural Meeting (14 February 1871)

**Part II.** J. W. Jackson, "On the Racial Aspects of the Franco-Prussian War Second Meeting (6 March 1871)

**Part III.** Hyde Clarke, "On the Prehistoric and Proto-historic Relations of the Populations of Asia and Europe..." Third Meeting (20 March 1871)

**Part IV.** W. Boyd Dawkins, "Report on the Results, obtained by the Settle Cave Exploration Committee out of Victoria Cave in 1870" Fourth Meeting (3 April 1871)

**Part V.** C. Stanilard Wake, "The Mental Characteristics of Australian Languages"; and W H. I. Bleek, "On the Position of the Australian Languages" Fifth Meeting (17 April 1871)

**Part VI.** H. H Godwin-Austen, "On the Stone Monuments of the Khasi Hill Tribes and on some of the Peculiar Rites and Customs of the People"; W. H. Pechey on the vocabulary of the Cornu tribe of Australia; and John Anderson, "Chinese Mohammedans" Sixth Meeting (1 May 1871)

**Part VII.** The Rev. Henry Callaway, M.D., "On Divination and Analogous Phenomena among the Natives of Natal" Seventh Meeting (5 May 1871)

**Part VIII.** F. G. H. Price, "A Description of the Quissama Tribe" Eighth Meeting (29 May 1871)

**Part IX.** Albert McDonald, "Mode of Preparing the Dead among

the Natives of the Upper Mary River, Queensland"; Hodder
M. Westropp, "On the Analogies and Coincidences among
Unconnected Nations"; and Henry H. Howorth, "The Westerly
Drifting of Nomads, from the Fifth to the Nineteenth Century"
Ninth Meeting (19 June 1871)

**Part X.** J. W. Flower, "On the Relative Ages of the Stone Implement
Periods in England"; and R. F. Burton, "On Anthropological
Collections from the Holy Land"

**Part XI.** The Rev. Langham Dale, "On a Collection of Stone Implements and Pottery from the Cape of Good Hope" Eleventh
Meeting (4 December 1871) (*Journal of the Anthropological Institute*, Vol. I [1872], Parts I–XI: 1–348)

It is an evocative coincidence that *Descent* was published in the same year
as the founding of the Anthropological Institute, but the relationship of the
text to the Institute and to its agenda may not be immediately apparent. The
Institute was keenly aware of Darwin's work on human evolution. Vice-
President Charnock announced, on 6 March the Institute's acquisition of the
two-volume, 1871 first edition of *Descent*. In the early 1870s, like Wallace's
group in Section D of "Biology," the Institute was defining its aims and settling issues regarding human origins, descent, and progressive civilization
(Stocking [1987] 257–58). With this in mind, linking *Descent* to Wallace's
1866 Address suggests that, in aim and organization, Darwin might have been
attempting to answer, or had inadvertently satisfied, the need for a unified,
*anthropological* document, one subsuming under the theoretical heading of
evolutionary biology an assemblage of sub-disciplines in the natural sciences
(biology, geology, and its sub-specialties), and in what is today defined as *social
science*, a heading that includes cultural anthropology, history, psychology,
geography, economics, and even philosophy. Even if Darwin had not intended
*Descent* to be a kind of manifesto of evolutionary biology, there is no doubt
that its publication was a critical and serendipitous event.

Darwin was not alluding to Alexander Pope's 1734 *An Essay on Man*
when he wrote to Wallace, on 26 February 1867, about his plans to publish
"a little essay on the origin of Mankind" (*L&L* Vol. 3 95), and again on March
1867, in which he refers to "my essay on Man" (*L&L* Vol. 3 95); nevertheless, he had a purpose comparable to Pope's. It is almost oxymoronic to call
an *essay on man* "little," but he did so again in a letter to A. De Candolle of
6 July 1868, in the phrase "a short essay on 'The Descent of Man'" (*L&L* Vol.
3 98). Whether intentionally or not, Darwin's "essay on Man" unified the scientific theories of his times pertaining to man. In a single interdisciplinary

context, Darwin deftly employed the hypothetical-deductive method, to support his views on human evolutionary biology. He cites an extraordinary 530 contemporary naturalists, from a wide range of fields. Conceptually organized, *Descent* has three interrelated areas of concern:

I. Evolution and the Origin of Man (Comparative Anatomy, Zoology, Embryology, Botany, Geography and Geology)

II. Evolution and the Physical Development of Man (Variation, Modification, and Inheritance)

III. Evolution and the Mental Development of Man (Intelligence [emphasis on Language], Morality, Sociology, and Religion).

Informing the three evolutionary concentrations — the origin and physical and mental development — are the principles of selection, natural and sexual, along with secondary factors responsible for human modification and variation. The parenthetical elements show that, in *Descent*, Darwin was able to incorporate efficiently under biological headings a number of the sub-disciplines that Wallace had cursorily enumerated in 1866. Thus, comparative anatomy, comparative embryology, zoology, and, to a lesser degree, geography, and geology, provide evidence to support the evolutionary Origin of Man; comparative zoology and the idea of heritable traits support the Physical Development of Man; and through comparative zoology, ethnology, neuroscience (phrenology notably excluded), philology, semiotics, pre- and modern history in the study of customs, sociology, politics, and even religion are depicted as having originated in the processes of evolutionary biology. Darwin, in essence, had assimilated at least a dozen discrete fields under what can be described as *evolutionary anthropology*.

# Works Cited

Aarsleff, Hans. *The Study of Language in England, 1780–1860.* 1967. Minneapolis: University of Minnesota Press; London: Athlone, 1983.

"An Act for the Abolition of the Slave Trade." Vol. XI of *English Historical Documents, 1783–1832.* Edited by A. Aspinall and E. Anthony Smith, general editor David C. Douglas. 12 vol. New York and Oxford: Oxford University Press, 1969.

Andrews, Peter. "Ape." In *Encyclopedia of Human Evolution and Prehistory.* Edited by Ian Tattersall, Eric Delson, and John Van Couvering. New York and London: Garland, 1988. pp. 39–41.

_____. "Hominidae." In *Encyclopedia of Human Evolution and Prehistory.* Edited by Ian Tattersall, Eric Delson, and John Van Couvering. New York and London: Garland, 1988. pp. 245–47.

_____. "Hominoidea." In *Encyclopedia of Human Evolution and Prehistory.* Edited by Ian Tattersall, Eric Delson, and John Van Couvering. New York and London: Garland, 1988. pp. 248–55.

Barnard, Alan. *History and Theory in Anthropology.* New York and Cambridge: Cambridge University Press, 2000.

Barton, George A., and Harold H. Rowley. "Race." *Dictionary of the Bible.* Edited by James Hastings. Rev. ed. of Frederick C. Grant and H. H. Rowley.

New York: Charles Scribner's Sons; Macmillan, 1963.

Blumenbach, Johann Friedrich. *Über die naturlichen Verscheidenheiten im Menschengeschlechte ... (Selections).* In *Readings in Early Anthropology.* Edited by J. S. Slotkin. Viking Fund Publications in Anthropology, 40. Chicago: Aldine, 1965.

Bonwick, James. *The Last of the Tasmanians; or, the Black War of Van Diemen's Land.* London: Sampson, Low, Son & Marston, 1870.

Brantlinger, Patrick. *Dark Vanishings: Discourse on the Extinction of Primitive Races,* Ithaca, NY, and London: Cornell University Press, 2003.

Bridges, E. Lucas. *Uttermost Part of the Earth.* New York: E.P. Dutton, 1949.

Brooks, Alison. "Aurignacian." In *Encyclopedia of Human Evolution and Prehistory.* Edited by Ian Tattersall, Eric Delson, and John Van Couvering. New York and London: Garland, 1988. pp. 63–4.

Browne, Janet. *Charles Darwin: Voyaging.* Vol. I of *A Biography.* New York: Alfred A. Knopf, 1995.

Caesar, Julius. *The Gallic War and Other Writings.* Translated with an Introduction by Moses Hadas. New York: Random House, 1957.

Chambers, Robert. *Vestiges of the Natural*

*History of Creation and Other Evolutionary Writings*. 1844–1845. Edited with a new Introduction by James A. Secord. Chicago and London: University of Chicago Press, 1994.

*Chambers' Biographical Dictionary*. Edited by J.O. Thorne. 1897. New ed. Edinburgh and London: W&R. Chambers; New York: St. Martin's, 1962.

Clarkson, Thomas. "An Essay on the Slavery and Commerce of the Human Species, Particularly the African. Translation from a Latin dissertation, Which Was Honoured with the First Prize, in the University of Cambridge, for the Year 1785, with Additions." London: J. Phillips, 1786. *Online Library of Liberty*, http://oll.libertyfund.org.

_____. *The History of the Rise, Progress, and Accomplishment of the Abolition of the African Slave-Trade by the British Parliament*. 2 vols. London: Longmans, 1808.

"Clarkson, Thomas." In *Chambers' Biographical Dictionary*. Edited by J.O. Thorne. 1897. New ed. Edinburgh and London: W&R. Chambers; New York: St. Martin's, 1962. p. 82.

Cook, James. *The Explorations of Captain James Cook in the Pacific, As Told by Selections of His Own Journals, 1768–1779*. Edited by A. Grenfell Price. Introduction by Percy G. Adams. Mineola, NY: Dover, 1971.

Cooper, John M. *Analytical and Critical Bibliography of the Tribes of Tierra del Fuego and Adjacent Territory*. Smithsonian Institution, Bureau of American Ethnology. *Bulletin*, 63. Washington, D.C.: Government Printing Office; Whitefish, MT: Kessinger Reprint, 1917.

Crawfurd, John. "On the Physical and Mental Characteristics of the Negro." *Ethnological Society's Transactions* (1866) 4: 21–39.

Darwin, Charles. *The Autobiography of Charles Darwin*. 1876. Edited by Nora Barlow. New York: W. W. Norton, 1959.

_____. *Charles Darwin's Beagle Diary*. Edited by R. D. Keynes. 1988. New York and Cambridge: Cambridge University Press, 2001.

_____. *Charles Darwin's Natural Selection. Being the Second Part of His Big Species Book, 1856–1858*. Edited by Robert C. Stauffer. Cambridge: Cambridge University Press 1975.

_____. *Charles Darwin's Notebooks, 1836–1844: Geology, Transmutation of Species Metaphysical Enquiries*. Transcribed and edited by Paul H. Bartlett, Peter J. Gautrey, Sandra Herbert, David Kohn, Sydney Smith. British Museum (Natural History). Ithaca, NY, and London: Cornell University Press, 1987.

_____. *The Correspondence of Charles Darwin*. Vol. I: 1821–1836. Edited by Frederick Burkhardt and Sydney Smith. Cambridge: Cambridge University Press, 1985.

_____. *Darwin Correspondence Project*. http://www.darwin.project.ac.uk

_____. *The Descent of Man; and Selection in Relation to Sex*. Introduction by H. James Birx. 1871. Amherst, NY: Prometheus, 1998

_____. *The Expression of the Emotions in Man and Animals*. 1872. New York: D. Appleton and Company, 1896. Whitefish, MT: Kessinger Reprint.

_____. *The Foundations of the Origin of Species: Two Essays Written in 1842 and 1844*. Edited by Francis Darwin. Cambridge: Cambridge University Press, 1909.

_____. *Journal of Researches into the Geology and Natural History of the Various Countries Visited by H.M.S. Beagle Round the World, Under the Command of Capt. Fitz Roy, R.N.* London: Henry Colburn, 1839. Second ed. London: John Murray, 1845. *The Complete Work of Charles Darwin Online*. Directed by

John van Wyhe. http://www.darwin-online.org.uk.

_____. *The Life and Letters of Charles Darwin, Including an Autobiographical Chapter.* Edited by Francis Darwin. 3 vols. London: John Murray, 1887. In *The Complete Work of Charles Darwin Online.* Directed by John van Wyhe. http://www.darwin-online.org.uk.

_____. *The Life and Letters of Charles Darwin.* Edited by Leonard Huxley. 3 vols. London: Macmillan,1913. In *The Complete Work of Charles Darwin Online.* Directed by John van Wyhe. http://www.darwin-online.org.uk.

_____. *Narrative of the Surveying Voyages of His Majesty's Ships Adventure and Beagle Between the Years 1826 and 1836, Describing Their Examination of the Southern Shores of South America, and the Beagle's Circumnavigation of the Globe. Journal and Remarks.* 1832–1836 [2nd edition]. *Journal and Remarks. Proceedings of the Second Expedition.* Vol. III of *The Narrative of the Voyages of H. M. Ships Adventure and Beagle.* 3 vols. and appendix. London: Henry Colburn, 1839. In *The Complete Work of Charles Darwin Online.* Directed by John van Wyhe. http://www.darwin-online.org.uk.

_____. "Natural Selection, Being the Second Part of the *Big Species Book* Written from 1856–1858, the Long Version of the *Origin*." In *Darwin on Evolution: The Development of the Theory of Natural Selection.* Edited by Thomas F. Glick and David Kohn. Indianapolis and Cambridge: Hackett, 1996. pp. 127–51.

_____. *The Origin of Species by Natural Selection.* Sixth Edition. 1859. Amherst, NY: Prometheus, 1991.

_____, et al. "Queries Respecting the Human Race, to Be Addressed to Travelers and Others." *Drawn Up by a Committee of the British Association for the Advancement of Science, at the Glasgow meeting* (August 1840) 10: 447–58. In *The Complete Work of Charles Darwin Online.* Directed by John van Wyhe. http://www.darwin-online.org.uk.

Darwin, Erasmus. *Zoonomia; Or, the Laws of Organic Life.* Vol. I. Project Gutenberg. http://www.gutenberb.org/ebooks.

Day, Matthew. "Godless Savages and Superstitious Dogs: Charles Darwin, Imperial Ethnography, and the Problem of Human Uniqueness." *Journal of the History of Ideas.* Vol. 69, No. 1 (January 2008): 49–70.

Degler, Carl N. *In Search of Human Nature: The Decline and Revival of Darwinism in American Social Thought.* New York and Oxford: Oxford University Press, 1991.

De Paolo, Charles. "Darwin, Charles, 1809–1882." *Encyclopedia of Life Writing: Autobiographical and Biographical Forms.* Edited by Margaretta Jolly. 2 vols. London and Chicago: Fitzroy Dearborn, 2001. Vol. I: A–K, pp. 260–61.

Desmond, Adrian, and James Moore. *Darwin's Sacred Cause: How a Hatred of Slavery Shaped Darwin's Views on Human Evolution.* Boston and New York: Houghton Mifflin Harcourt, 2009.

Doyle, William. *The Oxford History of the French Revolution.* New York and Oxford: Oxford University Press, 1990.

Eiseley, Loren. *Darwin's Century: Evolution and the Men Who Discovered It.* 1958. Garden City, NY: Anchor; Doubleday, 1961.

*Encyclopedia of Human Evolution and Prehistory.* Edited by Ian Tattersall, Eric Delson, and John Van Couvering. New York and London: Garland, 1988.

Fagan, Brian M. "Egypt and the Near East: Tomb Robbery by the Nile, Giovanni Belzoni." *Eyewitness to Discovery:*

*First-Person Accounts of More than Fifty of the World's Greatest Archaeological Discoveries.* Edited by Brian M. Fagan. Oxford and New York: Oxford University Press, 1996. pp. 75–8.

Farb, Peter. *Humankind.* New York: Bantam, 1980.

FitzRoy, Robert. *Narrative of the Surveying Voyages of His Majesty's Ships Adventure and Beagle Between the Years 1826 and 1836, Describing Their Examination of the Southern Shores of South America, and the Beagle's Circumnavigation of the Globe. Proceedings of the Second Expedition, 1831–1836, Under the Command of Captain Robert Fitz-Roy, R.N.* [1st ed.]. Vol. II of *The Narrative of the Voyages of H. M. Ships Adventure and Beagle.* 3 vols. and Appendix. London: Henry Colburn, 1839. In *The Complete Work of Charles Darwin Online.* Directed by John van Wyhe. http://www.darwin-online.org.uk.

_____ and Charles Darwin. "A Letter, Containing Remarks on the Moral State of Tahiti, New Zealand, &c." *South African Christian Recorder.* 2(4) (Sept. 1836): 222–38. In *The Complete Work of Charles Darwin Online.* Directed by John van Wyhe. http://www.darwin-online.org.uk.

Gabriel, Mordecai L, and Seymour Fogel, editors. "Genetics Chronology." *Great Experiments in Biology.* The Prentice-Hall Animal Science Series. Edited by H. Burr Steinbach, Mordecai L. Gabriel, and Seymour Fogel. Englewood Cliffs, NJ: Prentice-Hall, 1955. pp. 225–28.

Ghiselin, Michael T. *The Triumph of the Darwinian Method.* 1969. Mineola, NY: Dover, 2003.

Godwin, William. *Enquiry Concerning Political Justice.* 1798. Edited by Isaac Kramnick. Hammondsworth, Middlesex, UK: Penguin, 1976.

Gruber, Howard E. *Darwin on Man: A Psychological Study of Scientific Creativity.* Second ed. Foreword to the first edition by Jean Piaget. London and Chicago: University of Chicago Press, 1981.

Hawkes, Jacquetta. *The Atlas of Early Man: The Rise of Man across the Globe, from 35,000 to A.D. 500.* London: Dorling Kindersley, 1976.

Heawood, Edward. *A History of Geographical Discovery in the Seventeenth and Eighteenth Century.* New York: Octagon, 1965.

Hellemans, Alexander, and Bryan Bunch. *The Timetables of Science: A Chronology of the Most Important People and Events in the History of Science.* New, Updated Ed. New York and London: Touchstone; Simon & Schuster, 1988.

Herbert, Sandra. "The Place of Man in the Development of Darwin's Theory of Transmutation." Part I. *Journal of the History of Biology* (1974), 7: 217–58.

_____. "The Place of Man in the Development of Darwin's Theory of Transmutation." Part II. *Journal of the History of Biology* (1977), 10: 155–227.

Herschel, John F.W. *A Preliminary Discourse on the Study of Natural Philosophy.* 1830. Foreword by Arthur Fine. Chicago and London: University of Chicago Press, 1987.

Hopkins, John S. *Darwin's South America.* New York: John Day, 1969.

Hull, David L. "Darwin's Science and Victorian Philosophy of Science." In *The Cambridge Companion to Darwin.* Edited by Jonathan Hodge and Gregory Radick. Cambridge: Cambridge University Press, 2003. pp. 168–91.

_____. Introductory chapters to *Darwin and His Critics: The Reception of Darwin's Theory of Evolution by the Scientific Community.* Edited by David L. Hull. Chicago and London: University of Chicago Press, 1973. pp. 1–77.

Humboldt, Alexander von. *Personal Nar-*

*rative of Travels to the Equinoctial Regions of America during the Years 1799–1804*. Edited and Translated by Thomasina Ross. 3 vols. London: Bohn's Scientific Library; Whitefish, MT: Kessinger Reprints, 1851.

Huxley, Thomas Henry. "On the Geographical Distribution of the Chief Modifications of Mankind." *Journal of the Ethnological Society of London. Scientific Memoirs III* (1870): 1–7; http://aleph0.clark u.edu/SM3/GeoDis.html.

_____. "On the Methods and Results of Ethnology" (1873). http://www.gutenberg.org.

_____. "On the Natural History of the Man-Like Apes." *Evidence as to Man's Place in Nature*. New York: D. Appleton & Company, 1863. pp. 9–68.

_____. "On the Relations of Man to the Lower Animals." *Evidence as to Man's Place in Nature*. New York: Appleton, 1863. pp. 71–132.

Jarrett, Derek. *Pitt the Younger*. Introduction by A. J. P. Taylor. London: Weidenfeld and Nicolson, 1974.

Johnson, Samuel. *Dictionary of the English Language*. Edited by Alexander Chalmers. 1843. London: Studio, 1994.

*Journal of the Anthropological Institute of Great Britain and Ireland*. Volume I. London: Trübner and Company, 1872. Parts I–XI, pp. 1–348.

King, Philip Parker. *Narrative of the Surveying Voyages of His Majesty's Ships Adventure and Beagle Between the Years 1826 and 1836, Describing Their Examination of the Southern Shores of South America, and the Beagle's Circumnavigation of the Globe. Proceedings of the First Expedition, 1826–1830, Under the Command of Captain P. Parker, R.N., F.R.S.* [1st ed.]. Volume I of *The Narrative of the Voyages of H M. Ships Adventure and Beagle*. 3 vols. and Appendix. London: Henry Colburn, 1839. In *The Complete Work of Charles Darwin Online*. Di-

rected by John van Wyhe. http://www.darwin-online.org.uk.

Kohn, George Childs, ed. *Encyclopedia of Plague and Pestilence from Ancient Times to the Present*. 1995. Rev. ed. Foreword by Mary Louise Scully. New York: Checkmark, 2001.

Kuklick, Henrika. "British Anthropology." *Encyclopedia of Social and Cultural Anthropology*. Edited by Alan Barnard and Jonathan Spencer. London and New York: Routledge, Taylor & Francis, 1996. pp. 76–79.

Lamarck, Jean Baptiste. *Zoological Philosophy: An Exposition with Regard to the Natural History of Animals*. 1809. Translated and with an Introduction by Hugh Elliot. 1914. New York and London: Hafner, 1963.

Leakey, Richard E., and Roger Lewin. *Origins: The Emergence and Evolution of Our Species and Its Possible Future*. 1977. New York: E. P. Dutton, 1982.

Lubbock, John. *Pre-Historic Times As Illustrated by Ancient Remains and the Manners and Customs of Modern Savages*. London and Edinburgh: Williams and Norgate; Whitefish, MT: Kessinger Reprints, 1872.

Lyell, Charles. *The Geological Evidence of the Antiquity of Man*. 1863. Mineola, NY: Dover, 2004.

_____. *Principles of Geology, Being an Attempt to Explain the Former Changes of the Earth's Surface*. First ed. Introduction by Martin J. S. Rudwick. 3 vols. 1830–1833. Chicago and London: University of Chicago Press, 1990–1991.

MacGillivray, John. *Narrative of the Voyage of H.M.S. Rattlesnake, Commanded by the Late Captain Owen Stanley ... During the Years 1846–1850. Including Discoveries and Surveys in New Guinea, the Louisiade Archipelago, etc., To Which is Added the Account of Mr. E.B. Kennedy's Expedition for the Exploration of the Cape*

*York Peninsula.* 2 vols. Vol. 1. London: T. W. Boone, 1852.

Malthus, Robert Thomas. *An Essay on the Principle of Population.* 1798. Edited with an Introduction by Anthony Flew. Harmondsworth, Middlesex: Penguin, 1976.

_____. *An Essay on the Principle of Population.* 1803. Introduction by T. H. Hollingsworth. London, Melbourne, and Toronto: Everyman's Library, 1982.

"Malthus, Robert Thomas." *Dictionary of National Biography.* Volume 36, Malthus-Mason. London: Smith, Elder & Company, 1893. pp. 1–5. Reprinted: Elibron Classics Replica Edition. Chestnut Hill, MA: Adamant, 2006.

Marks, Jon. "Race (Human)." In *Encyclopedia of Human Evolution and Prehistory.* Edited by Ian Tattersall, Eric Delson, and John Van Couvering. New York and London: Garland, 1988. p. 493.

Mathieson, William Law. *British Slavery and Its Abolition, 1823–1838.* New York: Longmans, 1926.

Mayr, Ernst. *The Growth of Biological Thought: Diversity, Evolution, and Inheritance.* Cambridge, MA, and London: Belknap, 1982.

Melville, Herman. *Moby-Dick: An Authoritative Text, Reviews and Letters by Melville. Analogues and Sources Criticism.* A Norton Critical Edition. Edited by Harrison Hayford and Herschel Parker. New York: W.W. Norton, 1967.

Montagu, Ashley. *Man: His First Two Million Years: A Brief Introduction to Anthropology.* New York: Dell, 1968.

"Old Lima Haciendas of Peru." http://www.peruvian-pasos.com.

*The Oxford English Dictionary.* 21 vols. and Supplement. 1933. Oxford at the Clarendon Press, 1971.

"Phrenological Remarks on Three Fuegians." Appendix 17 of *The Narrative of the Voyages of H.M. Ships Adventure and Beagle.* pp. 148–49. In *The Complete*

*Work of Charles Darwin Online.* Directed by John van Wyhe. http://www.darwin-online.org.uk.

Pope, Alexander. *An Essay on Man. Pope: Poetical Works.* Edited by Herbert Davis. London and New York: Oxford University Press, 1966.

Popper, Karl R. "Conjectures and Refutations." In *Science: Men, Methods, Goals.* Edited by Boruch Brody and Nicholas Capaldi. New York: W.A Benjamin, 1968. pp. 178–200.

Prichard, James Cowles. "On the Extinction of Some Varieties of the Human Race." *Edinburgh New Philosophical Journal.* (1839) 28: 166–70.

_____. *Researches into the Physical History of Man.* 1826. Edited with an Introduction by George Stocking, Jr. Chicago and London: University of Chicago Press, 1973.

Rousseau, Jean-Jacques. *Discourse on the Origin and Foundations of Inequality Among Men* (1755). In *Rousseau's Political Writings.* A Norton Critical Edition. Translated by Julia Conaway Bondanella. Edited by Alan Ritter and Julia Conaway Bondanella. New York and London: W. W. Norton pp. 3–57.

_____. *On Social Contract or Principles of Political Right.* In *Rousseau's Political Writings.* pp. 84–173.

Sachs, Aaron. *The Humboldt Current: Nineteenth-Century Exploration and the Roots of American Environmentalism.* New York and London: Penguin, 2006.

Schlozer, August Ludwig von. "A New Year's Letter from Jamaica." In *The Enlightenment: A Comprehensive Anthology.* Edited by Peter Gay. New York: Simon & Schuster, 1973. pp. 688–89.

Schmid, Randolph E. "Before Lucy Came Ardi, New Earliest Hominid Found." Associated Press article on *Yahoo! News.* (October 1, 2009): 1–3. http://news.yahoo.com.

Sharpe, Granville. "Short Sketch of Contemporary Regulations ... for the Intended Settlement of the Grain Coast of Africa, Near Sierra Leone." 3rd ed. 1787. Reprinted: New York: Negro Universities Press, 1970.

"Sharpe, Granville." In *Chambers' Biographical Dictionary*. Edited by J.O. Thorne. 1897. New ed. Edinburgh and London: W&R. Chambers; New York: St. Martin's, 1962. p. 1166.

Sloan, Phillip R. "The Making of a Philosophical Naturalist." In *Cambridge Companion to Darwin*. Edited by Jonathan Hodge and Gregory Radick. Cambridge: Cambridge University Press, 2003. pp. 17–39.

Smith, Adam. *The Wealth of Nations*. Books I–III. 1776. Edited with an Introduction by Andrea Skinner. Hammondsworth, Middlesex: Penguin, 1976.

Stepan, Nancy. *The Idea of Race in Science: Great Britain, 1800–1960*. New York: Macmillan, 1982.

Stocking, George W., Jr. "From Chronology to Ethnology: James Cowles Prichard and British Anthropology, 1800–1850." Introductory essay to *Researches into the Physical History of Man*. 1813. By James Cowles Prichard. Edited by George W. Stocking, Jr. Chicago and London: University of Chicago Press, 1973. pp. ix–cx.

_____. *Race, Culture, and Evolution: Essays in the History of Anthropology*. New York: Free Press; London: Collier-Macmillan, 1968.

_____. *Victorian Anthropology*. New York: Free Press, 1987.

Szalay, Frederick S. "Eocene." In *Encyclopedia of Human Evolution and Prehistory*. Edited by Ian Tattersall, Eric Delson, and John Van Couvering. New York and London: Garland, 1988. pp. 180–81.

Tattersall, Ian. "Classification." In *Encyclopedia of Human Evolution and Prehistory*. Edited by Ian Tattersall, Eric Delson, and John Van Couvering. New York and London: Garland, 1988. pp. 136–38.

Tylor, Edward. *Primitive Culture: Researches into the Development of Mythology, Philosophy, Religion, Language, and Customs*. 2 vols. London: John Murray; Whitefish, MT: Kessinger Reprints, 1871.

Van Wyhe, John, director. *The Complete Work of Darwin Online*. http://www.darwin-online.org.uk.

Vogt, Carl, and James Hunt. *Lectures on Man: His Place in Creation, and in the History of the Earth*. Published by the Anthropological Society. London: Longman, Green, Longman, and Roberts; Whitefish, MT: Kessinger Reprints, 1864.

Wallace, Alfred Russel. "Anthropology." *Presidential Address of the Department of Anthropology, Section D, Biology, of the British Association for the Advancement of Science*, annual meeting (23 August 1866). Published in the *Report* series of the *B.A.A.S.*, Volume 36: 93–94. Reprinted in *The Alfred Russel Wallace Page*. Edited by Charles H. Smith. http://www.wku.edu/—smithch/wallace/S173.htm.

_____. *Infinite Tropics: An Alfred Russel Wallace Anthology*. Edited by Andrew Berry. Foreword by Stephen Jay Gould. London and New York: Verso, 2002.

_____. *Letters and Reminiscences*. Edited by James Marchant. Vol. 1. London: Cassell, 1916. In *The Complete Work of Charles Darwin Online*. Directed by John van Wyhe. http://www.darwin-online.org.uk.

_____ *The Malay Archipelago*. 1869. Tenth ed. London and North Clarendon, VT: Periplus, 1890.

_____. *My Life: A Record of Events and Opinions*. By Alfred Russel Wallace. New ed., condensed and revised, with

Facsimile Letters, Illustrations and Portraits. London: Chapman and Hall, 1908.

_____. *A Narrative of Travels on the Amazon and Rio Negro, With an Account of the Native Tribes and Observations on the Climate, Geology, and Natural History of the Amazon Valley*. Biographical Introduction by G. T. B. New Ed. Whitefish, MT: Kessinger Reprints, 1853.

_____. "On the Law which has Regulated the Introduction of New Species." (1855). In *Infinite Tropics: An Alfred Russel Wallace Anthology*. Edited by Andrew Berry. Preface by Stephen Jay Gould. London and New York: Verso, 2002. pp. 36–49.

_____. "On the Tendency of Varieties to Depart Indefinitely from the Original Type." (February 1858). In *Infinite Tropics*. pp. 52–62.

_____. "The Origin of Human Races and the Antiquity of Man Deduced from the Theory of 'Natural Selection.'" *Journal of the Anthropological Society of London.*

Vol. 2 (1864): clviii–clxx. Reprinted in *Infinite Tropics*, pp. 176–190.

_____. *The World of Life* (selections). In *Infinite Tropics*. pp. 17, 69–73, 256–59.

Wilberforce, William. "Appeal ... in Behalf of the Negro Slaves in the West Indies" (1823). In *Slavery in the West Indies*. 1923. New York: Negro Universities Press, 1969.

"Wilberforce, William." In *Chambers' Biographical Dictionary*. Edited by J.O. Thorne. 1897. New ed. Edinburgh and London: W&R. Chambers; New York: St. Martin's, 1962. p. 205.

Wilford, John Noble. "German Fossil Found to Be Early Primate." *The New York Times* National ed. Vol. CLVIII. May 16, 2009: A11.

Wilson, John. "Remarks on the Structure of the Fuegians." Appendix 16 to Volume II of *The Narrative of the Voyages of H. M. Ships Adventure and Beagle*. pp. 142–47. In *The Complete Work of Charles Darwin Online*. Directed by John van Wyhe. http://www.darwin-online.org.uk.

# Index